Engaged in Learning

Engaged in Learning
Teaching English, 6–12

Kathleen and James Strickland
Slippery Rock University

HEINEMANN
Portsmouth, NH

Heinemann
A division of Reed Elsevier Inc.
361 Hanover Street
Portsmouth, NH 03801–3912
www.heinemann.com

Offices and agents throughout the world

The authors and publisher wish to thank those who have generously given permission to reprint borrowed material:

Excerpts from *Power and Portfolios: Best Practices for High School Classrooms* by Jim Mahoney. Copyright © 2002 by Jim Mahoney. Published by Heinemann, a division of Reed Elsevier Inc., Portsmouth, NH. Reprinted with permission.

Figure 4–10 is reprinted from *Tutoring Writing: A Practical Guide for Conferences* by Donald A. McAndrew and Thomas J. Reigstad. Copyright © 2002 by Donald A. McAndrew and Thomas J. Reigstad. Published by Boynton/Cook, a subsidiary of Reed Elsevier Inc., Portsmouth, NH. Reprinted with permission.

Figure 4–11 is reprinted from *A Community of Writers: Teaching Writing in the Junior and Senior High School* by Steven Zemelman and Harvey Daniels. Copyright © 1988 by Steven Zemelman and Harvey Daniels. Published by Heinemann, a division of Reed Elsevier Inc., Portsmouth, NH. Reprinted with permission.

Excerpts from *Reflections on Assessment: Its Purposes, Methods, and Effects on Learning* by Kathleen and James Strickland. Copyright © 1998 by Kathleen and James Strickland. Published by Boynton/Cook, a subsidiary of Reed Elsevier Inc., Portsmouth, NH. Reprinted with permission.

Figure 7–1 is reprinted from *Standards for English Language Arts* by the International Reading Association and the National Council of Teachers of English. Copyright © 1996 by the International Reading Association and the National Council of Teachers of English. Reprinted with permission.

Library of Congress Cataloging-in-Publication Data
Strickland, Kathleen.
    Engaged in learning : teaching English, 6–12 / Kathleen and James Strickland.
        p.   cm.
    Includes bibliographical references and index.
    ISBN 0-86709-502-4 (alk. paper)
    1. English language—Study and teaching (Secondary)—United States.
    2. Language experience approach in education—United States.   3. Teacher-student relationships—United States.   I. Strickland, James.   II. Title.

LB1631 .S823   2002
428′.0071—dc21   2002009733

Editor: Lisa Luedeke
Production: Vicki Kasabian
Cover design: Jenny Jensen Greenleaf
Typesetter: TechBooks
Manufacturing: Steve Bernier

Printed in the United States of America on acid-free paper
09 08 07 06   VP   3   4   5   6

For Peter R. Stillman,
editor and friend

Contents

Foreword by Peter Stillman   xi

Acknowledgments   xv

1 **Education Begins with Philosophy**   1

Different Approaches
Beliefs Shape Perception
Curriculum in a Traditional Classroom
Curriculum in a Constructivist Classroom
Student-Centered Classrooms
What Happens When They Get to the Next Grade?

2 **Asking Questions, Facilitating Inquiry**   18

A Different Approach
Complicated by Our Expectations
Teacher-Talk: How Much?
Calling on Students
Facilitating Discussion
Risk Taking
Active Listening
Small Group Discussion
Facilitating Inquiry
I-Search Research
Using the Internet to Research
The Format of the Paper

3 **Reading and Literature**   36

Surveys and Interviews
Reading Logs

How the Subject Changed from Reading to Literature Studies
Teaching Reading by Connecting with Literature
Experiencing Success with Reading
The Place of Vocabulary Instruction
Supporting Readers During Reading
Supporting Readers After Reading
Literature Circles

4 Writing Workshop   79

Teaching Prewriting
Writer's Notebooks
Organizing Thoughts
Drafting and Responding to Writing
Keeping Track of Writers
Conferencing
Peer Response in Writing Conferences
Parading and Modeling for Students
Revision: Imagining the Better Text
Minilessons
Editing
Sharing: Writing That Goes Somewhere

5 Computers, Websites, and Technology   116

Writers Writing
Revision on the Computer
Editing
Web Publishing
Technology for Delivery of Information
Electronic Reading
Networking for Communication
Technology for Storage
The Future with Technology

6 Assessment and Evaluation—Codependent but Different   139

Assessment, Evaluation, and Reporting
Definitions Are Important
Checklists—Simple, Fast, Succinct
Rubrics
Test Is Not Necessarily a Four-Letter Word
Time and Resources—The Constraints of Testing
Teaching to the Test or Teaching for the Test

The Mixed Messages of Grading
Portfolios

7 The Politics of Standardization and Testing   177

Media Reporting of Achievement
Standards: Raising the Bar or Placing the Blame?
Where Does Thinking Come In?
Public Opinion Linked to Rhetoric, Not Facts
More Rebuttals
Measuring Accountability
Criterion-Referenced Testing
Problems with Standardized Testing
So, Now What?
Additional Resources

Works Cited   209

Index   217

Foreword

Typically the foreword writer observes about a book such as *Engaged in Learning,* I wish I'd had the opportunity to read it back when I started teaching. In this case, however, I wish I'd written it. Back then, when John Warriner was to English teachers what Mickey Mantle was to Yankee fans. The catch is, of course, that no right-minded publisher would have touched it. (The other catch is that I couldn't have written it with nearly the grace and wisdom that the Stricklands bring to bear.) Yet Jim and Kathleen's book would have been a boon for those of us entering classrooms for the first time back then, nothing much in our heads beyond Bloom's taxonomy and who wrote "Annabel Lee." Teaching pretty much amounted to conforming to a fixed mode of conduct. There seemed little to believe in, other than the rightness of precedent, which decreed that students were as hollow as chocolate rabbits. Our job was to stuff them, no philosophical underpinnings required.

I remember wondering on a long-ago May morning what I had accomplished over the course of that school year—what good I had done beyond instilling a muddle of syntactic conventions, leavened with "Annabel Lee." I came up with nothing. I'd done a job, met expectations, been freshly awarded tenure, and couldn't name a single kid whom I'd taught to love anything. We can teach only so long without needing to believe otherwise. There may be no more dreary, pointless an occupation than teaching without risk, without in any way venturing to radicalize our understanding of how our species best learns. It is essential that we know why we do what we do—that we believe for good reason in our every act in the classroom. It is essential that we perceive beyond the day not only what we want students to learn but also how we expect that learning to enrich their lives long past their years in school. We must, that is, teach to a consciously derived philosophy, rather than a set of mandates.

I sat down at a typewriter that same May morning and wrote a two-sentence resignation letter. What I should have done instead was to begin writing a book like this one.

The Stricklands do not offer a disquisition on the philosophy of learning. They do, however, provide in the opening chapter an informed and even-handed persuasion that we read and reflect, that we reconcile our teaching practices with what we come to believe—that we trust ourselves, our methods and convictions. They ask as well that we trust students to help us shape their own learning, the classroom becoming a place where teaching and learning flow both to and from student and teacher. As I have just put it, this may sound like so much happy fluff. In fact, it is edgy and fraught with noise and risk. The authors pull no punches about this in arguing for English (and by implication, *all*) classrooms becoming transactional domains, where the construction of meaning is cosponsored by students and teacher.

True literacy, the Stricklands reason, is best cultivated in an environment where language is in near-constant use, with reading, writing, speaking, and listening understood as closely linked dynamics rather than discreet subskills, and worse, the subject of lectures. Theirs is not a broad-scale assault on tradition; it is an affirmation of what, I believe, our humane, teacherly instincts are naturally drawn to.

Good teachers may already live this book, which I mean to be an argument for good teachers reading it. It is rich in information that no one individual could reasonably hope to tease out of their own classroom experiences—not list-y, what-to-do-on-Monday prompts, but resources, graphic illustrations, topical suggestions from teachers in the field, tips on formatting lessons, structuring learning situations, even pointers on when and why to shut up. These useful features are most often embedded in thematic context. From the unit titled "The Place of Vocabulary Instruction," for example, one comes away with a variety of approaches as detailed by four or five seasoned English teachers, framed by suggestions for why and how to cast this aspect of language learning into a transactional mode. In short, a mix of practice and theory, which characterizes the whole of *Engaged in Learning*.

I confess that I nearly skipped the chapter "Computers, Websites, and Technology," inasmuch as I would never dream of going to a movie with such a title, even if it starred Julia Roberts. And we all know how tedious and jargon-ridden such discourses threaten to be. The authors' approach, however, is neither recondite nor zealous: there are indeed ways that computers can enhance interactive learning, and these ways are examined in a thoughtful, engaging manner. But computers pose problems, too, among them mistaken assumptions as to their near-magical effects on student writing, research, and zest for learning. They can in fact threaten the very sense of community we should be committed to nurturing. Here is a tool, the Stricklands establish, that can abet transactional learning only if we keep ever in mind that this is the goal. This is an especially reassuring discussion, both for those who are ambivalent about the place of computers in the English classroom, as well as those whose enthusiasm for them may be misdirected.

It's easy enough for the armchair humanist to point out the follies and iniquities that plague American classrooms today. It's another matter to be there, daily guiding students through vital learning experiences and additionally seeking the ever-evasive, a just rationale for assessing and evaluating them. Ranking students is at best arbitrary, at worst, audacious. How is one to avoid being seduced by the bell curve's allure, to resist shrinking people into letters and numbers? The more we are persuaded by a transactional, constructivist philosophy, the more unreasonable traditional means and ends of assessment become. Worse, English teachers are now charged with preparing students for elaborate, one-shot standardized literacy tests that are more often than not inimical to students' best interests, the acquisition of a literacy never meant to be empirically tested. Yet test we must, measure we must (if for no other reason than that as a society we are positively batty about data).

Thus, *Engaged in Learning* does not provide strategies that will result in the abolition of formal assessment and evaluation. The Stricklands do, though, provide two of the most thoughtful chapters about these challenging matters that I have read. Are there indeed just, constructive ways to assess students' efforts as well as our own? Yes, and they are clearly detailed. Are there ways to prepare students for standardized testing that amount to more than capitulation in the form of practice runs and drilling? Yes again, and they are consistent with the philosophy that undergirds the entire book.

Years back, a student teacher asked me on her last day, "How will I ever know if I'm doing the right thing?" All I could muster in response was "By knowing when you're doing the wrong things." This book would have provided a vastly better answer.

Peter Stillman

Acknowledgments

First and foremost, we'd like to thank all the teachers who have shared their knowledge and their classrooms with us.

Thanks to Jeff Golub for hosting the listserv discussion group through the University of South Florida that allowed us to have virtual meetings with wonderful teachers and preservice teachers from all across the country, especially Leslie Boon, Shannon Dosh, Xinia Foster, Joan Kaywell, Brittanny Lemieux, Barbara Martin, Linda Peters, Margo Powers, and Teresa Savin.

A special debt is owed to Amy Johnson, a superb teacher at Hampton High School, outside Pittsburgh, Pennsylvania. She not only shared her own expertise with us but also let us share her students' work in the book. So we'd also like to thank Amber Nock, Jason Dudas, Mallory McDonough, Nicole Nowosielski, Dan Thaner, Giavonna Ferraro, Scott Kelly, and Scott Baret. Another kind of debt is owed to Amy's students who agreed to help us with photos for the book: Carly Hudale, Katie Kennedy, Amanda Kushon, Colleen Kroll, Tommy Lyons, Teresa Plunkett, Karen Pyptyk, and Annie Walsh.

Thanks to Annelise Schantz, of Hudson, Massachusetts, who allowed us to share portions of her remarkable high school graduation speech.

Thanks to our IUP colleagues and friends, Jane Blystone, Bob Dandoy, Don McAndrew, and Amy Walker. Thanks to our CEL friends from NCTE, especially Rick Chambers, Jeff Golub, Barbara King-Shaver, Jim Mahoney, and Louann Reid.

Thanks to Jim Burke and Carol Jago for their continued support.

Thanks to our own students at Slippery Rock University who help us examine our teaching and our profession, especially Melissa Hinterlang, Hollie Kotwica, Michelle Reigel, and Christa Welch.

And finally we'd like to thank our friends at Heinemann, especially Maura Sullivan, who first suggested that we do a follow-up to *Uncovering the Curriculum*. We'd also like to thank our production editor, Vicki Kasabian, whose assiduous vigilance was worth more than gold. Maura and Vicki promised us a great cover, and for that we'd like to thank designer Jenny Jensen Greenleaf. Of course, our heartfelt appreciation is offered to the entire team, especially Abby Heim, Peggy Wishart, Charlene Morris, Eric Chalek, and our editor, Lisa Luedeke. We'd also like to thank two people who couldn't be with us on this project: Melissa Inglis, whose insights and friendship we still treasure, and Peter Stillman, who had faith in us as writers, gave us our first of many contracts with Boynton/Cook, and continues to inspire us.

1

Education Begins with Philosophy

Get them to talk about things they need to understand. Show them it's all right to ask questions and listen to the answers, and then to react or ask more questions. Suggest that they write about what happens to them, so they can come to grips with experiences and share them with others. Encourage them to read for information, to cope with the print that surrounds them everywhere, to enjoy a good story.

—Kenneth Goodman

Several years ago a friend and colleague gave us a pencil holder for our desk, a lovely gold cylinder boldly engraved with two words: *Trust* and *Risk*. These two words have become increasingly important to us over our years of teaching and seem to capture our philosophy of learning. If we want students to think and make decisions for themselves, we have to trust ourselves as teachers—trust that although we're doing things differently in our classrooms, our definition of learning and teaching is based on solid research and best practice; trust our abilities enough to empower ourselves; trust ourselves to make decisions about curriculum and instruction based on data. The risk comes in asking our students to trust us and to trust themselves; to be honest and self-reflective; to trust us with different approaches to learning and to suspend excessive concern for grades. We realize how difficult it is to create a classroom in which students are responsible for their own learning, using oral and written language to think and discover across the curriculum. We realize how risky it is to establish student-centered classrooms with student- and/or teacher-generated curricula and organic lesson plans. And trusting is just as risky for us as teachers. We must trust our students as well as ourselves, risk giving up control of the curriculum, risk giving up precious time to try new approaches and to give students time to discover, without constantly worrying about grading and testing (see Figure 1–1).

1

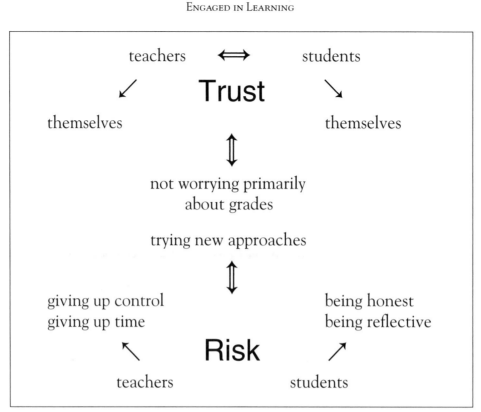

Figure 1–1. Trust and risk

As we try to practice what we preach—involving students in authentic learning and meaningful reflective activities—we constantly remind ourselves that good teaching always involves trusting students and taking risks. Many of us feel the pressure to employ mostly teacher-directed instruction, saying, "I only have so many weeks, so many classes a quarter or a semester; I have to give them information or they'll never get it. There isn't enough time to let them discover, reflect, connect—I have to tell them what they need to know." This comes from worrying about covering everything we're expected to address and worrying whether this class will get as much as the previous semester's students did. What happens if we don't cover something that is asked about on the state and federal standardized tests? That's why we must remember that learning is not the transmission of a body of knowledge from a teacher or from a text to the learners in a classroom. We must trust our students; empower them to make decisions about their learning, to set goals, and to work at a pace that is appropriate for them. As teachers, we must risk giving up control and giving up time.

Instead of worrying whether our students have learned a narrowly defined body of knowledge that the testing services and standards police believe students should possess, we should be concerned with whether our students understand their own learning and have found a place for literacy in their lives. Grant Wiggins (1993) elaborates, "understanding is not cued knowledge; performance is never the sum of drills; problems are not exercises: mastery is not achieved by the unthinking application of algorithms. In other words, we cannot be said to understand something unless we can employ our knowledge wisely, fluently, flexibly, and aptly in particular and diverse contexts" (200). As much as our students, we have to risk making mistakes, and risk the consequences of being educators at a time when many in the community neither understand our philosophy nor our methods of teaching. Growing means taking risks.

Many teachers search for a book that understands the realities of day-to-day classroom teaching and will offer down-to-earth suggestions that make sense about what to do on Monday. We understand that desire because we've shared in the quest for the holy grail of lessons, the magic elixir that will motivate disinterested students and transform leaden performances into golden achievements. At the risk of making another unwarranted generalization, the last thing many teachers think they need is one more book on the theory of learning. Although we will discuss strategies, methods, and even lesson plans, we first need to investigate how students learn. Whether we like it or not, the way someone teaches is the direct result of that person's philosophy of learning. Our beliefs inform our behavior.

Different Approaches

Kirk, a new high school teacher who found himself having to teach Shakespeare's *Macbeth*, began with a lesson on the clans of Scotland, thinking that would catch the students' interest. He decided to show a video of *Braveheart* or *Rob Roy* to give his students the flavor of warfare at that time, and he felt that this would certainly spark their interest in territorial battles and the forest of Birnam Wood that comes to Dunsinane. The students were mildly interested, until one asked if the material about the clans would be on the test. Having found that it wouldn't, they stopped listening to his lecture. The promise of one of the Scottish movies caught some interest until some of the students began arguing about the relative greatness of the gore. Most had seen the video already. Frustrated, Kirk threatened pop quizzes on the assigned readings and lecture material, but things were already headed downhill.

Another teacher, Brittany, began her class with a story about how the young man she was interested in while in high school asked the most popular girl, instead of Brittany, to the big dance. It didn't matter that Miss Popularity strung him along until she could get her steady boyfriend to make up with her. As he confessed to her later, while begging for another chance, his friends put him up to it. Sure, he wanted to date the "Prom Queen," but it was his friends who kept pushing him and telling him to "go for it." Then Brittany asked her students to write in their notebooks about a time when they talked their friends into doing something dumb or misadventuous, or when they were talked into doing something they knew was a risk or a bad idea. Then she asked if anyone wanted to share what they had written. At first, everyone looked around at each other, and then a flurry of hands went in the air. After ten minutes of sharing, Brittany began reading the section in *Macbeth* when Lady Macbeth talks her husband into killing Duncan. Her students were following in their texts and when she began to tire of reading aloud, she invited someone to take over. One of the girls in the front began reading at the same time as a boy toward the back did; she turned to him, and he deferred to her, but picked up when she grew tired. When the passage was finished, Brittany asked her students to predict in their notebooks what was going to happen. The unit continued in the same fashion with discussions of everyday situations connected with the plot, journal writing, readings from the play, and predictions. Brittany provided written summaries of some of the scenes and sometimes played selections from videotapes of the play. Instead of a culminating exam, Brittany asked her students to write about a characteristic of Macbeth that exists in people today, supporting their arguments with specifics from the play. The students used class time to brainstorm ideas, organize, and revise their drafts. At the end, volunteers were asked to bring in anything else they could discover about Scotland. Ironically, one student's presentation gave credit to his friend in another class who said his teacher apparently knew "tons" about the clans of Scotland.

What are the differences between the approaches of these two teachers? Some would accuse Brittany of watering down the curriculum and pandering to students who were unwilling or unable to read difficult texts. Some would praise Kirk's efforts to cover the curriculum while giving his students an historical backdrop from which to view the drama. While both teachers "taught" the same piece of literature, only one connected it to the lives of the students and helped them see its reading as purposeful. That teacher tried to engage each students' past knowledge and experiences—their schema or "map" of the world that we each carry inside our heads, as Frank Smith (1994) explains it—and let that guide their discovery of what the play meant. The other saw the students as deficient in specific knowledge and attempted to fill them up with the proper details, educating his students according to "sound" behavioral principles of learning, practices sanctioned by educational psychologists. Both teachers obviously care very deeply for their students, but we wonder whose students will remember *Macbeth* long after the books are passed on to another teacher's classes.

Beliefs Shape Perception

Teachers like Kirk and Brittany teach the way they do because of their beliefs about how learning takes place. Like any other belief, these are strongly held convictions, resistant to inconsistencies or contrary observations. In fact, Thomas Kuhn (1963), a physicist, discovered how difficult it is to change belief systems or paradigms, even in the face of unexplainable deviations and contradictions between beliefs held and evidence uncovered by research. These widely-held beliefs are embedded in the textbooks that teachers select (and in turn shaped by the textbooks' tacit model of learning).

The system is self-perpetuating. New teachers and preservice teachers adopt a set of beliefs and learn the tradition from what is taught in their education courses, from their cooperating teachers who sponsor them during their student teaching, and from mentors who take them under their wing, guiding them through mandated curricula taught with prescribed textbooks. In fact, many a new teacher has been all but told to ignore their college professors' idealistic notions and to start adjusting to the reality of the outside world.

Hollie Kotwica's (2002) first year of teaching is pretty typical. Despite her university preparation, Hollie explains that she was

> expected to follow the direction of the other English teacher on the sixth-grade team. Administration made it clear that teachers should be "on the same page" if they were teaching the same subject. Filing cabinets full of worksheets from the other traditional English teacher were wheeled into my room, and daily lesson plans were placed in my mailbox, consisting of the systematic, direct approach of definitions, rules, drills, and practice, all of which I believed to be ineffective practices. However, the other teachers on my team insisted that the systematic, direct approach worked, and my teammates were not interested in the thematic approach to education. Being a new teacher, I was afraid to challenge the veterans, so I began my teaching career doing exactly what I never imagined I would do. I became a traditionalist, and I hated it! Every day I tortured my students and myself. Following what the traditional English teacher had given me exactly, I introduced the definition or rule of a grammatical concept by reading from our textbook, practiced sample sentences with the students, and had them complete follow-up worksheets to drill and practice the new skill. Even though we did this every day, the students still could not pass the tests, and their writing skills were not improving. Using the systematic, direct approach for teaching grammar

seemed to keep the students quiet because the work was mindless, but during drill and practice time, I could not keep the students on task. Since the work had no value and was a meaningless enterprise, the students frequently acted out. Thinking that my enthusiasm for the subject was the problem, I developed rather interesting approaches to grammar lessons. I frequently stood on the desks, dancing and singing to coax my students' attention. Cutesy pictures became the norm in my lessons along with dramatic interpretation of rules and definitions of grammatical concepts. I learned quickly that drama and colorful pictures were never going to carry my lessons. These practices simply entertained, but did not teach. Students can only learn through meaningful enterprise, and the activities that I was engaging my students in were clearly not meaningful. Discouraged, I felt like I had failed my students and myself. When the other teachers suggested that I "make the students more accountable" by taking off more points for grammatical mistakes on writing assignments, I could not take it anymore. From that day on, I decided to make a change. . . . To make these changes in my classroom, I would need to take risks.

Thus, in Kuhn's terms, with the exception of courageous teachers like Hollie, the system is self-perpetuating; it remains stable, even in the face of common sense and research data to the contrary. Education remains unchanged despite the fact that every time there's an election or a new president, the first item on the agenda is always education. One reason the system remains unchanged is that, even though each politician promises to make education the number one priority, they all begin oddly enough with testing (Bush 2002; Clinton 1997; Walsh 2001). None of them wants to begin at the real starting place—investigating how children learn and then moving on to providing support for it to happen!

Our definition of learning is an outgrowth of our philosophy, of our belief system. In schools today there are two major belief systems. One is based on behaviorist principles, the "taxonomy of learning" developed by Benjamin Bloom (1956), a follower of B. F. Skinner (1953), in turn a follower of John Watson (1912), the founder of behavioral psychology. The other is based on constructivist principles (Dewey 1922; Piaget 1954; Vygotsky 1978). One says that learning occurs as a result of stimulus in the environment; the other says learning occurs when a learner actively constructs meaning from elements in the environment. Both paradigms are visible and one or the other is dominant, depending on the current political and cultural climate.

Curriculum in a Traditional Classroom

Much of what is done in current traditional teaching and learning is based on Bloom's taxonomy, which holds that "stimulus-response" learning, or rote memorization, is the easiest type of learning and that applying and evaluating knowledge is the most difficult. Educators who looked to behavioral psychology to explain learning found a science concerned with the behavior of subjects "learning" to pass through mazes and hit buttons necessary to release food pellets. For early educational psychologists, simple observation of how learning occurs and inductive knowledge did not count as acceptable scientific methods. For research to be regarded as "scientific" in the behavioral sense, it had to be based on the study of animals, not human children, and in controlled laboratory settings, not in the home or real classrooms. Such investigations employing counting and measurement, with variables under control, concluded that motivation and reinforcement were necessary for what they considered learning—rote memorization and recall—to occur.

American schools seem to follow traditional approaches in the teaching of English language arts, based on behaviorist principles. Since behavioral psychology, in general, supports learning that takes place from part to whole, students in English classes always seem to begin with lessons that focus on grammar, mechanics, spelling, and vocabulary lists, followed by numerous skills exercises, each having one correct answer. The text used in secondary and college English classrooms is often a grammar handbook, a classic such as Warriner's *Grammar and Composition* or Strunk and White's *Elements of Style*, supplemented with workbooks and dittos for the practice of skills. When students write, they write essays on assigned topics, in prescribed formats such as "comparison and contrast," with a prescribed length assigned in numbers of words, and they write for a known audience—their teacher. If they read literature, it is chosen for them from a narrow set of what are thought to be the classics or what Arthur Applebee (1992) found to be the great American standards—*Romeo and Juliet, Macbeth, Julius Caesar, Hamlet, Huckleberry Finn, To Kill a Mockingbird, The Scarlet Letter, Of Mice and Men, The Great Gatsby, Lord of the Flies*, and *The Odyssey*. Despite Applebee's claim that teaching literature "has usually been defined rather broadly, around important authors and traditions rather than around a few essential texts," the fact that the same works are taught with regularity at public schools, Catholic schools, and independent schools alike argues for "specific texts [being] . . . singled out for special attention" by the anthology publishers and the standardized testmakers (31). Reading literature and writing essays is the curriculum taught by English teachers in English classes, and the rest of the knowledge needed for life in the twenty-first century is handled by others, teachers of history, math, and science who see themselves as responsible for their own specific content area, and certainly not responsible for the teaching of language skills. In traditional classrooms the teachers are the holders of knowledge, and it is their job to transmit this knowledge to students, who are expected to sit still, not talk unless called on, and concentrate on instruction that many find boring and frustrating. Traditional expectations are often difficult for students with high energy levels and short attention spans to meet; thus, failure to comply leads to further behavioral problems.

Such behaviorist orientation controls classrooms in high schools and universities in which students are expected to memorize information and regurgitate ideas and facts that were transmitted to them through lectures and textbooks. In the behavioral paradigm, an educated person is said to be one who has learned the necessary "facts," one who is culturally literate, one who knows what his or her culture has tacitly agreed are the important facts to possess.

Curriculum in a Constructivist Classroom

As teachers tried to deal with puzzles unexplained by behavioral psychology, other disciplines helped shift the informed model of learning away from the "transmission" model of teaching advocated by behaviorists, one in which teachers are little more than "scripted technicians" passing on a curriculum established by others outside the classroom. For example, cognitive psychology offered insight as to how the human mind learns, developmental psychology emphasized the importance of experiences during early childhood, psycholinguistics provided connections between thought and language, sociology underscored the communal aspect of learning, and anthropology highlighted the study of culture from an insiders' point of view. As a result, over the past twenty years or so, the standard model of learning has moved toward a "transactional" model of learning, a constructivist philosophy of instruction in which learners actively engage with their teachers, their classmates, and their environment to create a curriculum (Smith 1988).

As a student, secondary school teacher Melanie Bills remembers she didn't

always sit in rows, always take tests, always do this or that. Especially in high school, I was fortunate to have what many would consider innovative teachers who were willing to experiment with their methods in class. The one class that I truly think made the greatest impact...was my AP English class my senior year....I took *her* class because I knew her to be a bit out of the ordinary. I saw the way her classroom looked physically: the words from floor to ceiling, the colored cellophane on the windows, the desks arranged in a circle. I really wanted to be *in* that room. Once in her class, I quickly realized how different this English course was compared with others I had taken. As a class, we did freewriting on the first day and frequently thereafter, we had writing families to share our drafts of papers with and to receive feedback from....It was extremely creative, open, but still tough. She still *really* pushed us to work. (Siebert et al. 1997, 110)

Some of the differences between transactional and transmission models of education can be illustrated by contrasting a traditional and a constructivist classroom (see Figure 1–2). In a transactional classroom, the teacher facilitates the students' construction of knowledge through active engagement in authentic learning tasks reflecting students' interests and needs. If learning is a process of actively constructing meaning, not an accumulation of skills, then English instruction takes place in the context of real reading and writing, reading whole pieces of literature independently and in groups, supported by oral reading and shared reading strategies, and writing for a variety of purposes across the curriculum, responding to the literature that they are reading, making observations, and keeping journals. In general, a transactional classroom emphasizes adjusting the curriculum to meet the needs and interests of the students, instead of pressuring students to meet the demands of a prescribed and rigid curriculum. Students learn by constructing meaning from the world around them. Watch how people make sense of their world—from solving the murder in a game of "Clue" to assembling a swingset for the grandchildren to understating tax code—and see how important constructing hypotheses and testing them out are to learning.

How methodologies of instruction can come from both philosophies, and how they work their way to defining practice, is much more difficult to illustrate in a chart. Just as one can register to be a Democrat or a Republican, one's political beliefs are usually on a continuum and the overlapping middle ground allows compromises to be made so the parties can work together toward common goals. We may register as fundamentally subscribing to the principles of either a behaviorist or constructivist philosophy of teaching and learning, but our methodologies and practice are on a continuum. Do constructivists ever lecture? Of course; sometimes it's helpful to provide students with information, not as an end in itself but as a part of the bigger picture. If desks are arranged in clusters rather than straight rows, does that signal a constructivist classroom in which students are working together, constructing learning as a community? Not if they're working on exercises that are busy work with no authentic purpose. As Melanie Bills says, "more important than the labels we attach to pedagogies is the ongoing spirit of innovation that leads good teachers to continue to find ways to guide their students" (Siebert et al. 1997, 110).

Since the way a teacher believes his or her students learn is what determines whether that person is a behaviorist or a constructivist, one's philosophy can't be a little bit of both, because they are opposite belief systems; however, each teacher could use practices that are common in the other paradigm. It's not a matter of black and white or good and evil, but rather what beliefs good teachers hold about how to best help students learn. The best constructivist and behaviorist teachers have in common a belief in their students, a concern for their welfare, and a

Transmission Philosophy Traditional Classroom		Transactional Philosophy Constructivist Classroom
1. Behaviorist model—based on stimulus/response learning of behavioral psychology	Basis of Philosophy	1. Cognitive/social model—based on research in developmental psychology, linguistics, sociology, and anthropology
2. Teachers are dispensers of knowledge. Teachers lecture and give the impression that there is one correct answer or interpretation—the teacher's.	Teacher Role	2. Teachers are facilitators. Teachers demonstrate what it means to be a reader and a writer by reading and writing in and outside of the classroom and by respecting student responses.
3. Students strive for "right" answers and see success and learning as high test scores and good grades.	Student Role	3. Students are risk takers. They see learning as an opportunity for open-ended response and critical thinking.
4. Prescribed curriculum; determined outside the classroom and driven by tests and standards.	Curriculum	4. Curriculum generated by teacher and students based on inquiry and need. Emphasis is on meaning-making and students' schemas help to connect to new understandings
5. Emphasis on discreet skills, such as vocabulary, grammar, and spelling; skills must be mastered as a precursor to reading and writing.	Skills	5. Skills such as vocabulary, grammar, and spelling are taught in the context of authentic literacy experiences; skills are tools for the effective reader and writer and are learned as a result of reading and writing.
6. Desks in rows, texts are basis of curriculum. Teacher lecturing in front of room, bulletin boards empty or decorated with school schedule and fire drill rules. Students take notes, respond when called upon.	Physical Environment	6. Environment is designed to promote literacy development. Variety of language materials are readily available for student use and student work is displayed. Classroom becomes a clustering of literature and writing groups where peer groups and individuals work and teachers/peers conference.
7. Teachers evaluate primarily by grading products or by giving tests. These tools focus on what students do not know. A successful teacher hopes for a bell curve.	Evaluation	7. Teachers are "kidwatchers," evaluating and assessing student progress based on observation, focusing on what students can do.

Figure 1–2. Contrasting models of education: A traditional/transmission classroom versus a constructivist/transactional classroom

continuing search for the best way to teach, based on who they are and how they see the world.

Notwithstanding whatever paradigm is dominant in our profession or in our schools, most of us are developing along a continuum, moving toward more authentic teaching and learning. Since none of us is 100 percent one philosophy or the other, each of us is moving, we hope, toward becoming a more transactional teacher. As teachers make changes in their teaching, they learn that change—any change—grows out of a perceived need, involves trusting, making attempts, and taking risks, and results in various successes and failures.

Moving along that continuum means embracing certain beliefs about language learning, such as:

1. Students learn by constructing meaning from the world around them, something quite different from learning by imitation. At the traditional–transmission end of the continuum, students are believed to learn by listening to lectures, copying notes, memorizing information, and reproducing the items on a test. Real learning is not a matter of simple transmission— telling what is; it depends on making hypotheses, testing them, making mistakes, taking risks, using what is able to be transmitted to discover what might yet be. In an article titled "Question Authority," Gerald W. Bracey (2001) praises a school culture that encourages the asking of questions that stimulate thought and discussion and fosters high-risk research, which may not always produce results but sometimes results in Nobel Prizes. Bracey warns, "we'd better think more than twice about replacing a culture that values questions with one that worships high test scores" (191).

2. Language learning is not sequential. At the traditional–transmission end of the continuum, reading is taught as a progression of skills, objectively tested through comprehension questions, to be certain that students understand main ideas and note important details. Regrettably, the teaching of writing has often followed this same traditional premise of learning subskills instead of whole processes. Students spend time on learning editing skills—spelling, grammar, and sentence structure taught through drill and practice—instead of real writing. This is what Jeff Golub (1994) of the University of South Florida likes to call "pumping the brakes while the car is still in the garage!" (33). The rules by which language is generated, and learned, are too complex to be regarded as "habit learning" and behaviorist approaches trivialize language and learning (Chomsky 1957). Two aspects of language could not be accounted for by behaviorist explanations: "First, virtually every sentence that a person utters or understands is a brand-new combination of words, appearing for the first time in the history of the universe. Therefore,

a language cannot be a repertoire of responses; the brain must contain a recipe or program that can build an unlimited set of sentences out of a finite list of words. . . . The second fundamental fact is that children develop these complex grammars rapidly and without formal instruction and grow up to give consistent interpretations to novel sentence constructions that they have never before encountered" (Pinker 1994, 9).

3. Language learning is linked; reading and writing skills develop simultaneously along with oral language skills. Students learn to read while they are writing and they learn about writing by reading. They may also learn about reading and writing while listening, but not when forced to listen exclusively to class lectures by their teacher. It is no wonder that students rarely pay attention during a lecture, an activity designed to exercise the teacher's language abilities, not the students'.

4. Curriculum in a transactional classroom is not a prescribed course of study, instead learning occurs when students are engaged and teachers are demonstrating. When the curriculum is set by those outside the classroom— textbook manufacturers, school boards, test makers, politicians—how can it be pertinent to the teachers who must teach it and the students who must learn it? At the traditional–transmission end of the continuum, students are assumed to perform according to their teacher's own expectations, while transactional teachers provide their students with opportunities to demonstrate what decisions they, as language users, are interested in and capable of making.

5. Although missteps and errors are inherent in the learning process, learners need to be encouraged to be risk takers. To develop a conception of themselves as readers and writers, students need opportunities to transact with print, think, create, and make mistakes, in an atmosphere of mutual respect, as they engage in real learning. If teachers hope to establish a community of learners, they need to model the behavior they hope to develop (Zemelman and Daniels 1988).

6. Reading and writing are authentic context-specific forms of communication; secondary and postsecondary students use reading and writing for real purposes and for real audiences. Directing students to write without an authentic audience or meaningful purpose is like asking them to talk into a disconnected phone with no one at the other end to listen and respond. No one talks into a "dead" phone (another of Jeff Golub's wonderful metaphors). It's an artificial, unproductive exercise, leaving the speaker or writer unmotivated and uninterested. Authentic communication, on the other hand, invites engagement as students transact with their audience, from whom they receive honest feedback and response.

Thus, a constructivist does not follow a course of study merely because it's prescribed; instead the teacher allows the curriculum to evolve as learning occurs, when students are engaged in making meaning, learning what is worthwhile, useful, and important to learn, as Alfie Kohn (1999) tells us in *The Schools Our Children Deserve*. Central to this philosophy is the belief that learning—and the teaching that stimulates it—proceeds from whole to part and back to whole, and therefore language learning is integral and inseparable. Students learn language and literacy simultaneously in environments that permit them to read, write, listen, and speak for a variety of authentic purposes. A transactional–constructivist philosophy embraces the progressive ideal of teaching students, rather than subject matter, and respecting each student as an individual learner, each blessed with unique needs and abilities. Thus, transactional classrooms are student-centered, focusing around a curriculum that is organic, growing with and out of teachable moments as they exist in the classroom. As students work together and their teacher provides opportunities to interact, they become responsible for their learning. Though a student-centered classroom might seem unstructured to those used to a traditional classroom with straight rows of quiet students, transactional teachers provide a structure that includes the social aspects of learning—people moving around, groups of students talking and working together, the teacher conferencing with students individually or in groups. A student-centered philosophy of learning may even be particularly beneficial to students with learning difficulties, including attention disorders, as teachers encourage moving around in classrooms to work in groups, locate resources, and move from learning center to learning center (Weaver 1994).

Though teachers have a responsibility to facilitate the curriculum prescribed by their district, especially in states such as Texas and California that have statewide adoption of textbooks and curriculum, this doesn't mean they must always cover the curriculum sequentially using traditional means. Even in districts that give teachers little choice in what materials they will use and in what sequence each item will be taught, constructivist teachers can take what they know about learning and use methods and practices that support authentic, meaningful learning. Although it is definitely more confining, even prescribed curricula can be taught from a constructivist point of view.

For example, a teacher found that she had to cover Coleridge's famous poem, "Rime of the Ancient Mariner," and panicked. She turned to a network of teachers who belong to a email listserv organized by Jeff Golub, of the University of South Florida. The next day she had a dozen ideas of how to teach prescribed curriculum from a transactional perspective. Linda Peters (2001) suggested connecting them to the central message of the poem by having the students write about a time when they felt responsible for something bad that happened to someone else and how they decided to make up for it. After reading the poem, the discussion could return to these schema-activating writings and generate ways to make up with people we've wronged. In small groups, students could discuss whether their "wrong act" was intentional or accidental, and then debate whether the mariner's transgression was on purpose or accidental. They could discuss the concept of "burden," as in "burden of guilt." The students could also do reader's theatre with the poem by dividing the class and the poem into groups/sections and reading it/acting it out. Linda advises, "Everyone has to have a part, but not necessarily a character part. They can do sound effects, some can whisper, echo, etc. . . . Additional activities can include drawing ghost ships and some of the characters . . . painting the scenes in the poem on a butcher block paper 'mural,' including symbols. . . . selecting music that corresponds to the mood of each section of the poem and explaining their selection." Linda says she usually has the unit culminate in a written paper, but what's important is that students make a personal connection with the poem. Finally, she recommends making sure "the lesson ends on a positive note. All things matter, no matter how small."

Student-Centered Classrooms

As we said, transactional classrooms are environments in which students' own needs and experiences provide the motivation for reading, writing, listening, and speaking activities. Areas of study evolve and develop as students identify areas of interest and questions are raised through reading and investigation. Such areas of study are student-centered and depend on the teacher to facilitate learning based on student need and interest. Risk taking is encouraged in a transactional classroom and students learn from experience. Transactional teachers recognize that questioning is an integral part of understanding and subsequent learning, and they work to establish an atmosphere in which students are comfortable taking risks. Students must understand what is presented, processing the information and relating it to what is already known. At the point where one student is confused, the learning has stopped for that student and others in the class who may share the student's confusion. As commonsensical as this seems, it flies in the face of those who see an uninterrupted presentation of material as a well-organized lesson.

Because transactional classrooms involve a exchange between students and teacher, no two classrooms are alike. Each class is unique; however, similarities can be found in the structure, purposes, strategies, and atmosphere of a student-centered classroom.

1. The design of the classroom promotes literacy development; that is, literacy materials are readily available, and students work cooperatively with each

other in clusters—literature groups, writing groups, and discussion groups—that are formed for many different reasons, including shared interests, or as individuals transacting with each other and their teacher.

2. Students engage in literacy activities daily, selecting what they read and write about from a variety of sources.

3. Literacy is taught in the context of meaningful transactions; oral and written communication should "make sense."

4. Skills are taught in the context of language to students who need appropriate instruction rather than as isolated exercises given in "blanket coverage" format to whole classes.

5. Students are risk takers; they see learning as an exciting opportunity for open-ended response and critical thinking.

6. Teachers act as facilitators rather than dispensers of knowledge, modeling what it means to be a reader and a writer, sharing their literacy experiences with their students and as "kidwatchers" (Y. Goodman 1978), evaluating and assessing student progress based on observation, focusing on what students can do.

What Happens When They Get to the Next Grade?

As we support the ways people learn, our pedagogy changes. Workshop approaches, cooperative learning, process orientation, hands-on authentic learning situations are all part of today's classroom because of what we now understand about learning, what research has shown us about supporting learners. We believe that if anything about learning is to make sense, our methods of measuring progress and reporting such progress must reflect our pedagogy. Teachers have noticed increasing cases where a score on a multiple-choice test or an SAT score doesn't reflect what they know is happening in a particular student's academic life. These teachers are interested in finding ways to measure the depth of their students' thinking, how their students are putting the pieces together, and where to go when their students come to class tomorrow depending on them for support.

Nevertheless, teachers brave enough to challenge the notion of covering a curriculum, yet still often working in isolation, confess that they worry about what happens when their students move to the next level. Will they be prepared to handle whatever is covered in the next grade and to know whatever's on the next test? The truth is that coverage doesn't equate to performance or preparation. To clarify by using an analogy from another environment where coverage is important: when a house painter works, he or she prepares the surface and applies the appropriate paint, but how well the paint is absorbed is often beyond the control of the painter; a lot depends on the material he or she is painting. Sometimes another coat works; sometimes multiple applications or a change of color are needed. Merely repainting one section usually gives an uneven finish. Regardless, the paint is absorbed according to the nature of the material and there is variation even between sections of the same material. Our students' minds are like the painted surface; each student absorbs what is taught in different ways to different degrees. To hope for uniformity is unreasonable. One of the reasons why human beings are so fascinating is that every student, in fact, every person, knows different things and constructs different readings of every text. This is also the reason why what is tested is not always what's important to learn.

For example, many students read *The Red Badge of Courage* at some point in their lives. A test question could ask, *during what war did the story take place?* Knowing that the answer is the Civil War is not knowing the book. What an individual student understands of the war and of the novel is a matter of the individual's schema of the world. We're not even sure one could ask a literal interpretation question about badges, since their knowledge of badges might be limited to police badges and ID badges worn by hospital personnel (or school personnel in some cities), unless a student had experienced achieving badges in Scouting. The meaning of the story for each individual will be shaped and refined during interactions with other readers, including those with the teacher. Since test makers have no access to these discussions, they can only ask about the most obvious, trivial matters or about interpretations that may not be appropriate for the group of readers being tested. And since students are active learners, they should not be forced to memorize discrete bits of information about literature or look for "one-answer" readings of story. When afforded opportunities to engage with literature, students will discuss, discover, consider, represent, and reread to make meaning. In fact, some researchers suggest that reading is a meaning-making transaction between the reader and the text (Probst 1992; Rosenblatt 1978). The words on the page may be cues from the author, but readers make meaning through personal knowledge, associations, feelings, and experiences as they interact with the text. And since each reader—young person or adult—creates meaning in the act of reading, each classroom is unique, evolving and taking shape according to the personalities of the students who inhabit them.

Ten years ago the metaphor we used to describe the educational approach we were advocating was *un-covering the curriculum*, unwrapping the program, releasing the restrictive, dictated, scripted lessons to be covered in any given year. Now we see the metaphor as *engagement*, being committed to learning, and emphasizing the students' half of the transaction. The metaphor is an apt one: we engage rocket thrusters; we engage in conversation; when we decline an offer because we're otherwise engaged, it means we're engaged in some other important matter. The transaction depends upon a teacher and a learner who are both engaged in making learning meaningful. Therefore, it is the teacher, as a trained professional, who should make curricular decisions after assessing students' individual strengths and needs. The challenge is for teachers to take control of the curriculum from the demigods who impose a prepackaged set of lessons to be completed in a predetermined order; the challenge is to be engaged in learning.

For Further Exploration

1. Think about your experiences as a learner in high school. How did you feel about language learning—writing and literature? Would you consider your experiences to be traditional or constructivist? Why?

2. Based on your experiences as a learner, how do you or will you teach? What are your goals as a teacher of adolescents or young adults? What is your classroom like? Why?

3. Visit several secondary classes. What philosophy of teaching and learning are evident? What criteria did you use to label these classrooms? Did English classes differ from classes in other content areas?

4. Interview several secondary teachers. Ask them their views of teaching and learning. How do they define their philosophy and how do they think it impacts their approach to teaching? If possible, observe these teachers teaching. Do you see practice that is consistent with what the teachers articulated in your interviews with them?

5. Interview several secondary students. How do they view their role in the classroom? How do they see the role reading and writing plays in their learning? What have their experiences been in learning to read and write?

2

Asking Questions, Facilitating Inquiry

*Questions include; they invite. By their definition they demand a
dialogue; someone is asking another to respond. . . . we might say
that what gets asked is what gets considered. . . . a class is not only
defined by the questions we ask, but the extent to which our
students themselves help to shape or ask these questions.*

—Jim Burke

Many comedies, from Shakespeare to *Back to the Future* films, are based on the
premise of someone who arrives from another time, culture, or country not knowing the rules for behavior. Learning the rules that govern behavior in different
situations is part of normal social development. And so, unlike any foreign vis-
itors, students in classrooms across the country are highly sensitive to the rules
of classroom behavior and the consequences for following or not following the
protocol.

When we went to school the unstated but nevertheless well-known rules for
conduct were that students sit quietly in their seats arranged in rows, eyes forward
on the teacher and the chalkboard; students speak only when addressed and raise
their hands to ask or answer a question; and, sometimes students would have to
rise and stand next to their desk to speak when called on. This is what we might
characterize as the extreme of traditional classroom behavior. Information flows
in one direction, from teacher to pupil, and any questions that are asked by the
teacher are done to test the attention and understanding of the class.

This transmission model for the classroom was derived from the language
model of the nineteenth century, one in which teachers would convey some facet
of the curriculum through lecture or exemplary models. Pedagogy revolved around
recitations, declamations, disputations; students would memorize passages and recite when called on, conjugate verbs, or parse constructions in texts to demonstrate
their learning. Since the object of the teaching was to teach educated taste and

the art of thinking, students were often assigned a thesis to defend or dispute orally and later prepare in written form. The ubiquitous "research paper" survives as a remnant of the days when debating and forensic activity were popular.

A Different Approach

A different set of rules for behavior exists in a constructivist, transactional class-room, and the different protocol can be confusing to students who are expecting one world and find themselves in another. Since transactional classrooms have a different perspective on how language is used to negotiate learning between stu-dents and teachers, classroom rules are based on the premise that knowledge flows in two directions, between master and apprentice, expert and novice. Students sit in various arrangements, circles, small groups, rows, and sometimes don't sit at all. Instead of confirming reception of transmitted information by repeating, rephrasing, or regurgitating the information back to the teacher, learning is cer-tified through a negotiated transaction in language between students, teachers, peers, and texts.

The discovery of ways to demonstrate that learning has occurred is an essential part of the student's response in a constructivist classroom, and the teacher's role as facilitator of such student-centered response is equally important. These inquiry-based classrooms, ones in which teachers create environments that support students posing real questions and learning to conduct and write authentic research-based projects (though not confined to the study of English alone) are dependent upon a transactional sense of reading and writing. When teachers share decision making with their students, turning over some of the power of learning, if you will, some teachers feel a loss of control and want to regain a sense of feeling organized and competent. "Many of the students have not experienced this degree of autonomy before. The structure does not meet their expectations of what a classroom is like. [It] asks them to behave in ways that they do not usually associate with school behavior" (Wieland 1990, 2). Teachers in a student-centered classroom are or-chestrating the learning—providing space for the students to perform, giving cues, coordinating efforts, blending talents, and making it happen. Believe us, this takes much more work than dusting off some yellowed lecture notes! It takes establishing a community of learners in which everyone's ideas are respected and valued.

Complicated by Our Expectations

Teaching is complicated by our expectations. If we expect students to be lazy, or to cheat, or to take the shortcut, they will. If we expect students to be as cynical as we are, they will be. If we expect students to give their all, they will. But all this is tempered by *their* expectations. Since each student sees our classroom based on his or her previous experiences and situations, we are always dealing with each student's past. If they expect teachers to act superior, to trick them, to embarrass them, then they naturally live up to those expectations. Some students have learned how to fail rather than how to succeed. Students who have experienced significant failure (retention included) are afraid of success. Success today means teachers expect you to succeed the next day. Amy Walker (2001) experiences this in her class: "Many of my students are afraid to take the risks inherent in learning, and they are even more fearful of success. They worry that if they succeed a few times, the teacher might expect them to succeed all of the time. [One student] expressed this concern when he asked, 'If I do good today, do I have to do good next time?'" (144).

It's easier in terms of work and dignity to live down to people's expectations of you and fail. It takes the pressure off; you're left alone. In Sandra Cisneros' (1991) "Eleven," the narrator says that you might be eleven, but inside you are still the person who was ten and nine and eight. And sometimes the four-year-old appears. So our students might be in our class for the moment but are always living or reliving the class they had last year or two years ago or their third-grade experiences. Perhaps this is one reason that many teachers aspire to establishing the classroom as a community of learners but have difficulty achieving it. Creating a community involves understanding a lot about group dynamics, how groups form, operate, continue, and dissolve. Steven Zemelman and Harvey Daniels (1988) offer the insight that some behavior that teachers suspect is off-task and disruptive may actually be essential to building and maintaining group sensibilities. This behavior, called maintenance behavior, is "normal and necessary whenever humans try to work in groups; it not only meets the creature needs but provides the social lubrication that makes collaborative effort possible" (53). These social activities include "eating, gossiping, moving furniture, borrowing pencils, . . . expressing and responding to feelings. . . . all the complex support behavior necessary to make task behavior work" (52–53).

It is easy to see why this behavior might be seen as disruptive. Teachers have to resist at every turn the pressure they feel to always be in control. Jim Mahoney (2002) says it's about power:

Power plays a crucial role in schools—with students, with teachers, with building administrators, central office staff, the board of education, and with the community. Ask one question about school and see if it doesn't have something to do with compliance: somebody wanting somebody else to do something or be something. . . . It's not that students don't want to become good writers or to compose their lives, or to discover the magic of writing so that they might explore and create. It's just that they keep getting different signals from their teachers. The teachers too want their students to become strong writers and readers but too often they withhold the power to allow students to get there. And the problem is deeper than that. Even good teachers are so entrenched in the system that they don't see the problem at all. Many of them too are trying or have been trying to "figure it all out," to wrestle with the power they have but may not be using wisely. It is a lifelong process for teachers, [and] as students helped me, I was able to help them do the same. In collaboration, we were able to discover some truly literate classrooms. (1–2)

Teachers must be facilitators of inquiry. They must realize that "learning is something that occurs inside of learners when conditions are right" and that it's their job to try to see that the conditions are right (2). Teachers must act in a variety of roles and refrain from sending conflicting messages that work against social community building, such as not tolerating socializing, having to have the last word in encounters with students, interpreting student bids for power as revolution, suppressing all forms of conflict. In other words, the methods learned in classroom management often work against community building. Teachers have to develop writing and reading activities that develop strong feelings of membership in the groups. Each person in the group needs a role to feel they are a true voting part of the franchise. Group development takes time, so teachers should refrain from reorganizing them too soon. Groups need time to work out interpersonal maintenance kinds of things before they can function effectively together (Zemelman and Daniels 1988, 60–61). Conflict is an important stage of development in group identity—challenges between students, tests of the teacher's authority, failure to comply with teacher-set or group-set rules or procedures. However, teachers often interpret this behavior as signals that the "group thing" isn't working. Students also resist because they've been taught to function alone and in competition. Zemelman and Daniels recommend some things to combat the sense that most students have that "they have no feeling of control or power over anything that happens to them" (65). Teachers want to "help *students* initiate, self-monitor, and self-evaluate" (65). Teachers have to believe students will work well in communities—our expectations shape our experience. Differences don't always need to be resolved but students need to learn how to give and receive feedback without feeling threatened or intimidated. Classrooms need to places for "win-win" situations, as we used to say.

Building community means recognizing that a traditional driving force in school, besides competition, is conformity (Jonsberg 2000). Students adhere to the unspoken rules: "don't stand out from the crowd" and "don't wreck the curve, or make everyone look bad by excelling." In the movie *Finding Forrester*, the young man explains why he never excelled at his neighborhood school. It wasn't that he wasn't bright; it wasn't that the teachers were bad. He just wanted to fit in. To stand out would get you ostracized, cut off from the group, labeled "lame" as sociolinguist William Labov explains it. Part of the competition and conformity code is cultural and not open for adjustment in our class, but as teachers, we need to build community, getting everyone involved or else no one beyond the few "teacher-pleasing" students will participate.

Teacher-Talk: How Much?

Connie Weaver (1994) is fond of saying that in her classroom if there are twenty-five students then there are twenty-six teachers, including herself. In such a case it's not unexpected that a change noticed in a transactional classroom is the teacher's physical position in the room. Students, and probably everyone else, expects the teacher to assume the position at the front of the room, a location some refer to as the "Big Desk" (Atwell 1985). The position is sacred, no matter if the teacher is behind a lectern or desk, half-seated, leaning on the edge of the desk, or sitting lotus fashion on the desk itself. Most of us have spent our lives in traditional classrooms, and we know what does not work. When transactional teachers step out from behind lecterns and desks, and they stop being the traffic cop for discussion in the classroom, issues arise such as, *Who does the talking? To whom are comments directed? In what context? How do we ensure that the talk is productive? What does it mean to facilitate discussion? What do we do when students want us to give information?* All these questions and more are important to transactional teachers. Even knowing what we know, it is hard to change what is familiar unless we understand the role of talk in our classrooms.

To model the type of discussion that encourages students to think and to take risks, transactional teachers must establish trust and a sense of community and purpose. This type of discussion not only gives students opportunities, it also requires that students become more responsible and involved. Before any type of real discussion can take place, the teacher must establish a sense of community, a climate for conversation that is relaxed but focused. The tone of the response from the teacher must be sincerely warm and friendly—students know when their teacher is "faking it" or pretending to be interested when he or she has another agenda. Conversation, whether at a dinner party or in a classroom, is a profound social activity that is based on genuine respect—respect for other's ideas, feelings, and reactions—and humility—understanding that the speaker is only one person in the conversation, someone with opinions but willing and eager to learn from the ideas of others, including students.

Calling on Students

New teachers and even veteran teachers get conflicting advice from administrators, other teachers, university professors, and colleagues about whether they should call on students directly. Some tell them to call directly on students, adjusting the mix of those called on who have raised hands and those who haven't, a practice supposedly insuring that everyone's attention is kept on the lesson. And their supervisors include this classroom management ability in their evaluations of them. Years ago when our daughter was in high school, she asked us at the dinner table, "Do teachers call on students who don't have their hands raised just to embarrass them? If you don't have your hand up, you don't know the answer; so, why put us on the spot?" Before we could offer an answer, Laura continued, "It doesn't really matter though. When I don't know the answer, I bend over, get a tissue from my backpack, and blow my nose. They never call on you when you blow your nose." Laura had figured out the system and learned how to survive.

Putting students on the spot shows disrespect for them as members of a community of learners. We agree with Jeff Golub (1994), author of *Activities for an Interactive Classroom*, who advises never to call on anyone who hasn't volunteered to share (37–38); we speak outside class or during group work to those who are reluctant to share to see if we can help them become more involved and ask their permission to call on them. Barbara Martin (2001), a new teacher in Florida, subscribes to the practice of only calling on those who volunteer. "It has worked remarkably well [and] it's contagious when the kids feel that what they have to say is valid. . . . There are other ways to participate." She suggests pairing the quiet or nonparticipating students with more extraverted students in group activities. "All I really know" she says, "is that I hated being called on in class. It is very intimidating and the only thing I learned were strategies to *avoid* being called on. I honestly did not remember the lesson, but I still remember the feeling."

Traditionally, the sort of questions teachers asked were known-answer questions, ones that they believe have one possible answer; students raise their hands; and, the teacher calls upon one of the students, who may or may not have volunteered to be called on. This type of questioning is the IRE model (Cazden 1988)— *Initiate* (question is asked by the teacher), *Respond* (student gives answer), and *Evaluate* (teacher evaluates "correctness" of answer, usually according to what's in the teacher's manual or the teacher's head). If the student's response doesn't match as "correct," the answer is sometimes dismissed with a "sort of" and "anyone else?" reply. Sometimes the questions are asked more to find out whether students are paying attention or following along than to find out if they are ultimately understanding. And this raises the second problem with calling on students. Questioning often promotes passivity among students (Good 1981). For example, students perceived by their teachers to be low achievers are called on less frequently, afforded less time for their response, and provided with the appropriate answer rather than suggestions to clarify or improve their reply, when their response differs from what the teacher expected. Teachers are also more likely, according to Good, to criticize such students' failures than praise their successes. Soon students stop trying and become passive learners.

The language of teachers' known-answer questions has its own rhetoric that affords cues in their phrasing and continues through the line of questioning (Wells 1986). For example, when teachers ask, "Can anyone tell me how the woods symbolize death to Robert Frost?" the language of the question restricts the range of answers. Rather than eliciting genuine response to the experience of the poem, the question acts as an attempt by the teacher to transmit known information, coaxing the class to discover the answer that the teacher already has in mind. "Oh, come on. What happens to your body when you die? Does it stop....?" Consequently, students learn to listen carefully for these cues, trying to "read the teacher's mind," so they will be able to guess the answer the teacher feels is "correct." And if questioning has traditionally been used to check the level of understanding, then students have learned that asking questions is an admission of confusion or incomplete understanding. Students realize that some teachers resent what they perceive are "dumb questions" that interrupt their presentations and know that asking these questions opens the door for ridicule and condescension.

Known-answer questions sometimes aren't even questions; they are directions for organizing and managing class time: "And a summary of our discussion is due tomorrow, isn't it?" "Does everyone see how the eyeglasses represent an all-seeing presence in the story?" "Would you like to read, Jeremy?" This constant substitution of questions for imperatives instructs students in the rhetoric of school-talk. One has only to watch children "play school" to notice how quickly they pick up the language and behavior we employ.

Questioning in transactional classrooms should afford students opportunities to work out possibilities. When teachers lead discussions with answers in their heads that they either anticipate or have gotten from teacher's manuals, the discussion is constrained by the boundaries of their preconceptions. One of the lessons we've learned from our grandson Ryan, who has autism, is that there are multiple, alternative ways of viewing much of what goes on around us. One day while on a visit to the pumpkin patch with his preschool class, Ryan's attention was not on the round, orange gourds on the ground but on the criss-crossed wooden fence around the pumpkin patch. Ryan was fascinated by the repeating Xs the fence made. None of the other children noticed what Ryan saw that morning, perhaps because the teachers thought they should be looking at pumpkins. Questioning should have as much to do with thinking and hypothesizing as it does with answering, maybe more. Teachers need to step back and listen; they need to let students discover "answers" and often generate entirely new possibilities or new questions. Teachers need to learn how to do this because teachers haven't seen it modeled. It takes practice to learn how to facilitate discussions using open-ended questions. Framing sentences with the following openings helps when we're new to this.

- What would you predict will happen?
- What can you connect this to?
- What would you change?
- What was your favorite part?
- What did you notice in this?
- What did you realize about this?
- What did you feel when you closed the book?
- What seems like the most important idea?
- What didn't happen that you thought should have?

Facilitating Discussion

Every teacher shares the dream of having students who are "so involved in classroom discussions that they . . . jump into the talk passionately, stating opinions, questioning, arguing a point, providing evidence for their opinions, challenging, drawing out the ideas of others—almost as in a verbal swordfight" (Wieland 1990, 1–2). It may be difficult, however, to convince students that questions are honestly sought and welcomed and even part and parcel of how discussions are conducted.

Students learn what teachers want in their classrooms, and unfortunately, their learned behaviors are part of a model based on the transmission of knowledge and student passivity rather than on transactional learning and student involvement (Wieland 1990). To move from a teacher-directed model of questioning and discussion to one of a student-centered facilitator, discussions need to take place among groups of students, sometimes without the teacher present. Questions need to be seen as useful for finding out information and answers offered in discussions are seen as ways of explaining one's point in discussion. Some suggestions for successful class discussions, based on Sharon Wieland's (1990) research are:

- Remember that listening is one of the five language arts, along with reading, writing, speaking, and viewing. Teachers as well as students should be listeners. Instead of trying to summarize and shape each student's response, teachers need to let the class react to what was said. This will in turn help students listen to each other better.

- Be more aware of what body language communicates. Shaking one's head, opening one's eyes wider, biting one's lip, crossing one's arms, and furrowing one's brow tell students what their teacher really thinks. Teachers need to monitor what their bodies are saying.
- Learn to ask authentic questions. Thinking aloud as one ponders what a student has said can prove disarming to students who are conditioned to seeing everything as a criticism, so at the beginning of the year, it couldn't hurt to preface such remarks with, "I don't know the answer to this and I'm just thinking aloud here . . . . "
- Control the din only when it becomes impossible to think. Active rooms are noisy. Many teachers know the surest way to quiet a room is to put students in a group and tell them to discuss; conversely, the students working on individual projects will at some point turn to classmates and engage them in conversation, often about the topic they are working on. So, authentic activity gives rise to authentic conversation, which sometimes becomes loud.
- Turn control over to students. Instead of framing the task as, "I want you to tell me . . . ," students can be told to "tell each other . . ." and to share responses later with the entire class.

As teachers, we can teach students how to discuss by modeling what listeners and group members do; we need to be part of the community instead of the "sage on stage."

Risk Taking

In a transactional classroom, questioning is used in a very different context and for different purposes. In such a classroom, questioning supports risk taking; there is more than one way to look at something and differing views are encouraged. For example, when reading the Robert Frost poem previously mentioned, the teacher might start a discussion by asking, "Have you ever stopped an activity right in the middle of what you were doing? Try to remember a time when this happened? What were you doing? What caused you to stop? What interrupted you? Did you get back on track? What shook you up and got you back to the activity at hand?" Students could share their responses to these questions orally or in writing, with the entire class or in small groups.

The important thing is that transactional teachers believe that each student brings different experiences and schemata to any question, and therefore each student views questions or prompts from different perspectives. To respect this belief, teachers should treat whatever a student says as worthy of their attention as well as their classmates'; teachers should try to understand what the student means and to look at the question from that perspective or at least prompt the student to explain so the teacher and others can understand the student's perspective. Good teachers learn to listen actively to what a student is saying, an approach popularized by psychotherapist Carl Rogers (1969). This takes practice because most of humanity's misunderstanding result from mishearing what the other person said.

Active Listening

Teachers who ask questions often listen for a correct or predicted response. Students frequently give other replies. For example, a teacher asking about symbolism in Poe's "Raven" might respond positively, thanking the student, but then solicit other answers if the response was something like this: "It reminded me of a time when I was up late at night because I was alone in the house and I kept hearing all these creepy sounds." To improve the listening aspect of our teaching, we can practice saying back what the other said ("What I hear you saying is..."). A teacher who believes in active listening would draw out the previous student's response by saying back what was said, inflecting the statement as a question:

You were up late at night?
It bothered you to be alone in the house?
You heard creepy sounds?
The poem reminded you of this night?

It was unlikely that the student had fully considered the memory of being alone or drawn comparisons between personal experience and the poem when he or she offered the original response. With nonjudgmental active listening, the teacher draws the story out of the student, guiding and prompting the recall of circumstances and emotions. If students do not respond to the nondirective approach, teachers can try more direct questions that are still open ended:

Why were you alone?
Why might Poe's narrator have been alone?
How does Poe's narrator feel about being alone?
What would have made you feel better about being alone?
What would've made Poe feel better?
What words, phrases, or images in the poem reminded you of this experience; what exactly brought this back to you?

Active listening in class resembles a real conversation, one in which participants contribute something that they truly wish to share, and the others listen because they care about the person and the topic. Others present for the discussion will not only enjoy hearing their classmate's story, but will see their teacher supporting the development of their classmate's critical thinking in a nonintimidating way and, in turn, be encouraged to add their own response.

When students who are perceived to be "stronger" give replies that don't match the predicted response, most teachers give them opportunities to elaborate and clarify. Transactional teachers feel that *all* students should be given the same chance, including those who usually don't "play school" or see the world the way the teacher does. And so, transactional teachers frame the next comment or question on what the student meant by his or her response, instead of returning to a preconceived line of questioning, because their purpose is to stimulate thinking and response, not to elicit predetermined answers. Questioning in a transactional classroom is part of the meaning-making activity; it is a tool, but a nonthreatening and open-ended one.

Small Group Discussion

The fact that discussion is often thought of as a give-and-take situation among as many as thirty participants—the whole class and the teacher—is another problem. In a typical classroom, the numbers alone preclude what is needed for active discussion—attention, participation, and interaction. In whole class discussions, the teacher almost always talks too much as a consequence of assuming the role of moderator or discussion leader, the one whose role it is to keep the discussion moving forward. A more sensible way for teachers to include all students in discussions is to try small group discussion within the class. Unfortunately, this cannot happen immediately in the beginning of the semester because most secondary students are still uncomfortable with risk taking.

Before students will be comfortable joining in a discussion or responding to others, their teachers must refrain from dominating the discussion. And, as difficult as it is for teachers to let go of the leader role, it may be equally difficult for students to become active participants in a discussion. When students are just put in groups and simply asked to discuss something, the results are predictable. They initially sit and look at each other, and then one or two will try to guess what it is that they are supposed to say. Obviously, the climate is often strained and uncomfortable. Students need to be shown how to discuss matters in such a way that discussion groups will be productive, stimulating, and enjoyable. Providing students with a discussion model often helps them discover how to discuss while giving them the opportunity and responsibility of facilitating discussion.

There are many such models to follow, but in any discussion the participants must understand the purpose of the discussion and that all members of the group have a role to play. Assigning roles to each member of the group will help students all take part, especially early in the year when they are unfamiliar with the class and the community has not been established. The number and names of the roles don't really matter, but some of the popular roles are leader, note taker, time-keeper, questioner, and reporter (Hill, Johnson, and Schlick-Noe 1995). The role of the leader is to restate the question for discussion and keep everyone on track. This person's role includes not only keeping one individual from dominating but also drawing into the discussion others who haven't said very much. After the items for discussion and how long will be spent on each part have been established, the timekeeper's role is to set and keep the schedule. Often groups will leave a few minutes at the end to go back and sum up or return to an issue that they did not fully cover. The note taker's function is to jot down important facts and points as the discussion is underway. (The term *note taker* is preferred to the gender stereotyped term *secretary*.) The questioner's responsibility is to pose follow-up questions to either the small group or later to the whole class. The reporter, after conferring for a couple of minutes at the end with the note taker and the questioner, gives an account of the discussion to a larger group or the whole class.

At first the roles may seem somewhat stiff and formal, and students may pay more attention to the format than to the quality of discussion; but after awhile, the format becomes routine, and students have a forum in which to share ideas and respond to one another. If they take turns assuming different roles, the duties will become matter-of-fact as they go about their business. When students believe that what they have to say is important and that their ideas will be respected, they cannot help but be engaged in learning. As students become more confident about how to discuss, the formal roles will no longer be needed as members of the group function for the good of the conversation.

These roles are a little different from those assigned for literature circles that will be discussed later, roles that make different demands on readers during the act of reading; these general discussion roles seem to work well when the deliberation is about topics previously considered, assigned for homework, or brought up to engage schema.

Facilitating Inquiry

In a classroom where questions are for more than evaluation, students begin to ask questions themselves. Questioning becomes wondering, thinking about those things that students have a burning desire to know. We've found that secondary students often need to rekindle this natural tendency for inquiry that they had as small children. This is obvious in the beginning of the year when many students seem hard pressed to come up with topics to write about or even topics that they want to learn more about.

In the traditional classroom, a standard requirement is the research paper, a tired and often useless exercise that is left over from the old days, as we mentioned at the beginning of this chapter. However, in this information age, it is more important to form new understandings than to just paraphrase and summarize investigations someone else has already conducted. Granted, part of a secondary teacher's responsibility is to teach the process and form of research papers, but teaching the process and purpose of real researching must come first, which always begins with a desire to know. We begin here, helping students discover the topics that are seminal in their lives, ones which are worth the time and effort that real research demands. To do that, we abandon the traditional topics for research paper: gun control, euthanasia, capitol punishment, and other topics that students may have an interest in but generally no personal investment. We spend class time discussing and sharing topics which would be worth our while researching. For example, one semester we had spent time doing what many professionals in their fifties do—planning for our retirement ten or fifteen years down the road. Although we had participated in retirement savings, we were now at a point in our lives where it was important to understand how to best plan for the years when we wouldn't be getting a weekly salary. We began by framing these real questions about planning and investing. Another semester, the link between autism and vaccinations became an important issue to us since our grandson had been diagnosed with autism. We had a burning desire to understand what causes autism, which made it not only of interest to us, but worth our time and energy to investigate. Although some believe people can be given good prompts to research, much the way newspaper reporters are given assignments, we believe a desire for answers to the questions we ask ourselves is what drives our research; the information we gather and synthesize should have an impact on our lives. Isn't that the reason for research in the first place?

I-Search Research

Giving students an opportunity to investigate what is important to them results in what is often their first attempts at conducting original research. The format for such a process for research in the classroom is taken from Ken Macrorie's (1988) *The I-Search Paper*. In the process of doing an I-Search, students learn all the traditional required skills—the format, paraphrasing, attribution and citing, creating bibliographies, and so on. However, instead of merely completing an exercise for English class and reporting on someone else's efforts and discoveries, students learn how to conduct authentic and meaningful research.

The first step is helping students decide on a topic that will be worth investigating for a few months of their life. This is perhaps the most crucial step and one that belongs entirely to the student. We can help with process and putting together the product, but we can't know what is important enough for each individual to investigate, and unfortunately, oftentimes the students don't either. We need to remember that we're asking them to think in ways that have not traditionally been asked of them in school. Usually the teacher tells students what to do or at least gives a list of choices. To begin thinking about what topic would be most appropriate for each student has to be the student's decision. This takes some time, discussion, sharing, and often more than a single attempt. When students get stuck, we find that a conference with us or a peer can sometimes help. Often the sharing of ideas in class sparks a new idea. We also need to take time to teach a minilesson on what are some topics that will work and others that won't. For instance, researching the effects of nutritional supplements on body building has many possibilities for primary and secondary research, and the results can affect someone's decision about taking such supplements. However, researching the existence of angels will be difficult, because of the lack of credible sources. Research on angels may yield a flood of anecdotal evidence, but it will be based on belief and theory rather than any concrete evidence.

After the topic has been decided on, the students must then frame their research question or questions. What is it that they want to learn, to discover? Their questions will guide the research and should be addressed in the findings section of the research paper. Students are then ready for the actual research process. It is during this process that minilessons on interviewing primary sources will be taught as well as lessons on using the Internet to wade through both credible and unreliable sources.

Using the Internet to Research

Once upon a time, doing research meant a trip to the library; now it usually means a trip to the virtual library. The Internet's worldwide collection of computer resources bypasses any library, and with a click on the search icon, theoretically offers students access to any information imaginable. Even the most unsophisticated user can be successful with search engines. We believe students find the Internet more satisfying for its presentation of information for several reasons: websites are eye-pleasing, timely, and clickable. Books have bound sheets of off-white paper with black ink text running in lines from left to right, up and down the page—books always look like books. The Internet's websites have colorful graphics and eye-catching design. Rarely do scholarly books have colorful graphics, and their text is never arranged on a page in a range of fonts and typefaces. Websites are also timely. Most books take years to write and often six months to a year to actually produce. Websites are easily created and revised—information posted last week can be modified today. Websites are as current as their last update (usually found at the bottom of the page). Scholarly books aren't updateable, except in the case of revised editions. And the Internet is easily linkable, scholarly books aren't. The information on a website is designed to lead the user to other pages, controlled by a click, governed by the user's interest. Scholarly books are arranged according to how the author believes a reader should move through the material, usually sequentially by chapter and page.

Interestingly enough, these three features are what might also be termed the downside of the Internet. The colorful graphics and eye-catching design can be distracting, especially the annoying banners at the top of many web pages, placed there by sponsors and advertisers. Users expect web pages to be updated; they tend to wonder what the webmaster has been doing with his or her time if the page is unattended. Graphics also take a long time to load, so users sometimes report that the Internet is slow. An embedded series of links can lead one down a number of fascinating but useless paths. As our students report, the Internet is a good way to waste a lot of time. Of course, we recognize that everyone's notion of "time well spent" is relative; we are old enough to remember losing lots of afternoons wandering around in the library stacks.

Some other problems that arise from use of the new technology are the number of hits a search reveals. The only thing worse than receiving only a handful of sites is the avalanche of hits that result from searching for general terms—anywhere from one hundred thousand to results in the millions. As Bill Wresch (Wresch, Pattow, and Gifford 1989) predicted almost twenty years ago, the real skill that researchers will need to develop in this century is not the ability to find resources, but the ability to sort through and evaluate the resources available. No one could be expected to scroll through a million plus abstracts and summaries of websites. So, students need to know which search engines evaluate the millions of hits and present them in a way that indicates which are closer to what was asked for—rank ordering them or giving a rating, such as the number of red balls or stars—higher being closer. Teachers must teach these new skills if we expect students to use the Internet as a source of information when writing expository essays.

Reliability

A related problem concerns the reliability of sources presented by the Internet. Students need to understand that the Internet was not created to store information; libraries were. People write web pages to announce their personal expertise or hobby; a web page on the Internet today can be taken down tomorrow or next week.

The Internet is not an archive; it's temporary and transitory. Today it promotes the latest things, the "new" commercial items that the dot.coms are selling, but no one is evaluating the accuracy of information. So, how can students tell how reliable a site is? For example, how reliable is a site titled "Old Time Radio" by John? Or one titled, "How Television Works" by Michael Brain? One has a creator with no last name and the other could be a nickname, but how does someone know if this information can be trusted? Our students decided one way was to look for what we call the pedigree. Is the source, individual or institution, connected to a university or organization that has credibility? My students agreed that Cornell University after the author's name had more credibility than the "Feel Good Institute." Does the author tell his or her qualifications? Authors with an R.N. after their name might be credible sources for information on lupus or hypertension and a J.D. might give some reliable advice about tenant-landlord rights and obligations.

Currency may be another indicator for reliability. As mentioned earlier, websites are easily created and revised, but also posted and abandoned. Our students suggested looking to see if the site is up-to-date. Some announce dates at the top, like newspapers and journals; others give a "last updated" reference at the bottom of the site. Being new or current isn't a guarantee of reliability, but it is an indicator of a custodian. A third indicator is citing sources. Our students felt that the reliability of a website could be judged in the same way that their research papers will be judged. If students are asked to attribute what they know to sources that are stable and trustworthy, then it would be worth looking to see if there is evidence for assertions presented in the site. There might not be a bibliography at the end, but students could look to see if the site gives references and dates.

If students are asked to be aware of their own opinions and personal bias, then it would be worth examining websites for traces of bias and hidden agendas. Our students wondered if the information is accurate on many of the websites, given their commercial sponsorship, or subtle (and sometimes not so subtle) sales pitches. A website proclaiming the aphrodisiac qualities of chocolate, sponsored by the Hershey or Nestlé Company, might not be as objective as one would hope. The wisdom of ingesting supplemental B vitamins might be considered more reliable if found on the Consumers' Union website rather than one put up by a pharmaceutical company's research team. Even when appearing objective, most information in our culture possesses a hidden agenda of persuasion or a hidden bias (Harris 1997).

Students should keep several other considerations in mind. For one thing, the Internet has what might be considered the raw data of research—statistics, biographies, timelines—but it is lacking in comprehensiveness. Books or full-length analyses of events, people, and developments are generally not found on the Internet, though the ingredients for such analyses might be, such as news stories from the major news agencies and some journal articles. Another consideration is what might be called the ease of use. Books are organized linearly, have consecutively numbered pages to help readers keep track of where information was found, and feature a table of contents and sometimes an index to help locate items. The Internet relies on search engines to find information, and once a site is located, there are scrollable screens instead of pages; to find where they've been, users can click the "back arrow" or the GO tool on the menu bar to find traces of where they've been. If books are linear, the Internet is multidimensional, and one needs a Hansel and Gretel string of breadcrumbs to find the way home.

The Format of the Paper

Students need to see that research papers are set up in a style respected by the appropriate research community and one that allows the story of their research process to be told. They begin by writing about why this topic was important to research, otherwise dubbed the reason for the study. Since they will be telling the story of the birth of their research, writing in the first person only makes sense. The next part of the paper includes the research questions asked as well as the methodology or an explanation of how the researcher went about researching his or her topic. It also includes an explanation of how the research was analyzed. Of course, during the weeks that students are researching, the teacher demonstrates with his or her own research how data is collected and analyzed. Students then proceed to write their findings, a section that they should be able to write with conviction and heart, since they have discovered evidence that informs them personally. Finally, the students write a conclusion and assess the need for further research. This is a section that almost teaches itself, since real researchers always discover that research unearths more questions and that inquiry is a never-ending process.

Presenting the Research

After all that work, it's important to give students an opportunity to present their research. Of course the easiest way to do this is to present to the class, but because of the range of topics and interest addressed, it's also possible to include others who may have an interest—those who were interviewed, others that the student know would be interested, and so on. The way the research is presented is important. Reading papers aloud is boring and dry, but telling the story of the research is almost always interesting. Students find ways to present that are suitable for their research, everything from a traditional PowerPoint presentation to bringing in props and doing demonstrations. Others invite primary sources—veterinarians, dietitians, parents of autistic children—as experts that support their research finding. Such presentations take time, but the experiences in the language arts are obvious—reading, writing, listening, speaking, and viewing as both a facilitator and a participant.

As Suzanne Miller (1991), realized, "When students...[research and] discuss...with the support of an encouraging teacher, they can examine what they know, and learn to actively shape, question, elaborate, and remake knowledge....When students transform...their discussion of texts, they also move toward a personal sense of intellectual self-worth in their new images of themselves as readers, writers, and thinkers. If we want to open students to possibilities in texts and in their lives, we need to encourage teachers to talk with their students, who...sadly remind us, have very likely never heard their own voices in school" (11).

For Further Exploration

1. Observe several classes in which discussion is taking place. What model of questioning does the teacher use (IRE, open-ended, and so on)? Is the discussion facilitated by the teacher or the students? What was the depth of student interaction?
2. Practice facilitating a small group discussion on a reading, text, or poem. How do you prepare? What is your primary objective? How do you make sure all members of the group are included?
3. Often choosing a subject that is worth our time and effort is the most pivotal step in research. Ask students, what do they wonder about. What are some ways we can help students identify topics that they might like to research?
4. Listening is one of the five language arts. As teachers, how do we teach listening? How do we model it?

3

Reading and Literature

There are no kits of materials or systematic exercises for teaching children how the world uses written language. They learn—usually without anyone being aware that they are learning—by participating in literate activities with people who use written language. . . . Children learn about reading and writing by "joining the literacy club."

—Frank Smith

Many teachers, and certainly the vast public, believe that by the time students are in high school, they do not need to be taught to read. If they can't read, the argument goes, then they should be retained or placed in a remedial situation until they've mastered reading. Thus, often the only "reading teachers" in secondary education are Title I teachers and special education teachers. For years, English teachers have taken the stance that if students can't "keep up with the reading," they should get help. But we believe all English teachers should be reading teachers since students continue to be at different stages of reading development, even in high school and college. This is often because of past experiences with texts in English classes as well as in content courses. To provide instruction that meets the individual needs of each student, instruction must build on each student's strengths and support each student's growth in ways that are appropriate and meaningful. It's not enough to know whether a student can read, a teacher should know whether a student likes to read, the extent of the student's reading ability, and even what that student chooses to read.

Surveys and Interviews

A first step in understanding students as readers can be through interviews. This can be done by talking with them just as in writing conferences, or asking them to fill out a survey, akin to a written interview. During face-to-face conferences, teachers

36

can follow lines of questioning similar to those asked on the written surveys, shown in Figure 3–1. Face-to-face interviews reveal information that couldn't have been anticipated in a formal written survey, so teachers should be open to such additional opportunities and feel free to ask questions that arise during the conversation. These interviews can be more like discussions, so students don't feel put "on the spot," and teachers should share as well as ask for information.

In an informal conversation at the beginning of the year, one of Jim Mahoney's (2002) students said he never read the classic, *Huckleberry Finn*, because it was so boring; another student agreed, "It seemed so dumb, about this kid who runs away on the river with a runaway slave. I couldn't even understand what he was saying half the time." Another said that *Ethan Frome* "was the worst. Talk about dumb. Nothing ever happens. I read the first chapter and the last and then I got the *Cliffs Notes*." Another confessed, "Hardly anyone in my class reads the books. The teacher reads some of it in class and she discusses it and goes over each chapter. Then we have the test. You don't really have to read to get a good grade." When Jim expressed astonishment at what he was hearing, one of the students told him, "I used to like to read when I was little. I stopped in elementary school. My mother used to get me all kinds of books when I was little. I hate to read now. I just can't get into books right now." Her friend backed her up, saying, "Only about a third of the kids in my 11 Honors class actually read the books, unless we read it in class, the way we did with *The Crucible* and now *Inherit the Wind*" (104–105). This is candor; this is the challenge.

Whatever the format, questioning helps teachers find out how students look at reading, how they define what reading is, what strategies they might use when

---

1. Would you rather read a book or watch a movie?
2. What is the last book you read? Why did you read it?
3. Do you consider yourself a "reader"? How would you define that?
4. What's the best book you ever read or one of your favorites? When did you read it and why was it memorable?
5. What kinds of books do you like to read?
6. If you were to describe the place reading has in your life, how would you do so?
7. Do you ever discuss favorite books or movies with friends?
8. What would you consider a "good" book?
9. Do you ever go to libraries or bookstores?
10. Is reading important in your life? If so, how?

Figure 3–1. Reading survey

reading, and most importantly, how they feel about reading and about themselves as readers. One year, Burton, a student in our first-year composition class, was having trouble choosing a novel for an assignment. We suggested a Dick Francis novel, one in a series of mysteries that always involve horses and racetracks in some way. Burton took the book and dutifully read during class and at home. After a week, he brought the book back and said that he just couldn't get started with it. He kept reading the same pages over and over, he said. We told him that not every reader likes every book, so he should keep trying different ones until he found the right one. We sent him off with another suspense/adventure book, but after the weekend, Burton came to class excited because he found a book on his own. It was a novel from the R. L. Stine *Fear Street* series. We were happy for Burton but worried that someone in class would remark about the reading level of the book. Fortunately, no one did. And fortunately, no one in the English Department made an issue of our letting students make this kind of choice. Obviously, as college teachers, we want more for our students, but to nudge them forward, we must begin with their interests and comfort, helping them see themselves as readers. After reading his book and completing the writing assignment along with his classmates, Burton wanted to lend the book to us, proclaiming it a great story, confiding it was the first book he'd actually completely read. We have to talk with students if we're to have enough information to know where to begin.

Sometimes our good intentions lead us to administer attitude and interest surveys in the beginning of the school year, but then we do little with them. After all, with twenty-five students in a classroom, it takes time to get a full picture of each student's strengths/needs and classroom teachers have to keep teaching during that time. Teachers don't have the luxury of waiting until they've gathered all the evidence, but teachers can begin instruction based on what they know so far. Like anthropologists, teachers need to be constantly revising their assessments of their students, not waiting like a jury to hear all the evidence before taking any action. Hypotheses can be made in a teacher's journal or with anecdotal records, short notes used to record observations.

We must use assessment to drive our instruction. For example, a reading survey, like the one in Figure 3–1, which can be used pre- and post-, told us that a number of students freely admitted that they didn't see a place for reading in their life. One student's response was typical in that class: Jamie knew reading was important, but she didn't do it very often. She also felt "good" readers read fast, and she didn't see that as one of her strengths. From this information, we realized that, although it wasn't stated directly in the syllabus, a primary goal for the course would include providing experiences in which students could function as readers, and more important, see themselves as readers. Another group of students might indicate on their surveys that they already see a place for reading in their lives, see themselves as readers, and are ready for reading experiences that challenge their abilities. Whatever the case, we need to know our students early in the semester. By the end of the course, many of the students indicated on their post-surveys that they were proud of the fact that they had successfully read five novels in twelve weeks. More important, students like Jamie admitted that she now read "faster" and appreciated the books she read.

Sometimes it helps to have students examine who they are as literate people. Many teachers have a version of the "this is your life" type of autobiographical writing assignment, so why not make the subject of this memoir reading? As part of creating a portrait of themselves as young children, the students can examine their journey as readers and writers. If they have the opportunity or desire to interview people in their families, they may. A sample data-gathering sheet for interviewing parents and grandparents is given in Figure 3–2. Students can then write literacy memoirs, snippets of the past where they see themselves developing as literate human beings—the good moments and the bad.

Students often write a story of their literate lives and literacy memoirs that reveal important bits of information, such as these:

I remember my mom reading to me when I was little, usually in the evening. I'd sit on her lap or I'd snuggle down under the covers listening to her voice. I don't remember when that stopped, maybe when I learned to read myself.

When I was very young, I remember my bedroom floor was linoleum with nursery rhymes and pictures and the alphabet around the perimeter. I remember "reading" those nursery rhymes to my younger sisters.

My mom told me she bought me a Golden Book at the supermarket every week when she did the grocery shopping. I sort of remember the *Little Train that Could*

1. What was my favorite book?
2. Did anyone read to me?
3. Did I read to brothers/sisters? They to me?
4. How did I feel about books?
5. Did I change my reading likes?
6. How did I get books?
7. Did I have a library card?
8. How did I learn to read?
9. When did I begin to draw and write?
10. Did I ever listen to books on tape or on records?

Figure 3–2. Interviewing someone who knew you then

and one about a dog. She said I loved getting a new book and couldn't wait 'til she got home.

I loved Nancy Drew books when I was in fifth grade. I couldn't wait to start the next book as soon as I finished the one I was reading. I couldn't use them for book reports in school though—no serial books allowed.

I remember doing a book report in sixth grade. The book was about a teenager who overcame the odds against him, customizing a winning drag racer and, in the process, won the affections of the most beautiful girl in school. At the time, I was more interested in the parts about cars than I was about girls. My teacher dismissed the book report as "too juvenile" simply because of the book's title, *Boy Gets Car,* a word play on the popular expression, "The boy gets the girl," something even I understood in sixth grade.

I liked to read until a few years ago. Now it seems I just don't have time. Reading is assignments from textbooks and notes to study. I miss books but who has time for that now?

After writing and sharing memories, students can construct an understanding of literacy and how they've gotten to where they are now. More important, they can figure out where they will be going and how our class can help them get there.

Reading Logs

Another source for understanding students as readers is reading logs, which can be used for instruction or assessment and evaluation. Periodically reviewing logs can reveal the type of evidence of reading development that can be observed over time. Reading logs can provide hard evidence that can be shared with parents and that students can use to articulate their strengths, reflect on their growth, and set goals for further learning.

Reading logs as we use them are journals in which students record titles, authors, and perhaps genres of books they have read. In addition to writing title, author, and main characters, students are asked to reflect about the book in their reading log; such reflections help teachers assess comprehension, inferences, and depth of understanding of character development, plot, and theme. The entries can also furnish starting places to initiate reading conference questions, so teachers can assess levels of comprehension.

As teachers assess reading progress, simple lists of books can help identify interests, which in turn help teachers make further suggestions and remind both teacher and students that we learn to read by reading. The reading logs compiled in a class of students can offer evidence to themselves, their teacher, and the world of their individuality as readers. Some students' lists will reveal a diversity of titles and authors. Other lists will reveal a sophisticated choice of titles. Still others will astonish us with the number of books read. And even though some students' logs will not be as impressive in diversity, number, or choice, they can still tell us quite a bit about the reader. For example, the student in Figure 3–3 chose to include the page count, almost 4,000 pages, which shows the pride this student feels for her reading. The log also shows the presence of books recommended by classmates. An early choice, *Holes*, was the result of her friend Autumn's excitement after reading the novel.

Reading logs act as a motivational tool for readers; as students keep track of what they've read independently, books they've read together as a class, and books with partners or in literature groups, the growing list assures them of their abilities and encourages them to add more titles. As the list grows, so does their impression of themselves as readers, as members of what Frank Smith (1988) calls "the Literacy Club." Many parents are amazed at the sheer volume of reading that takes place over a few months' time in reading-based English classes.

Reading logs need to be meaningful to students. To be productive, teachers must encourage and put value on independent reading; that is, independent reading must be seen as "worth" something because the teacher provides time for it, counts it in grading considerations, and respects student choice. Some teachers ask students to bring their reading logs once a week to share thoughts and reactions

Title	Author	Pages
Superstitious	R. L. Stine	309
Whisper of Death	Christopher Pike	180
Holes	Louis Sachar	233
Strangers	Dean Koontz	681
Amanda/Miranda	Richard Peck	458
Hatchet	Gary Paulsen	195
Pigman	Paul Zindel	182
The Chocolate War	Robert Cormier	253
To Kill a Mockingbird	Harper Lee	284
Masters of Darkness	editor, Dennis Etchison	766
He Sees You When You're Sleeping	Mary Higgins Clark and Carol Higgins Clark	202
	Total	3743

Figure 3–3. April's log of books read

with classmates about their independent readings. Sharing helps readers feel part of a reading community, and the lists have a purpose beyond their use for the teacher. However, students can become competitive, comparing numbers of chapters or books read, so teachers need to downplay the number-of-books-read aspect and emphasize the reading process and responding to different books chosen.

Competitiveness is a real danger when schools participate in special programs in which students receive prizes, such as pizza, for reading a certain number of books. We agree that reading should be celebrated and that eating pizza is fun, but competition doesn't belong in a reading curriculum. One student, Natalie, confided to us that she remembers using information gleaned from the back of the book and inside its jacket to qualify for a pizza. These programs foster not only competition, but might encourage students to choose books based on how quickly they can be read (to accumulate the required number of points) rather than according to genuine interest. For example, the way points are awarded in a contest might determine whether a reader chooses five short books instead of one long, classic work. Natalie was only slightly embarrassed by her back-of-the-book subterfuge because she saw the program as a game rather than as reading for meaning. Reading is not a contest, and published programs such as Accelerated Reader can give students the wrong message about reading.

The same caution applies to well-meaning principals and supervisors who challenge students in their schools to read an extraordinary number of books in return for which the administrator will make a fool of himself (or herself) by dressing in a clown costume and taking pies in the face. Teachers should always remember why we read: it's not to accumulate points, to win pizzas, or even to advance to the next level after answering questions. Real readers read to enjoy, to learn, to share ideas, and to experience—classrooms in which this is celebrated are classrooms of readers.

Given the nature of classrooms, students want to see that their readings logs are "worth something" in terms of their grade. Nevertheless, when teachers review reading logs, they should remember why they were assigned. Reading logs offer a way to get inside the head of a reader and assess how that person is reading, not to assess the writing itself. Therefore, reading logs employed for this type of assessment can be replied to, but shouldn't be corrected. If a grade is to be given, it could be based on both completeness and depth of response. Instead of the teacher reading every entry, students could identify their three best, paper clip those pages, and invite an evaluation based on predetermined criteria. The grade is then clearly determined and students see that their effort "counts." A simple evaluation form, such as the one in Figure 3–4, recognizes effort and quality.

I have included	10 entries (2 points)	_____
	7–9 entries (1 point)	_____
	fewer than 7 (0 points)	_____
My responses were	reflective (1 or 2 points)	_____
	connected to other books (1 or 2 points)	_____
	looked at issues/ideas not directly stated by author (1 or 2 points)	_____
	TOTAL	_____

Grade scale: 8 points = A; 6 points = B; 4 points = C;
fewer than 3 = Incomplete/resubmit

Figure 3–4. Reading log evaluation

How the Subject Changed from Reading to Literature Studies

Most high school teachers would argue that reading isn't actually a part of their curriculum. High school and college teachers don't teach the process of reading, they teach the content of the reading—the literature. This shift from reading to content in secondary language arts—usually known simply as English—puts students who enter with reading difficulties at an even greater disadvantage. Our argument would be that teachers who ignore the reading process and contend that each student is already, or should be, developed as a reader are like the teachers in Robertson Davies' novel, *The Cunning Man*, who groom "boys of unusual talent . . . like racehorses." The honor student in the story confides, "My friend and I came in heavily for this sort of fine-tuning, but poor Charlie was a hopeless case and, although nobody was downright miserable to him, he felt the chill of exclusion as one who was simply not worth extra coaching." Unfortunately, some teachers are selective about who is worthy enough for their instruction on the sophisticated intricacies of literature and who should be grateful for being allowed to listen in.

This change in educators' approach to reading, in which literature becomes the race course of competition, is due in large part to an interesting twist of events that happened in the late nineteenth century, the full details of which can be found in Jim Berlin's (1987) *Rhetoric and Reality* and Sharon Crowley's (1998) *Composition in the University*. For this discussion, the intriguing development was the introduction of the "entrance exam" at Harvard in 1874. Apparently, the most prominent Ivy League school found itself admitting students, mostly from the best prep schools, whose writing abilities were deemed so poor as to require additional tutelage. At the time, Harvard's preeminent scholars were doing their best to avoid teaching remedial classes in writing. To raise the caliber of those admitted to study and keep teachers focused on loftier pursuits, the entrance exam would serve as an initial check of the students' abilities. Of course, every other college worth its salt followed suit. And when students were not admitted or sent to skills-intensive writing classes taught by lecturers and less distinguished faculty, the high school teachers and their curriculum were blamed.

Now the entrance exam itself required "each candidate … to write a short English composition, correct in spelling, punctuation, grammar, and expression" (Bizzell and Herzberg 1991, 3). And what was the subject of the composition? The topic was taken from literature that had been previously announced—a list of books. The works chosen for the first year were *Merchant of Venice, The Tempest, Julius Caesar, Vicar of Wakefield* (Goldsmith), *Ivanhoe*, and *Lay of the Last Minstrel* (Scott). By 1879, the composition requirement had become more rigorous and the topics more esoteric: "Write a short composition upon one of the subjects given below. Before beginning to write, consider what you have to say on the subject selected, and arrange your thoughts in a logical order. Aim at quality rather than quantity of work. Carefully revise your composition, correcting all errors in punctuation, spelling, grammar, division by paragraphs, and expression, and making each sentence as clear and forcible as possible. If time permits, make a clean copy of the revised work" (Crowley 1998, 67). The five prompts that year were "(1) The Character of Sir Richard Steele, (2) The Duke of Marlborough as portrayed by Thackeray, (3) The Style of 'Henry Esmond,' (4) Thackeray's account of the Pretender's visit to England, (5) Dueling in the Age of Queen Anne" (67–68). And lest anyone believe today's standards are slipping, over half the candidates regularly failed the exam. Harvard's notion of correctness and proper knowledge of literary texts must have seemed so foreign and bizarre "to young men whose preparation did not include practice in the sort of reading and writing skills that would be necessary to pass" (68).

So, high school teachers, of course, became responsible for preparing the students, since a responsible high school curriculum committee would, the reasoning goes, do a disservice to its pupils if it failed to cover these works in its curriculum. Of course, given the wealth of important twentieth-century works, we'd hardly expect the works of Sir Walter Scott or Thackeray to be high school classics today. And who would choose *Merchant of Venice* over alternative Shakespeare choices? But which Shakespeare work is the most worthy? Is *Hamlet* more meritorious than *Macbeth*? And aren't both superior to that secondary workhorse, *Julius Caesar*? Interestingly, the National Council of Teachers of English (NCTE) was formed as a professional organization in 1912 to speak for and defend secondary

44

teachers. Its first campaign was for the elimination of reading lists for entrance exams.

This was the beginning of teaching to the test. But it was much more insidious because the shift went from reading to being able to offer an expository essay on a work of highly regarded literature. In that light, what was asked of students was not that they read but that they read a special sort of material in a special sort of way. It had little to do with literacy.

And the same misguided agenda is still being put forth today as the Core Knowledge movement, an attempt to regulate what content is taught at each grade level, including what great works of literature are covered. Having dictated content for the first eight grades, attention is now being turned to the secondary curriculum. The theory underlying this movement is that in a civilized society we must share the same knowledge about our history, our literature, and our culture. If the purpose of public education is to create an informed citizenry, the argument goes, then it is up to the schools to pass on this core knowledge so that we can share the same cultural literacy.

Of course, this reasoning is seriously flawed because the Core Knowledge movement assumes that cultural literacy can be transmitted by direct instruction in schools. Most of what a culture shares is communicated to its members through oral storytelling in a variety of settings from religious ceremonies to front-porch gatherings. The oral transmission involves stories read to children, stories told in songs, and today through stories told through technological media including television shows, game cartridges, and computer simulations. Of course, it includes stories told in classrooms, but it is not limited to the literature assigned in classrooms. Cultures take care of communicating their stories; otherwise they don't survive as a culture. No one has to teach culture for culture to survive; those outside a culture may study it for curiosity, but that is not how it is transmitted and maintained within the culture. For example, no one would be asked on a cultural literacy test to identify the Weathermen, a subgroup of the Students for a Democratic Society (SDS) or to explain the origins of their name. And yet, this information was common knowledge for the hippie culture that was responsible for the Woodstock nation and the dream of peace, love, and music. That particular culture has not survived, though there are probably numerous cases of the hippie culture being the subject of academic investigation and dissemination. On the other hand, the Native American culture has been able to find a way to stay alive in the face of what might be seen as cultural genocide.

Yet, British and American literature is regularly chosen as reading material for students either to offer them a passing acquaintance with the literary masters, those deemed worth knowing by the Core Knowledge gurus, or else to expose them to the enrichment of the arts that comes with reading Browning, Keats,

Shakespeare, Faulkner, and Hemingway. School boards and Boards of Education are so intent on controlling the literature being "taught" that some have reacted the way that Florida has, mandating, according to one Florida teacher, "that each child be issued a literature textbook.... [which, in turn] will outlaw classroom sets [of trade books to]... "force" teachers to use only the literature text instead of...other materials that I have been implementing in my classroom" (Dosh 2000). And having no way to assess whether students have been properly acquainted, exposed, or enriched, the transmission traditionalists resort to comprehension tests, which see if the students read the story as assigned and if they comprehended it "correctly." In school, tests and the questions become more obscure and tangential to the reading experience—"tricky" in the parlance of the school. Teachers' manuals give teachers the inside scoop on the major themes and symbols that should be covered. This inside information is obtained from the university professors who devote their lives to an author or a period or a theoretical approach—much of what ends up in *Cliffs Notes*—style guides to interpretation—and thus, the details of what the culturally literate student should know become codified. How can we reverse this misrepresentation of what is important? For one, we can restore the interpretation to the reader, much as reader response theory does.

Teaching Reading by Connecting with Literature

Literature-based reading instruction has a significant effect on language development. Response to literature is an *active* transaction between the reader and the text (Rosenblatt 1978). The words on the page are cues from the author, but readers build meaning through personal knowledge, associations, feelings, and experiences as they transact with the printed text. The more a reader knows of a variety of stories, the better he or she is able to relate to, understand, and predict what will happen next. This development of "story schema" helps readers adjust their expectations about characters and events in new stories and broaden their conception of how the world works. At every level of reading, students' experiences with literature help them build the story schema needed to recognize the conventions and patterns of language. Literature-based reading instruction, unlike traditional reading instruction, helps students discover the ways authors create meaning, rather than superimposing a "single reading" of story or a teacher manual's concept of literary analysis (Huck 1977). If readers create meaning *as they are reading*, then neither literary analysis nor one-answer comprehension questions nor memorizing facts about literature are appropriate responses to reading. Students are individuals and have individual readings and interpretations that we cannot predict or constrain. As active learners, students need opportunities to engage with literature—discussing, discovering, considering, representing, and rereading to make their own meanings (Piaget 1971; Probst 1992).

Students need to interact with the characters and the elements of a story, and active learning involves connecting the world of reading to the world in which they live. Sometimes adults and curriculum designers want adolescents to react to literature the way adults might. For example, *The Great Gatsby* is one of those stories that is part of the curriculum. We wonder how this became a classic to teach to adolescents. Two story lines feature adultery, and the central story is one of betrayal and loss. Some adolescents may have had heart-breaking experiences, but they haven't yet been damaged the way Fitzgerald's characters have. They have had what we used to term "puppy love"—early experiences of love and loss, but hardly the sort that propels the characters in Gatsby. So, instead of dealing with the adult themes of this classic, the test makers ask trick comprehension questions— what was Gatsby's real name? What did the eyeglasses symbolize? We would be better to chose stories that our students can connect with, or at least value their reactions when they might appear superficial to adult sensibilities.

Students simultaneously learn language and literacy in environments that permit them to read, write, listen and speak for a variety of authentic purposes. In traditional classrooms, when students are asked to respond to worksheets and take tests that assess "mastery" of comprehension questions that focus on minute details, such as the color of Daisy's car in *The Great Gatsby*, they are deprived of opportunities for active involvement in the reading process. In a transactional classroom, students are psychologically engaged, both independently and as a class, in the process of actively reading and writing about a variety of literature—classics, contemporary favorites, librarians' selections, articles in popular magazines, and grocery store paperbacks. If we are to use literature in these ways, we need to continue to be teachers of reading, so we can give all students the tools that all readers need.

One of our students, who was himself adopted, read Barbara Kingsolver's (1993) *Pigs in Heaven* and argued for an ending that seemed right to him: the adopted mother would have full custody rights. He proposed this by inserting a scene in the story in which Annawake, lawyer to the Cherokee nation, drops her opposition to the adoption after she receives a message in a dream from her brother, telling her that he was taken from his family and she shouldn't take Turtle from her family. Our student did not see that the Cherokee in the story are portrayed as a family unit, each one responsible for the raising of the community's children, regardless of who gave birth biologically. His reading was from a perspective that held that adopted children belong with their adopted parents, because that's who he is.

One of Carol Jago's (2000) students at Santa Monica High School in California tells that she related to the main character in her reading of *The Odyssey*. She said that she experienced Odysseus' longing to be home since her own family lived far away in Mexico. In the story, when Odysseus was moved emotionally at hearing songs of his homeland and his soldiers' brave exploits, she connected that with a time when she watched a television program on the Discovery channel about her home in Puebla, Mexico. She and Odysseus were both saddened when hearing their own story. When she saved money to fly home at Christmas, she says she had to pass up many temptations and distractions to accumulate enough money. She felt this was similar to what Odysseus was enduring when he confronted the lure of the Siren's song, Circe's festivities, and the Lotus flower of forgetfulness. She, too, feels Odysseus' desire to escape hospitality and imprisonment because she longs to leave the American family and school that she feels both confined by and grateful for. This is the sort of interaction teachers should model and encourage in readers.

Experiencing Success with Reading

When literature is used as a vehicle for teaching literary conventions rather than reading, students who have had difficulties in the past are discouraged when faced with a challenging work of literature. One technique that helps students experience success with reading is called "jigsawing," which we learned about from Barbara King-Shaver (1991), of South Brunswick High School in Monmouth Junction, New Jersey.

Jigsawing makes various groups of students responsible for different chapters of a class novel. After each group does a close reading of their assigned parts, the groups take turns constructing the plot of the story and carrying on an analysis of the characters in their assigned chapters. Thus the class is actively constructing meaning in the act of tying the story together to complete the jigsaw puzzle. This approach works best with novels that are episodic in nature, but it can be used with any novel that seems difficult for students to read, for example, Mary Shelley's *Frankenstein*, Homer's *Oddysey*, Brontë's *Jane Eyre*, or Dickens' *David Copperfield*. As King-Shaver points out, when doing jigsawing, students use the four language acts—reading, speaking, listening, and writing—and, in a meaningful way, experience a novel they might not otherwise have read. This technique complements other activities involved with reading that ask students to demonstrate their understanding of the novel such as scripting a presentation, enacting a scene, or creating a piece of artwork (Wilhelm 1995). Amber, a ninth grader from Pennsylvania, created a map of places and events after reading Christopher Paul Curtis' *The Watsons Go to Birmingham* (see Figure 3–5).

To help students activate background knowledge and focus on key ideas, anticipation/prediction activities can be done with students to activate prior knowledge and arouse curiosity about issues addressed in the text. For example, a teacher asks students, without mentioning the name of the work of literature, how they

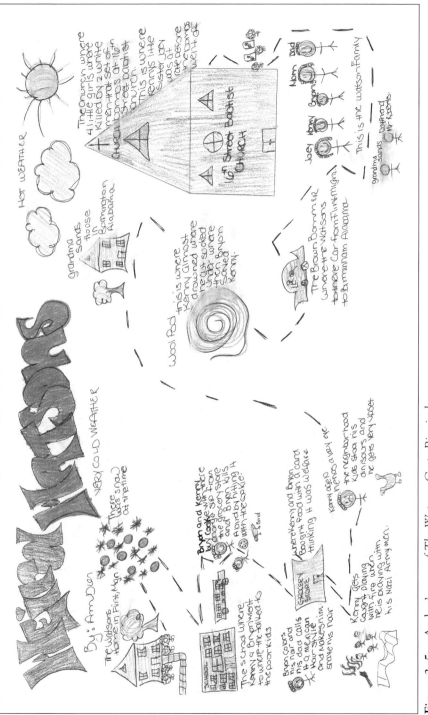

Figure 3–5. Amber's map of *The Watsons Go to Birmingham*

49

would feel if their parents were to get a divorce and their mother suddenly started dating another man. The students respond to the situation in writing, and they include how they would feel if they found out that their mother's new boyfriend had taken over their father's job, and they suspected that the new man in her life had something to do with their father being fired. At this point, when the students begin reading Shakespeare's *Hamlet,* they are better able to connect the play's plot to the themes of divorce and murder; they are better able to read the play.

Clear expectations can help students set a purpose for their reading and self-monitor their comprehension. One way is to develop a list of expectations on the chalkboard or on an overhead projector transparency as students simply tell what they expect to learn from the next reading assignment. This works when reading expository texts as well as selections with plot lines. The "great expectations" list can be done at the end of class to prepare for the reading given as homework or it can be done as an in-class activity. In this case, the students read a selection or portion of a text and the teacher asks them to recall everything they can remember.

Recalled ideas are shared in brainstorming fashion and recorded on the board, on a transparency, or in their notebooks. Next, the teacher and/or students provide a purpose for further reading by predicting what will happen. With this purpose in mind, students return to the next portion of the text. These strategies enhance comprehension by actively involving students in their reading through prediction and helping them realize the importance of being able to recall important details. Postreading activities may include summarization, discussion, evaluation, or other skills that the teacher deems important.

Amy Johnson, a ninth-grade English teacher in the Hampton school district in western Pennsylvania, uses anticipation guides when preparing students to read both expository and narrative texts. Before reading "Death on the Mountain," an article from *Life* magazine, Amy has each student answer fifteen true or false questions based on their knowledge of mountain climbing. The students then read the article, either silently or as a class, answer the questions about the reading again, and see how much the article added to their knowledge base (Figure 3–6)

Amy said the students responded well to the anticipation guides.

We spent time debating whether or not the statements were correct before we started reading. I was amazed at how quickly they got down to the business of reading the article—they usually don't become so engrossed in their reading assignments. As they read, I noticed they were checking their predictions and making notes about the reading in the margins.

Once everyone was done reading, we quickly confirmed whether the statements were true or not. I was amazed—many students raised their hands to

ANTICIPATION GUIDE

Dowling, Claudia Glenn. "Death on the Mountain." *Life* Aug. 1996: 32–46.

Before Reading		Directions: Before reading the article about Mt. Everest, read each statement below. If you believe the statement is true, put a check in the <u>Before Reading</u> column. Read the article to confirm your predictions. After reading, check the statements that are true in the <u>After Reading</u> column.	After Reading
———	1.	At 29,028, Mt. Everest is the highest mountain in the world.	———
———	2.	Climbers must use oxygen tanks in order to climb Mt. Everest.	———
———	3.	There are three unwritten rules of the heights: First, save anyone you can. Second, save the person who has the best chance of surviving. Third, save yourself.	———
———	4.	The altitude above 28,000 feet is known as the Death Zone.	———
———	5.	Bodies are left on the mountain because it is impossible to remove them.	———
———	6.	There is no way to communicate with the rest of the world from Mt. Everest.	———
———	7.	Those at high altitude breathe 50 times a minute (4 times the normal rate at sea level).	———
———	8.	Climbers tested at Camp IV take 50% longer to understand a sentence than a six-year-old.	———
———	9.	Sir George Everest was the first man to reach the top of the mountain.	———
———	10.	People have tried to hang glide and paraglide off Everest, ski and snowboard down it, and climb it one-legged.	———
———	11.	Companies such as Rolex, Starbucks, and Vaseline have turned down opportunities to sponsor expeditions to Everest because of concerns of having the company names associated with such a dangerous endeavor.	———
———	12.	It costs approximately $65,000 to climb Everest, about the price of a Range Rover or a gown by Chanel.	———
———	13.	The government of Nepal charges climbers $5,000 a person for a permit.	———
———	14.	4,000 people have attempted to climb Mt. Everest, 660 have succeeded, and 142 have died in the attempt.	———
———	15.	The death rate is 3.5%, which is 140 times higher than U.S. highway fatalities.	———
———	16.	Scientists have discovered a thrill-seeking gene in human DNA.	———

Figure 3–6. Anticipation guide

confirm the validity of the statements. Usually when I asked traditional-type questions, students just stared at me. Now, they seemed much more willing to volunteer their thoughts and ideas. I attribute this not only to the subject matter, but also to the format of the anticipation guide. Moving through the anticipation guide helped me quickly assess whether or not the kids "got it." Once I knew my students had a literal understanding of the article, we could discuss some of the bigger issues. In the past, I did most of the talking during discussions about reading assignments. This time, the after-reading statements [see Figure 3–7] helped focus students and draw them into the discussion. It also asked them to pose some statement questions to the class, which led to some surprisingly enthusiastic conversation.... For example, I was surprised when students brought up a topic I hadn't considered myself—the environment. Several students were concerned about the trash that litters Mt. Everest, particularly empty oxygen canisters. Students wrote statements such as these that they posed to the class:

> God doesn't want man messing up his creations.
> I would help get the garbage down.
> People should be paid to pick up empty oxygen tanks.

I found their statements to be better discussion-starters than the ones I wrote. In fact, as a class, students were much more interested in discussing their own statements, not the teacher's. (1–3)

Anticipation guides are just as appropriate when preparing students to read a piece of fiction. Amy Johnson (2002) says she likes to use a technique called story impressions as anticipation guides for fiction. Here's how it's done:

The teacher creates a list of words or "impressions" from a narrative text. They are generally put in chronological order. Students then read the list and freewrite a prediction about what happens in the story [see Figure 3–8]. After the majority of students are finished, the teacher may ask volunteers to share their predictions [see Figure 3–9]. This can lead to interesting discussion. After a few are read, the teacher then directs students to read the story to confirm the accuracy of their predictions.

The point is not to predict the story accurately; there is no such thing as a right or wrong prediction. Instead, the idea is to get students actively thinking about the elements that might be in the story before they begin reading. It is important that you make this clear to students. Recently a student handed me her story impressions prediction for "The Lady, or the Tiger?" and said timidly, "I think I did it wrong. Everyone else had something else. Mine was so different." I responded by telling her there was no right or wrong answer. "Did you think about what the story might be about?" I asked. She nodded. "Are you curious to read the story now?" I continued. She nodded again. "Then you did it correctly!" I affirmed.

AFTER READING DISCUSSION STATEMENTS

Dowling, Claudia Glenn. "Death on the Mountain." *Life* Aug. 1996: 32–46.

Directions: Read the following statements. If you agree with the statement, place a check next to the statement. If you disagree, leave it blank. Be prepared to justify your decision with information from the reading assignment and your own experiences.

————   1. Man should climb Everest "because it is there." (Andrew Irvine and George Leigh Mallory)

————   2. The 1996 tragedy could not have been prevented. No one is to blame.

————   3. "Life of mountains is stronger than life of people. Mountains will win every time." (Anatoli Boukreev)

————   4. The Nepalese government should limit the number of climbs each year.

————   5. Anyone with time and money can summit Everest.

————   6. Commercial expeditions should be banned. Only experienced climbers should attempt the climb. They should prove "they deserve to climb Mount Everest." (Ed Viesturs)

————   7. "People are very spoiled. They respect themselves, not mountains." (Anatoli Boukreev)

————   8. Man should continue to push the limits of Mt. Everest by finding new, daring ways to break Everest records such as hang gliding, skiing, or snowboarding.

————   9. I would climb Mt. Everest with no reservations.

For numbers 10–12, write your own discussion statements in the space provided. These statements will be used as part of our class discussion.

————   10. _____

————   11. _____

————   12. _____

Figure 3–7. After reading statements

> **The Lady, or the Tiger?**
> Semi-barbaric king
> Amphitheater
> Agent of poetic justice
> Choose one of two doors
> Lady or tiger
> Reward or retribution
> Adminster justice
> Daughter of king
> Young man, lowness of station
> Love affair
> Prison
> Trial savage tiger
> Fairest, loveliest of damsels
> Princess hated her
> Secret of the two doors
> He knew she would succeed
> His eye met hers
> "Which?"
> Decision
> Slight, quick movement to the right
> The lady, or the tiger?

Figure 3–8. Story impressions

Giavonna
English 9-2
Miss Johnson

The Lady, or the Tiger?

I predict this story to be about a semi-barbaric king who goes to a show at the Amphitheater. This man is chosen to come on stage and choose one of the two doors. Behind each door is either a lady or a tiger. He will either receive a reward for the door he chose or he will regret choosing that door. The king's daughter is in love with a young man and is soon to be married. Then someone is sent to prison and there is a trial. The trial is for the tiger. He will either live or die. The king, at the trial spotted a beautiful lady. The king's daughter hated the woman that her father was talking to. Then the king told his daughter about the secret of the two doors. At the end of the trial the woman got to keep her tiger. The king moved toward the lady their eyes met. Then it was time for the king to make a decision. He had to choose, either the lady, or the tiger.

Figure 3–9. Story prediction

Actually, when I read her paragraph, I noticed she was closer than most students in her prediction about the story. Once again, the point is not to get kids to predict the story correctly; it is to get them engaged and thinking about what they are going to be reading.

Sometimes teachers argue that doing a story impressions activity will "give away" the story's ending. Perhaps that is somewhat true, but I don't see that as a problem. Research indicates the more front-loading teachers can provide their students, the better they will understand the reading. My purpose is not to entertain students with stories with surprise endings. My job is to help kids deal with difficult text, and I value that much more than the threat of giving away part of the story.

I've found that using story impressions is also useful for guiding students through a story. Because the list of words in story impressions is in the same order as they appear in the story, it helps move readers through the text. Recently I used story impressions with my remedial reading class. After we shared our predictions, students began independently reading. One of my students seemed surprised when he encountered one of the words from the list. "Hey!" he spoke aloud. "It says 'Stratosphere Tower.' That was on the list you just gave us!" For that student, story impressions definitely helped him look for key words, phrases, and ideas. (4–5)

The Place of Vocabulary Instruction

Some teachers believe struggling readers need help with vocabulary and preteach whatever words in the text they believe are unfamiliar to the students. Sometimes teachers are led to this assumption by the textbook manufacturers, who boldface or note words in a reading selection that are given in a glossary. As mentioned earlier, anthology editors are far too arbitrary to decide that some words, whose meaning can be derived from the context of the story, should be included in a glossary at the bottom of the page while others aren't. The uncertainty of whether words will appear at the bottom of the page teaches a strategy that isn't replicated in authentic reading—interrupting one's reading to glance at the bottom of a page—and one that isn't even reliable enough to warrant using it. Luckily, English is a language with enough redundancy that most unfamiliar words can be decoded in context.

However, since no one sits down to write a tenth-grade appropriate work of literature, there will always be some words that cannot be gotten from context. So, teachers still need more effective ways to teach vocabulary for secondary students. In the reading, students can increase their vocabulary by using their Post-It notes that they probably have for their literature circle work. When they come across a word that is one they don't know or is somehow interesting, they write it on a Post-It. When class meets and vocabulary time comes, we share our words in groups or with the class as a whole. Each word is discussed in context, and people try to figure out the meaning. If it is still unclear, the one who brought the word volunteers to find out what it means by the next class meeting. This allows student choice, instead of vocabulary being assigned by the textbook publisher or the teacher; it makes the activity authentic because the words are found in the context of real reading—it's a reading activity rather than a vocabulary in isolation activity; and, it lets the students be the ones who help the other students learn the word. The words can be displayed on the chalkboard or a posted list or even by a collection of Post-Its. Margo Powers (2002) of Florida creates word walls for vocabulary with her students; they're doing "words we love" for February. Each student brings in a word they "love," or at least like strongly—*pandemonium, quandary, infidel,* and *buttress* have turned up—to present to the class through a graphic organizer done on an overhead transparency, which includes synonyms, antonyms, dictionary definitions, and examples in sentences. Each word presented is written on a cut-out heart for Valentine's Day and posted on the wall in the classroom. This idea can be continued or done in other months, for example, "stormy weather words" written on cut-out clouds for April's showers.

Joan Kaywell (2002) of the University of South Florida believes "the best way to enhance [students'] vocabularies is through reading," so she suggests teachers get their students "reading to find the vocabulary." If there are twenty-five words to be learned, Kaywell suggests distributing them to the class and giving points for each word found in their outside reading and subsequently brought in to be shared with the class. Kaywell says there are plenty of variations on this, distributing the words in groups and making the group find at least ten, for example. The grading points can be awarded in any number of ways, but "it's the reading that we want our students to do so they actually do increase their vocabularies."

Vocabulary is an important item in anthology textbooks. Stories and poems contained in anthologies frequently give meanings for words that the editors believe might be challenging. We remember reading Shakespeare's plays in versions that gave a half page of notes explaining vocabulary and meaning; it not only took forever to get through an act, but it conditioned us as readers to keep checking the bottom of the page for clues instead of concentrating on creating our own reading of the play. Teachers should preview readings to see what words couldn't be gotten from context and judge how important each is to understanding the story. When we watched Bob Dandoy, a veteran English teacher at Karns City Area School, teach a short story, "The Sniper," by Liam O'Flaherty, we wondered how much vocabulary preparation students needed to read this story. For example, the textbook editors decided that *ascetic* and *fanatic* would be difficult to understand, but most readers would be able to guess at the meaning from the context of the story: "His face was the face of a student, thin and ascetic, but his eyes had the cold gleam of the fanatic." Moreover, a more difficult word, *paroxysm,* is not explained, yet even that can be guessed at through context—"A paroxysm of pain swept through him." We feel the inclusion of a glossary at the bottom of the page disrupts a reader and draws undue attention to an individual word.

Amy Johnson (2002) says

When I began my current teaching assignment, my department head gave me a stack of materials, including *Vocabulary Workshop*, the popular standardized test prep vocabulary program, which I dutifully followed, completing exercises in which students defined words, completed the sentences, found synonyms and antonyms, and chose the right answers. When I gave the test, many did not do well at all; I decided it just boiled down to sheer laziness. After all, all they had to do was memorize the words! How hard was that?

I had put my finger right on the problem: I was asking students to memorize words instead of encouraging them to relish the power of words. I should have been helping them by finding rich examples of words, showing them words used in multiple and varied contexts, and revealing the power of words for more effective and elegant communication. No wonder they weren't motivated.

Vocabulary programs like this get several things wrong. First, students have trouble making personal connections to some of the words. Why should they get excited about words they can't connect to their own lives? Students can't see any reason to learn, let alone use, a word like *obstreperous*. Second, these exercises are totally unconnected to anything else students are doing in school. We might be reading *Great Expectations* one week and talking about great words like *jilted* or *retribution*, then stopping everything to "do" the required, but totally unconnected, words in the developmental vocabulary program. Isolated exercises just don't seem to work. Finally, students themselves see these programs as useless exercises they just have to "do" to pass English class.

I've changed my approach to vocabulary. No more lists of words to memorize—instead, I focus on a few important words and teach them with examples and multiple exposures throughout the year. I've also connected words to what we are learning. For example, during a unit on *Romeo and Juliet*, I expose students to a variety of words related to hatred and discord such as *vendetta, enmity, strife, grudge, vengeance,* and *adversary*. Not only are these words directly connected to the themes of *Romeo and Juliet*, the words are also very applicable to the everyday lives of teenagers. While they may not have a personal *vendetta*, they have seen lots of movies where characters are motivated by *vendetta*. Also, many students have experienced *grudges* or know what it feels like to have *enmity* for an *adversary*. When I can tap into their personal lives and show students how they can use new words to express their feelings, I am helping them realize the power of vocabulary. (7–9)

Amy also encourages students to use a word map to understand and remember the word as a concept rather than a simple definition. One of her students, Jason, explored the word *thwart* in the word map that is shown in Figure 3–10.

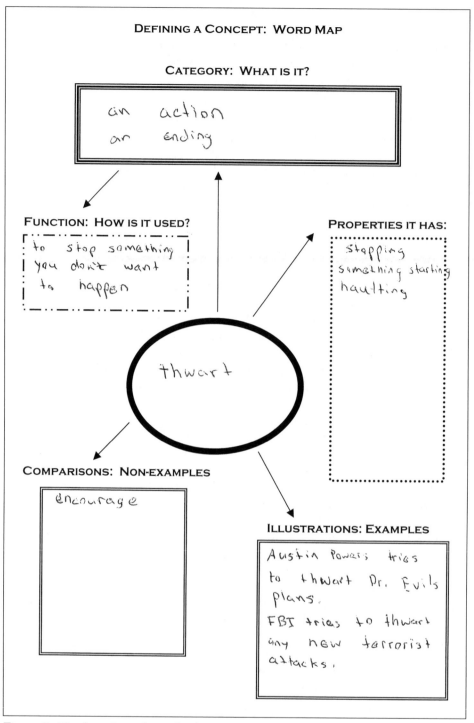

DEFINING A CONCEPT: WORD MAP

CATEGORY: WHAT IS IT?

an action
an ending

FUNCTION: HOW IS IT USED?

to stop something
you don't want
to happen

PROPERTIES IT HAS:

stopping
something starting
haulting

thwart

COMPARISONS: NON-EXAMPLES

encourage

ILLUSTRATIONS: EXAMPLES

Austin Powers tries
to thwart Dr. Evils
plans.
FBI tries to thwart
any new terrorist
attacks.

Figure 3–10. Jason's word map for *thwart*

Amy also says

I have found that using story impressions [see Figure 3–8] can help me introduce vocabulary in context. For example, students preparing to read "War" by Jack London worked on a story impression activity. One of the words on the list is *carbine*. Some students did not know that it was a type of gun. We talked about it briefly as a class and then students continued to write their story impressions. I knew that when it came time to read the story, students would understand the word *carbine* when it was used. Therefore, the story impressions activity also helps expose students to vocabulary in context without a traditional prereading vocabulary drill. (4)

Supporting Readers During Reading

There are several activities that teachers can provide to give readers support during the reading of a text.

1. Read to the class or a group of students. Just as students must be actively engaged in learning to learn, they must be actively engaged in reading to read. Hearing the words read aloud is a wonderful way to demonstrate the engaging aspect of reading; it mirrors the way readers hear the text in their heads, hearing the words and letting them wrap the reader/listener in them. This is an aspect that struggling readers don't "get"—proficient readers get lost in the world of reading. They aren't decoding words to decipher a message; they aren't skimming the material looking for information to use in a project. They're transported to the world of the story; some might say they're in a different place and time. One way to teach this engagement is to model it. Just as young children love to be read to, at home and in the primary grades, our students still enjoy it. But the message comes from some quarter of our society that says as children become older, teachers and parents should be less willing to read to them. "You're a big boy (big girl), you can read it yourself now," goes the incantation. Being read to conveys the enjoyment of reading and encourages a positive attitude. Jim's brother Don read to his two boys, Ken and Benjamin, from the time they were young all through high school. Often the family would take turns reading aloud from the group's chosen novel. Both boys were highly successful students and are now lifelong readers. We believe growing up in a reading household was in part responsible for their development. We can do the same in our classrooms.

In the classroom, a first strategy to provide this sort of support could be a language experience; the teacher reads a story with as much emotion and storytelling resources as possible. Teachers unable to muster the theatrics might try books-on-tape. While commercial audiobooks are often abridged and take other liberties with the text, making them unfit for read-along activities, they are read by professional actors who are trained in mesmerizing an audience with their voices. One vivid example is the audio version of the Harry Potter series; along with many other children and adults, we believe the audio version is even more enjoyable than the printed one, largely because of the vocal acting skills of Jim Dale, the actor performing the reading.

2. Have students read along with other readers. Some reading, such as poetry, can be read aloud in unison. The teacher's voice leads and provides a model as the group reads along with the teacher. This promotes fluency, helps develop word recognition and comprehension as it supports all students encountering unfamiliar sight words, and it builds confidence and flow for word-by-word readers, offering an excellent way to practice oral reading without the anxiety of a solo performance.

Another read-along activity can be created with a personal cassette tape recording. Teachers can provide students with an audiotaped version of the text to be read so that they can listen to the text while reading the written version. In this case, we would prefer homemade recordings, so that the recording follows the text exactly. An abridged recording might only confuse word-by-word readers and undermine their confidence.

3. Have students read aloud in class. Students rarely see adults in school reading for enjoyment, and they are rarely read to. One method is for the teacher to read one chapter or segment of a book aloud to the class to create a common experience with the literature and provide a model of good read-aloud behavior. The class can then read the rest of the book on their own. Another method is for the teacher and students to share reading a book/novel together by having a rotating volunteer (or the teacher) read aloud, as the rest of the class follows along. Karns City teacher Bob Dandoy uses the reading aloud technique as a component of his reading/writing workshop approach in teaching "The Sniper." First, he asked the class to read the story and write an immediate response in their notebooks. We were impressed that the teacher did everything that he asked of the class instead of filling out reports or marking papers while the students worked, demonstrating to the students that he placed value on the activity that he asked of them. Harvey Daniels (2002), founder of Best Practices High School in Chicago, believes students need to see adults making meaning, sharing literary tastes, connecting with their lives, and talking about the thinking that reading inspires. This also helps to combat the mistaken impression students have that school is a place where young people go to watch old people work, as our friend Jim Mahoney (2002) quips.

After writing in their notebooks, Bob asks the students to reread the story aloud in class, each person reading a paragraph or so, as much or as little as they wish. No one is called upon and no one complains that they've already read the story. Amazingly, no more than seconds expire before the next reader takes over. Some call this "popcorn" reading because the voice of the reader moves around the room, the way kernels pop randomly.

At this point, Bob asks students to choose a phrase, a sentence, or line or two that struck them as important, and he directs them to write the line at the top of a page to freewrite about for five to ten minutes. No one complains that they've already written once about the story. The first was a freewrite; the second is a focused freewrite, which they then share by trading writings with classmates or by reading aloud and sometimes they do both (students may read someone else's aloud, with the author's permission). Bob believes that we gather more with each rereading of a piece and we share our interpretations to negotiate the meaning of the story with others.

It must be stressed, however, that Bob's approach is different from round-robin reading (in which every student reads a paragraph or two in turn, progressing around the room). We believe round-robin reading is never appropriate; it puts students on the spot. As Natalie, one of our students has told us, readers end up counting the paragraphs and practicing their part, instead of attending to the meaning of the text. Besides, in the reading world outside the classroom, such practices are nonexistent. Furthermore, as we mentioned earlier, students will read aloud in class if the choice to read is theirs—if everyone is free to read as much or as little as they wish, if there is no penalty for not doing so, and if no one is called upon. Should you notice that an individual never volunteers, a word outside of class may be all that is needed to ascertain the reason behind the reluctance and/or give the student the confidence to try.

Bob never finds a need to test his students on what the story meant (on some literal level), or who the main characters were, or what the setting was. This brings up related questions. How much background is needed to read this story set in Dublin, Ireland? Can adolescents figure out the Republicans are fighting with the Free Staters? As adults, we possess more knowledge (some more than others) than our students about Ireland and the fighting in the streets. Would a lecture concerning the "times" and the geography of Ireland be essential to understanding the story? What wars could our students relate to? For students in the suburbs and rural towns like Karns City, urban warfare might be as foreign as Ireland and its troubles. For urban students, like those in sections of Pittsburgh, the rooftop battle could be between two rival gangs. Bob understands that each reader activates what he or she knows about two rival groups fighting and killing. The city students might be able to activate a gang schema to understand, but the country students similarly know about school rivalries, in-school cliques, first-person video games, and the *Star Wars* battles. The important thing is that each reader constructs meaning. The author's intent in writing this story is almost tangential; any comments that an author makes about his or her own work become just the remarks of one more reader. Understanding expands as readers share their responses with each other. In much the way Brittany teaches *Macbeth,* Bob not only covers the curriculum, but his students are engaged.

4. Have students read with a partner. At the simplest level, a student works with a partner, reading together at the same time from the same book. This works for self-selected reading and whole class readings. Variations on this strategy involve pairing with someone outside the classroom for the shared reading—a parent, a sibling, a student from a different class or grade. Readers can then stop at various points during their reading and verbalize their thoughts and questions to their partner and make connections as they read a text line by line. These "thinking aloud" processes give readers and teachers insights into different readers' approaches to processing text. Moreover, this strategy invites students to create new understandings, draw conclusions, and enter the world of the text by drawing from their own past experiences and knowledge.

A variation on the thinking aloud activity would be to alternate the pattern of questioning between student and partner or student and teacher. After the student and partner have both read the first segment of a passage silently—a paragraph, a page, a chapter—one asks as many questions as he or she can. The partner answers whatever questions he or she can clearly and completely, saving the difficult ones for the teacher. It is the partner's turn next to ask the questions about the same segment. The teacher fields the remaining questions, but then also gets a turn at asking questions. This strategy provides a communal shared-reading experience, while it promotes good questioning, recall, and comprehension. In addition, students become actively involved in monitoring their own comprehension. Making bookmarks with Post-It notes for vocabulary or quick response can help students remember questions and parts to discuss after reading.

5. Promote rereading. One of the true ironies of teaching is that teachers get better and better at reading and comprehending the works of literature chosen to be studied simply because they reread the same works year after year. For example, almost no one truly appreciates *Moby Dick* the first time through; however, after teaching and reteaching Melville for ten years, almost any reader would warm up to the astonishing characters and the fantastic adventure. Thus, one of the most profitable strategies to support readers of every ability is simply rereading passages, even though the amount of material to be covered pressures teachers to feel that they can't afford the time rereading passages requires. Two classroom activities employ the rereading strategy—plays and readers' theatre. One of the best ways to encourage authentic practiced or repeated reading is through performance of a work, which is especially applicable when doing drama. Students will eagerly practice a passage several times if they know that somewhere down the road they will be asked to perform it. Shakespeare's plays and modern dramas are natural choices. But even novels or poems with dialogue and a variety of characters can be rewritten by the students as a script and turned into readers' theatre pieces. After rewriting, the students can perform the story by reading off their script and using a minimum of props. The point is to read, not memorize, so it is low risk and students have an opportunity to reread for an authentic purpose. In addition to increasing fluency from repeated reading, these activities promote reading with expression and help the word-by-word readers develop a natural speaking style.

6. Make time for reading. Teachers should create reading times in class to show that they place value on reading and also expect students to continue this behavior on their own time, a reciprocal demonstration of value by the student. Sustained Silent Reading (SSR), in which students read silently from self-selected materials for extended periods of time for their own purposes, offers students the opportunity to discover reading for themselves and helps in reading enjoyment and motivation. Teachers can support struggling readers by creating an environment that brings comfort to reading—enforcing silence during SSR shows the seriousness of the reading; not restricting readers to student desks shows the individual nature of reading poses; and most important, participating as a member of the community by reading along with students during SSR, instead of engaging in other activities such as correcting papers or holding conferences, signaling that SSR is regarded as filler or "seat work."

7. Use direct teaching when applicable. If a student is unable to comprehend at a level that allows success, the teacher could engage a more systematic approach— summarizing a passage, questioning, clarifying, and predicting. This comprehension technique, known as a DRTA (Directed Reading Thinking Activity), usually follows a seven-step sequence:

a. *Choose a text.* Although the choice of what to read normally belongs to the reader, the teacher needs to chose a selection that has appropriate places to stop to help readers focus.

b. *Activate prior knowledge.* Reading the title, talking about the topic, or listing what readers might already know sometimes helps to activate schema. A simple question like, "What comes to mind when you think about mountain climbing?" generates a great deal of previously known information that will aid reading a story about that subject.

c. *Make predictions.* Have students look at pictures, headings, captions, and so on to try to anticipate or predict what they will be reading about.

d. *Read a predetermined section.* Have students check their predictions by reading a section of the text, either orally (volunteers) or silently to themselves.

e. *Confirm or revise prior predictions.* Stop after reading the section for students to confirm, revise, or make new predictions. Encourage students to explain what in the text caused them to confirm and/or revise their predictions or what led them to make new predictions. Simple questions like, "What do you think will happen next?" often help readers think aloud.

f. *Repeat steps d and e.* Continue until students have finished reading.

g. *Ask questions.* The teacher or students can ask questions about the reading that promote thinking or discussion. Rather than comprehension questions that are literal recall questions, these questions will require students to return to the text to support their ideas.

Supporting Readers After Reading

Almost no one wants to take a comprehension test after reading a novel, a poem, or a play. And yet, students become conditioned to expect multiple-choice tests and don't regard other postreading assignments as good tools to judge their understanding of a reading. Students grow to like these sorts of tests because they can complete a literal reading to get a grasp of the basics and then answer the picky little details that you'd only know if you read the book such as "What kind of car did the mother drive?" Comprehension tests may be difficult for some, easy for others, may trip up those who didn't finish the assignment, and/or may reward readings that match those of the test makers. But comprehension tests only give a teacher evidence of reading, completing an assignment; they do not provide an indication of level of understanding.

But there are many other ways to evaluate a student's understanding. To get at more than a literal understanding, a test or assignment needs to ask the student to interact with the text and its world. But unlike writing, which produces an artifact in the process to serve as evidence of completion, reading has no such associated end product. After reading, many people like to have a discussion (if we believe the growing popularity of book clubs). So why not use the natural "after reading" inclinations that real readers have?

1. Use book talks. Many teachers are fond of book talks, brief introductions to reading selections, offered to highlight some aspect of the book to encourage others to read it. Why not allow students to give book talks to each other? When a student or group of students finishes a work, teachers could offer a block of time to "book talk" to the rest of the class. These talks would offer anecdotal evidence to teachers concerning a student's progress, and offer another form of engagement for the reader and potential readers. We'd suggest that teachers allow students time but not demand participation, especially not requiring participation at a specified date and time. Real readers finish on their own schedules and hate to be rushed to finish or told to wait until their scheduled appearance. A requirement of one book talk per marking period with five sign-ups every week should give students enough flexibility and choice. (Book talks ought to first be modeled by the teacher, so the students can see how to give enough information. A minilesson could demonstrate techniques to entice an audience through book talks.)

2. Create levels guides. Other solutions are more structured. For example, a teacher could give students declarative statements instead of questions and challenge them to find evidence in their text that supports their responses to the statements. Students will be engaged in higher-order thinking to comprehend at the three levels of learning: the literal, interpretive, and applied levels. Having students themselves come up with possible statements gives them more responsibility and makes them more engaged in the reading. Amy Johnson (2002) tells of her success with this technique:

> One day I was leading what I thought was a great discussion about literature when I looked out at the class and noticed that most of my students had glazed eyes or were sleeping. I asked myself why the kids weren't responding. Why aren't they participating by discussing the guide questions? Why aren't they making profound statements? Why aren't they making personal comments? Where is the witty repartee? Why am *I* doing all the talking? I stared out at a sea of blank faces and realized that if I didn't do something quickly, I would spend the next thirty years talking to a group of disinterested teens, just like that monotonous, droning teacher in *Ferris Buehler's Day Off*.
>
> Around the same time I was exposed to different discussion techniques besides the traditional guide questions. I realized why the kids weren't responding. Why would they give an answer to one of the questions? If it wasn't the "right" one the trusty teacher's edition confirmed, I would just tell them "No, that's not it" and prod more until someone came up with the right answer. And if no one could give the correct answer, I would finally tell my class what it was. It didn't take long for my students to figure out that it was easier for them to just sit silently and wait until I gave them the right answer.
>
> That's why I decided I had to change things. I wanted my students to be active participants in their own learning. I had to rethink how I handled discussion in class and make some changes—fast!
>
> First, I changed all of my reading guides. Instead of questions, I formed a levels guide consisting of literal, inferential, and application statements [see Figure 3–11]. I asked students to consider whether they agreed with the statement, instead of answering a question. It sounds easy, but it isn't. Students must

"The Road Not Traveled"
by Robert Frost

LEVEL I: EXPLICIT IN TEXT

Directions: Check the items you believe say what the author says. Sometimes the exact words will be used; other times other words may be used.

—— 1. The speaker wishes he could travel both roads.
—— 2. The second road is covered more in grass.
—— 3. The first road is less attractive than the second.
—— 4. There are footprints in the road where people backtracked.
—— 5. The speaker believes he can return one day to try the first path.
—— 6. The speaker took the road on which most people traveled.
—— 7. The speaker thinks that his choice did not make a difference in his life.

LEVEL II: INFERENCES

Directions: Put a check on the line beside any of the statements below which you think are reasonable interpretations of the author's meaning.

—— 1. The speaker makes his decision easily.
—— 2. The roads symbolize the choices we make in life.
—— 3. The speaker regrets his decision.
—— 4. Most people take the first road because it is a little easier.

LEVEL III: APPLICATION/THEMATIC

Directions: Place a check in the blank beside any statements that are supported by statements in level II and by previous experience or study. Be sure you can defend your answers.

—— 1. Our lives can go in different directions, even if we start at the same place.
—— 2. He who chooses the beginning of a road chooses the place it leads to.
—— 3. The choices we make have consequences.
—— 4. Our lives are the result of the choices we make every day.
—— 5. It does not take much strength to do things, but it requires great strength to decide on what to do.
—— 6. Destiny is no matter of chance. It is a matter of choice: it is not a thing to be waited for, it is a thing to be achieved.

Figure 3–11. Levels guide

be able to justify their decisions with support from the text. This becomes increasingly difficult as students move up the levels to inferential and application statements.

Second, I required students to create their own discussion statements. This worked particularly well because it empowered them; they loved to read their statements to the class and solicit comments from classmates as to whether they agreed. Not only was this student-centered, the quality of discussion tended to be high-order in nature.

Like any activity, levels guides and discussion statements can get old if they are overused. I probably use each activity once or twice in a nine-week period. Any more than that and students get bored. (5)

3. Use graphic organizers. Sometimes making a visual representation from a variety of maps and diagrams helps to promote reasoning, understanding, and logical thinking. Students could create semantic maps that represent text concepts graphically. For example, they could draw maps that retell the events of a text. So, after reading *Romeo and Juliet*, they could map the major actions and the reactions that move the plot along. Typical maps branch out like a tree, with the main topic as the central trunk and branches containing levels of information, labeled to indicate major ideas or categories and specific supporting details. However, given license to invent, students create even more interesting maps. Amy Johnson's students created their own ways to demonstrate their personal understanding of the plot of Shakespeare's play (see Figures 3–12 and 3–13).

Creating a map, alone or in groups, will help students understand how concepts are related. And these maps could be used to teach literary notions of foreshadowing and theme. Venn diagrams can help students think about how two items are alike and different—two characters, two settings, two themes, or two episodes. Students might arrange a list of words into a Venn diagram of interlooping circles showing the uniqueness and interrelationships among the concepts being studied. Students could draw connecting lines between terms to indicate relationships. After students have completed their maps or diagrams, the teacher and class could discuss what each did and why and help anyone having difficulty understanding relationships or recognizing cause and effect, both implied and explicit. A way to model this for students in class would be to use well-known pieces of literature or even picture books. Conducting a minilesson with *The Three Little Pigs* and *The True Story of the Three Little Pigs* (told from the Wolf's perspective) would demonstrate the procedure in an enjoyable but concrete fashion. High schooler Mallory's diagram in Figure 3–14 (see page 70) illustrates the technique.

4. Send postcards from characters. The title character in Alice McDermott's *Charming Billy* was forever writing short notes to other characters in the story,

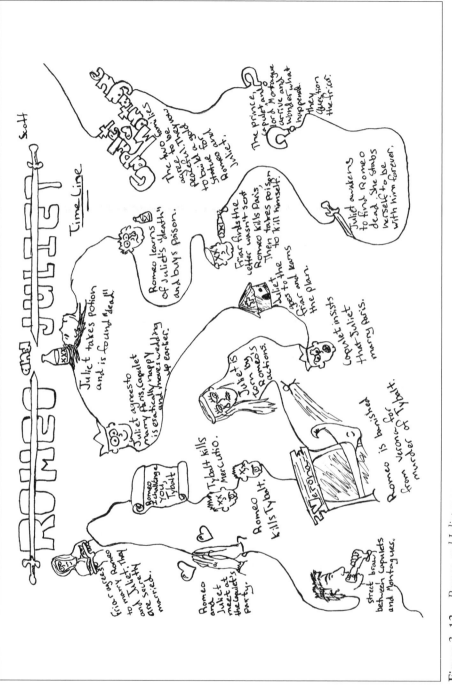

Figure 3–12. *Romeo and Juliet* map

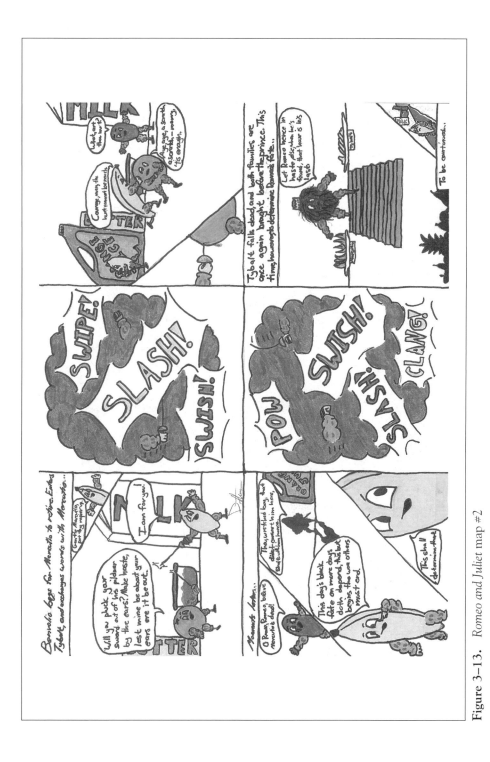

Figure 3–13. *Romeo and Juliet map #2*

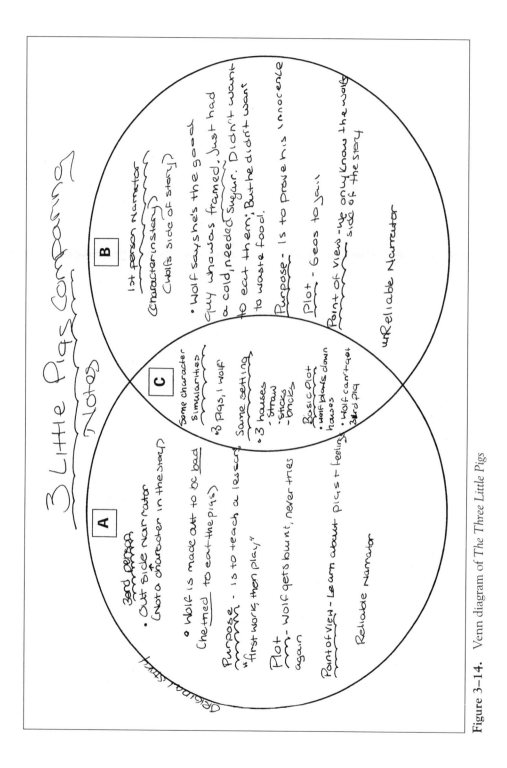

3 Little Pigs Compare

Notes

A (True Story)

- 3rd person
- Outside narrator (not a character in the story)

• Wolf is made out to be bad (he tried to eat the pigs)

Purpose - is to teach a lesson "first work, then play"

Plot - Wolf gets burnt, never tries again

Point of View - Learn about pigs + feelings

Reliable Narrator

C

- Same character similarities
- 3 pigs, 1 wolf
- Same setting
- 3 houses
  - straw
  - sticks
  - bricks

Basic Plot
- Wolf blows down houses
- Wolf can't get 3rd pig

B

- 1st person Narrator (character in story)
- (wolf's side of story)

• Wolf says he's the good guy who was framed. Just had a cold, needed sugar. Didn't want to eat them; But he didn't want to waste food.

Purpose - is to prove his innocence

Plot - Goes to jail

Point of View - we only know the wolf side of the story

uRReliable Narrator

Figure 3–14. Venn diagram of *The Three Little Pigs*

notes scribbled on the backs of envelopes, napkins, or pieces of scrap paper. Students could imitate this behavior in the story they are reading and write notes on behalf of one character to other characters, discussing events and concerns that character would be having in the story thus far. Teachers could structure the activity further by having the notes "sent" to others in class, who would then reply in character. Or, the notes could be created as postcards, written on the blank side of 5″ × 8″ index cards that have photos cut from magazines pasted on the lined side. The photo chosen and whether the postcard's greeting was in keeping with the plot and the characters would tell teachers as much as a "pop" quiz would about who is comprehending the reading.

5. Rewrite the ending. Readers often want to debate the endings of stories. So, a natural after-reading activity is to discuss the story's ending. When we read *Pigs in Heaven* with our students, one said that the ending was too pat, objecting to the happy ending. Everything worked out—the maternal grandfather (Cash) marries the adopted child's grandmother (Alice), and as a reunited family, the adoption crisis is solved. Unfortunately, class discussion stopped when their teacher reacted by agreeing that the ending was somewhat contrived, wondering what the chances were that a custody fight would be solved by a romantic involvement straight out of Dickens. No one spoke up to endorse the happy ending, and so their teacher assumed that the class felt the same. Students' sense of classroom discussion tells them that teachers ask questions and endorse the "right answer" when they hear it, and then discussion is over. By agreeing with the first response, their teacher ended the discussion, however unintentionally. Yet, by asking a text-extending question in a written assignment such as "How else might this story end?" the discussion was revisited. Another student, Michelle, wrote

> If the book were to end differently, I think that Taylor would have been torn apart. If the law really would logically have taken control, then Turtle would have been taken away. It was obviously pointed out that the adoption was illegal. If this were to happen, I think that many people would have been hurt. This is why the book almost needed to have a "happy" ending. In real life, the law would not know Taylor as we did, so they wouldn't really look into her character so much as her crime. By the end of the book everyone was so tied together, there was no way to end it without breaking that tie.... I just noticed a quote ... on the back of the book, "Kingsolver makes you care about her characters to the point of tears; she is bitingly funny—and she writes like a dream." This really helps me to make sense as to why the ending was so "happy"; it's like a dream!

The teacher never heard this response in class and might never have heard it unless she asked or gave the students multiple opportunities.

Rewriting doesn't have to be restricted to the ending. Movie producers love to rewrite novels, changing the main character's gender, or race, or ethnic background. Others change the historical time. For example, *High Fidelity* was originally set in England, not Chicago; *Ten Things I Hate About You* is a modern telling of Shakespeare's *Taming of the Shrew*; and *Clueless* is Jane Austen's *Emma* in California. Sometimes it works; sometimes it doesn't. Students could interact with a story by changing the main character's gender, race, ethnicity, or social standing and then consider what would change in the story as a result. They could consider changing the time period and finding out what the story would be like if it were told in an earlier or later time.

6. Give an award to a character in the story. Students are quite familiar with awards for athletes and celebrities. Have them imagine that a character in the story they've just finished reading has been chosen to receive an award. It is their job to decide what the award is and who it is from.

For example, a character in *City of Lights*, Louisa Barrett, is headmistress of Macauley School for Women, a private secondary school. In the story, she helps several young women with problems outside of the regular curriculum, including handling a death threat due to racial prejudice and an unwanted pregnancy. Louisa might receive an award from the New York State Women's Rights Commission (the book takes place in 1901) for her efforts at raising the expectations of women in terms of their futures and their education in general.

And since the assignment doesn't have to be solemn, the award could be tongue-in-cheek. For example, in the novel *In the Lake of the Woods*, the sheriff could receive an award for solving the mystery. However, it would be more fun to give it to the main character, John Wade, a politician defeated in a landslide vote fueled by media revelations about his disgraceful behavior in Vietnam. He disappears at the end of the book, and his wife disappeared in the beginning of the book. He could receive an award from the United Magicians of Maine for the Ultimate Magic Trick award.

Since the students present the award, they also have to make a little speech introducing their character at the awards banquet. In the speech, they tell about the person's background and what the character did that was so deserving of the award. The students are to use details from the novel and details that fit with the person's character and personality. They can tell stories about the person, but these should be the kind of stories that make the audience applaud the person as deserving the award. Furthermore, if we're pretending that the character is real, that the time is the present (even if the novel is a historical one), and that the students would be chosen to give the award, then they should introduce themselves as well and come up with a plausible explanation of why they were chosen. For example, the teacher could model, "Good evening. My name is Jim Strickland, and I've been asked to say a few words about Louisa Barrett. I wish I could say I was one of Louisa's oldest friends, but I only came to know Louisa through my participation on the Board for her Macauley school. And yet Louisa Barrett was a name I had heard mentioned ever since I moved to Buffalo, New York, five years ago . . . ."

7. Investigate a life. Another after-reading activity might involve engaging a reader's natural curiosity about the person behind the story and suggesting an in-depth study of the author and his or her works. For example, students who enjoyed *Of Mice and Men* might want to learn more about who John Steinbeck was, what other stories he wrote, where and when he lived, and what hobbies he indulged in. Finding out more about the writer sometimes strengthens the positive experience of the reading just completed, and it helps students make text-to-text connections through familiarity with the author.

Literature Circles

A special type of after-reading activity, structured as a group response in which each participant discusses a story from a given perspective or role, is one way of thinking about classroom-style book clubs called Literature Circles (Daniels 2002; Hill, Johnson and Schlick-Noe 1995).

Book clubs are nothing new. For years, adults have been choosing books to read in groups, reading them on their own, and then meeting at someone's house for coffee, cake, and wonderful conversation about the books. But until lately, the techniques of book clubs and reading groups haven't been a part of the elementary and secondary language arts classroom. In literacy education, we've championed personal response and reflection in the analysis and interpretation of literature, but we hadn't connected reader response in literature (Rosenblatt 1978) to old-fashioned book clubs. One person who deserves credit for raising our national awareness of reading together in a group is television personality Oprah Winfrey. More than a smart business woman promoting book clubs on TV, Oprah's shown America how enjoyable and exciting reading groups can be.

Literature circles in classrooms operate in a fashion similar to book clubs. They offer a choice of selection, a respect for individual's ideas and interpretations, and a desire to construct "meaning." In classrooms, one difference is that a teacher helps participants learn how to discuss and provides choices and opportunities to grow as readers. Harvey Daniels (2002) explains the philosophy, organization, and management of literature circles in the classroom in *Literature Circles: Voice and Choice in Book Clubs and Reading Groups*, and outlines some key ingredients:

1. *"Students choose their own reading materials"* (18). The teacher or students can give book talks, as discussed earlier, so that students make an informed choice when indicating their preferences about what they want to read.

2. *"Small temporary groups"* (18). After students pick a first, second, and third choice of books, the teacher can group them into literature circles of 4–6 students according to their selections and a functional mix of students of varying developmental abilities. Since groups are not ability based, they can alternate and rotate with different book choices.

3. *"Different groups read different books"* (18). Sometimes selection becomes a constraint when a limited numbers of copies of a certain title are available in the school, but students can get into the act, suggesting and locating available books. However, we've had literature groups in which everyone read the same title, and although choice was compromised, the students loved beginning their experience with literature circles this way. (We began with a sure winner—*The Giver* by Lois Lowry, and then moved into choice.)

4. *"Groups meet on a regular, predictable schedule"* (18). Time must be allowed for literature circles to become a valued part of classroom time. Teachers must provide blocks of time to talk. Twenty minutes will be necessary for younger groups, forty-five minutes for those who are experienced participants.

5. *"Kids use written or drawn notes to guide both their reading and discussion"* (18). Participants in literature circles should be prepared for circle time. While reading, we suggest they mark places of interest and responses with Post-It notes. These notes serve as reminders and can help students locate references during discussion. Students can also prepare for discussion by responding in their journals or completing role sheets with specific responsibilities, such as Questioner, Summarizer, Connector, Literary Luminary, Illustrator, Researcher, and Word Wizard.

    The Questioner will come prepared with several open-ended questions to prompt discussion. The Summarizer usually opens the discussion with a short overview of the day's reading. The Connector shares personal connections between the characters, action, and plot, and experiences in his or her own life or connections to books and movies he or she has read or seen. Such examples prompt other readers to share their connections. The Literary Luminary chooses passages to be shared and read aloud in the groups, explaining why he or she felt they were worth a closer look. The Illustrator, a popular role once discovered, draws a scene or part of the book he or she feels strongly about, sharing the drawing while remaining quiet. After group members have had a chance to bring their interpretation to the drawing, the illustrator shares his or her original intention. The Researcher looks up information that is mentioned in the text, and the Word Wizard discusses vocabulary. Daniels explains these roles and others in depth in his text and provides handouts or role sheets to use as guides in class. These roles teach students discussion possibilities but eventually are not needed, as students internalize the nuances of participating in discussion groups. (For more information on the use of roles, see Daniels' book or visit the website, *www.literaturecircles.com.*)

6. *"Discussion topics come from the students"* (18). Teachers should not provide questions to answer or study guides to complete. Students should be given the responsibility for coming up with not only the questions, but multiple ways of looking at the text. Amazingly, when given a chance, students often come up with many of the same questions that the teacher would have provided, along with others that the teacher's experience wouldn't have inspired. In *Teaching as a Subversive Activity*, Neil Postman and Charles Weingartner (1967) reveal how heavily teacher-talk is filled with questions, most of which are disguised imperative directions. Postman and Weingartner challenge teachers to limit themselves to three legitimate information-seeking questions a day and allow students to relearn what questioning is all about.

7. *"Group meetings aim to be open, natural conversations"* (18). This is where the theory of reader response becomes practice. Reading is a personal experience and we need to provide time and respect for personal responses. In literature circles, students move away from finding right answers and learn to construct meaning in supportive literate communities. We need to remember that we can only read from our own perspectives and that perspective is shaped by our experiences, which are based to a great extent on our age. When teenagers respond to *Pigs in Heaven,* they react to the sequences about cheating lovers. Why? Because that's what they're most interested in at their age. As teachers, we hope they will react to the struggles between cultures conveyed through the perspectives of the two adults from different backgrounds. Rather than lecturing about this particular meaning, teachers can trust that the roles in literature circles will nudge some students to look at the story from a perspective other than their own.

8. *"The teacher serves as facilitator"* (18). The teacher has an important role in literature circles, but it is not one of lecturing or clarifying the meaning of the literature. Instead, the teacher supports, organizes, and manages, and provides the structure and opportunities for real learning to take place. Sometimes the teacher becomes a fellow reader, but we like to save this role for larger group discussions because we find that our presence changes the dynamics of a group. After a while, especially in after-school book clubs, we can become full participants and part of the group.

75

9. *"Evaluation is by teacher observation and student self-evaluation"* (18). Because this type of learning is not measurable with numbers and letter grades, assessment techniques are authentic and include observation (kidwatching), performance assessment, conferences, videotaping, portfolios, and artifacts. We've found that the most valuable tool in literature circles has been the self-assessments. Students begin to look at their own performances, participation, depth of thinking, and begin to take responsibility for goal setting and risk taking.

10. *"A spirit of playfulness and fun pervade the room"* (18). Those of us who have already joined what Frank Smith (1988) calls the "literacy club" know that we read because it is fun. Schools everywhere say that their goal is to help students become lifelong readers, but if that goal is to be realized, then reading has to be fun! Readers have always looked for someone to talk with about the books they've read and to share opinions and ideas. Literature circles are providing our students with an authentic way to read and share their reading, to do what real readers do.

11. *"New groups form around new reading choices"* (18). We know the value of sharing ideas and experiences with different readers, and literature circles disband naturally and reform as other groups. But sometimes we like book clubs to be more permanent, the way adult reading clubs tend to be. There is a time for both. For example, after- or before-school clubs keep a core group of the same members, but are usually open to new members joining at any time, which of course can change the dynamics. As teachers, we should be careful that literature circle book clubs never become reading groups based on ability.

Amy Johnson (2002) tried literature circles for the first time this year. She said,

> I usually begin their study of literature by introducing story elements. Students read several short stories and react by writing a reader's response. Because of the number of stories we read each year and the fact that study guides, anticipation guides, and other reading tools can become monotonous if overused, I decided to use literature circles. I put students into groups of four people, and I assigned one of the following stories to each group: "All the Years of Her Life" by Morley Callaghan, "Split Cherry Tree" by Jesse Stuart, and "By the End of Summer" by Grant Moss, Jr. Students had to read each story and prepare one of the following literature circle roles: discussion director, literary luminary, illustrator, or connector.
>
> The next day students met in their groups. First, the discussion director led the group in discussion of the story and students worked together to understand

the story. The literary luminary clarified vocabulary and also looked for literary devices. The illustrator shared his or her drawing that represented a scene, idea, or theme in the story. Finally, the connector linked the story to other stories or real life. Once groups had finished their discussions, they had to present the story to the class in a unique way. Many created skits. Others created a drawing to demonstrate the themes. One group even scripted and performed a puppet show. Once all the groups made their presentations to the class, each group rotated roles and read the next story until all three stories were read by each group.

As a teacher, I thought this was a success. My students also liked the activity, as some of them shared with me:

> Literature circle discussions and presentations helped my understanding of the story because I could ask questions to my group and not have to ask in front of the entire class. Also, when I am part of the work and I have a certain role, I find myself trying harder. I think that if I would have discussed the stories in traditional ways I wouldn't have understood them as well. In lectures and study guides I find myself not listening and not trying as hard as I could because I don't have a special part in the discussion that no one else has.

> Using the roles helped me in many ways. First, the literary luminary would point out key paragraphs so I understood the story better. The discussion director would ask questions, and once answered, that story or story segment was clarified. Working in groups helps me because I got some new opinions and views. The others in the group could also help me on confusing parts by explaining them to me.

> I think literature circle roles helped me because it made me look into the story deeper than I would have. I would have to look hard to find some of the answers to the questions. Instead of reading it just to read, I would read and think about what I was reading. I think the literature circle roles really helped. (11–12)

If, as Frank Smith (1994) explains, reading is "a creative and constructive" activity, there is no one way to teach reading in secondary classrooms. Providing students with opportunities to read, thereby providing opportunities for students to develop as readers, is a big undertaking and never easy, but it is the responsibility of all teachers.

For Further Exploration

1. Observe a class using literature circles or participate in one yourself. How were the texts chosen? How was the circle facilitated? Was there equal participation by all members? Was the experience an "authentic" reading experience? Why?

2. Write an anticipation guide for a text chapter or nonfiction article. Try writing one for a poem or a piece of fiction. If possible, use the guides

with students. What was the response? Did it facilitate interest and provide purpose?

3. Try teaching a story or textbook chapter using the Directed Reading Thinking Activity (DRTA). Plan when you will pause for interaction and how you will involve students. What are the advantages of this strategy? What are some pitfalls you must try to avoid?

4. Try teaching vocabulary in ways that come from real interaction with text. How do these activities differ from memorizing lists of words and testing?

4

Writing Workshop

*Writing has so much to give, so much to teach, so many surprises.
That thing you had to force yourself to do—the actual act of
writing—turns out to be the best part. It's like discovering that
while you thought you needed the tea ceremony for the caffeine,
what you really needed was the tea ceremony. The act of writing
turns out to be its own reward.*

—Anne Lamott

The teaching of writing in American schools is still stuck in a traditional mode focused on the alignment of a completed theme or essay with what is considered standard edited English. This traditional method of teaching writing focuses on the product—the finished piece, the composition, fixated with the format of the essay and research paper, and obsessed with polite usage and correct style. Traditional–transmission teachers act as though teaching writing is really a matter of teaching students how to carefully edit their prose. Traditionalists believe that competent writers know what they are going to say before they write, that the most important task before writing is to organize content, that discourse exists in four discrete categories of description, narration, exposition, and argument, and that the composing process is linear. Time in this type of class is spent on what we used to call the "mechanics" of writing—grammar, spelling, and usage.

Yet many teachers today, those who engage in writing with their classes and consider themselves writers, prefer focusing on the *process* behind the creation of the product—from prewriting to drafting to revising, editing, and publishing—and downplay didactic formal grammar and usage instruction (see Figure 4–1). While the "mechanics" are important to a writing's final, published version, writing spans the entire process from prewriting, the stage when the ideas that will form the writing are conceived, through drafting multiple versions of the ideas and revision

Product Approach	Process Approach
• the finished product	• the process of getting to the product
• writing is taught	• writing is learned
• individuals work alone	• writers work collaboratively
• teacher's process: assign, collect, mark, return	• writer's process: generate, draft, revise, edit, publish
• taught atomistically	• taught holistically
• writing done outside class instructional setting	• writing taught workshop style, allowing for time, choice, response, structure, and community

Figure 4–1. Comparing the features of the process approach to writing

as the expression of the ideas is reworked and refined, to editing and publishing a polished version. If we believe that writing is recursive, turning back upon itself as often as the processes advance forward, then it makes more sense to teach writing in a setting that not only allows time for exploration and shaping of the writing, but time for the writing itself. Thus, one of the primary differences between a process writing pedagogy and a more traditional method of teaching writing concerns the understanding of *what* constitutes writing.

The entire writing process becomes important because of the investment writers make. This change in perception is even clearer when students are writing about topics of their own choosing to an audience of real readers, rather than an assignment given by and read exclusively by their teacher. This approach was made popular by educators such as Donald Graves (1983), and it has been widely supported by professional organizations such as the National Council of Teachers of English, and many other educators and researchers (Atwell 1998; Britton et al. 1975; Emig 1971; Flower and Hayes 1980; Tchudi 1985; Zemelman and Daniels 1988).

The exploratory nature of the composing process is

easier to see in the beginning when a writer is taken with the urge to write, but even a piece of "finished" writing may not be the end of the writer's thought on the subject. The composing process is essentially a meaning-making process. As the writer begins percolating and drafting, there's often only a vague sense of intention or purpose. The full thrust of ideas has not yet emerged and part of the cycling/back and forth among percolating, drafting, and revising involves the writer in shaping purposes and refining intentions. Donald Murray (1978), one of the foremost students of this process, which he calls *internal revision*, has collected over 2,000 statements from professional writers, all of whom essentially repeat E. M. Forster's remark: "How do I know what I think until I see what I say?" The meaning that thus emerges from one's text, and has been the focus of rereading it, is a result of this forward-backwards motion of the composing process. This interaction—returning to reread the text from a different angle of vision—plays a key role in helping the writer push forward to create meaning. (Mayher, Lester, and Pradl 1983, 36)

But another difference between a process approach to writing and a more traditional method is the location of the actual writing. In a traditional setting, the writing takes place at home or in the library, outside of the locus of instruction. Think of the scene in the classic holiday movie, *A Christmas Story* ("You'll shoot your eye out!"), in which the teacher gives the class a writing assignment, "What I'd Like for Christmas." Ralphie goes home and feverishly composes his argument for the air rifle, turns it in the next day, and then waits an eternity for the teacher to return his masterpiece, covered in red pencil marks with a big C$^+$ circled at the top. This is the classic traditional cycle: assign, collect, mark, return. An emphasis on process allows time in school to do writing, instead of simply making it a homework assignment (although writers are certainly encouraged to continue and revise their work on their own time at home). Writing requires effort and requires practice, which means that writers need blocks of time that they can count on to work on their writing—whole periods, several days, sometimes even weeks. Class time is devoted primarily to the writing itself, but time is allowed for prewriting, collaborating, conferencing, revising, editing, and publishing. A process approach also recognizes that class time is needed for some direct instruction, through individual minilessons or one-on-one conferencing, but most of the time is given to writers for writing. By allowing time for writing to be done in class, the process approach validates the time spent, valuing the work as worthy of class time. Because of its similarity to the hands-on method used in the arts, this strategy is generally referred to as a workshop approach.

In addition to the element of time, some of the other characteristics of a workshop approach used in process writing are choice, response, structure, and community (see Figure 4–2). These are discussed in greater detail throughout this chapter.

Teaching Prewriting

Writers' workshop teachers recognize that not every writer is the same, so the types of prewriting strategies will vary with writers as well. For example, visual learners, those who like to think in drawings and models, might do better with

TIME—Writing is hard work and requires practice. Writers need chunks of time over several days, even weeks, to work on their writing. Time in writing workshop is used primarily for the act of writing itself, but also includes time for generating topics and ideas, conferring, revising, editing, publishing, and sharing. Part of the time allocation in writing workshop classrooms is for direct teaching through individual conferencing or minilessons, but most of the time is used for writers to write.

CHOICE—Writers must be given opportunities to write about topics of their choice. Such topics grow out of students' interests, experiences, and questions. As teachers of writing, we must facilitate such choice through activities and strategies that help writers identify what is important and worthwhile to write about. We also must remember that writers must not only decide what to write about but also decide what pieces they want to share through publication.

RESPONSE—Writers need response and it is through response that teachers have opportunities to teach or to support writers. When we listen to students talk about their writing, we listen in order to identify what writers know. We respond to the potential in the writer's voice, not to identify problems. We teach writing by helping students generate options as they stand back from their writing and with us, revisit it. Honest response sparks interest in writing and confidence in one's ability to write.

STRUCTURE—Writing workshop classrooms organize themselves around a predictable and efficient structure. All participants understand the procedures and their responsibilities. Structure does provide for options, however. Writing is a process but is not a formula and is not sequential; writing is recursive. All pieces do not need to go through several drafts, and not all need to be revised. Writers decide what should be published. The structure of the workshop is not to control the writer, but to provide the framework for writers to do what writers need to do.

COMMUNITY—Writing workshops can only function in a community where all respect each other's ideas, viewpoints, and accomplishments. Such a community grows out of demonstrations and mutual respect among all participants. Writers in a community value themselves and their talents and contributions as well as those of others. Teachers need to trust students and students need to trust teachers in order for writing communities to function.

Figure 4–2. Elements of a workshop approach to writing

creating webs and diagrams to organize their thoughts; more auditory learners, those who respond to verbal directions and thinking out loud, might find prewriting easier with a partner who will take notes or make a web while listening to them talking it out (Boon 2000). It is important to recognize that there is no one prewriting strategy that will work for all writers, and so we suggest teaching a variety of strategies to allow writers to find their own favorites rather than what works best for us. We need to guide them by showing possibilities rather than expecting them to stumble along on their own. In fact, Aristotle's classic system of training orators had over two dozen generating strategies. Good writing teachers must avoid giving the impression that there is a lockstep pattern to success in writing.

But regardless of learning styles and prewriting strategies, nothing is potentially more intimidating than a blank page. Some writers have a fear of making a false move, writing the wrong thing, or making a bad start. Others are somehow overwhelmed by the infinite choices that are possible. "Write about anything that you want" can be as stultifying as giving a prompt that the writer has no interest in. It's not unusual to have writers spend almost an entire class period trying to get the first sentence right, typing a tentative beginning, backspacing, typing an alternative, deleting a word or two, and finally erasing the entire line. A more productive strategy seems to be generating as much text as possible, withholding judgment as to its suitability or worth until later. The secret to writing is to begin. The trick to beginning is to just start—without worrying about making false steps—knowing everything is disposable. Some writers suggest beginning that honestly, "I don't know where to begin. I could write about the problems of television programming or the renewal of patriotism. But I could write about. . . ."

Later, they find their topic. This is the basis of freewriting, a nondirective prewriting technique advocated by Peter Elbow (1973). When freewriting, students are invited to write as quickly as they can, allowing their minds to jump from one idea to the next as quickly as the connections are suggested. Our minds work on the principle of association, and freewriting takes advantage of the chaotic connections that one's subconscious mind makes, leaping from one thought to the next, often without making explicit the reason for the connection. When freewriting, one suppresses concerns about grammar, punctuation, coherence, or a grade. A writer simply writes.

Freewriting seems a way to reach the reluctant writer or the hesitant writer, a way to free the writer from constraints. The procedure for freewriting directs students to begin writing whatever comes to mind about their subject (or even their lack of a subject). If they get stuck, they are directed simply to write that they are stuck, "and now I cannot think of anything else to say, so I guess I'm stuck, I wonder what will get me unstuck, like the time I was stuck in the snow. That happened when I was coming home after a basketball game. Basketball games were major social events when I was in high school...." After trying this technique a few times, most writers realize that at some point, their mind will leap to another idea or topic. Writers are simply directed to write; the only stipulation is to keep writing and resist going back to delete or revise. When we begin to teach freewriting, we usually ask students to write for a certain amount of time—five or ten minutes—or a certain length—filling a page or a computer screen. Often students will exceed the time or length suggestions. But for some, the end of the page or the end of the time frame provides a goal to strive for, and having done that, it gives a sense of accomplishment separate from anyone's estimation of the worth of the writing itself. And making students feel good about themselves as writers goes a long way to encouraging further growth.

Some students are comfortable with freewriting and are able to continue shaping that writing through various stages of drafts. Others prefer a more structured approach. Therefore, writers' workshop teachers can offer some variations in brief minilessons. Freewriting is unpredictable and one technique that can give direction to a piece of freewriting is known as nutshelling—a synthesis stage to pull together what has been written—what Elbow (1973) calls finding "the center of gravity" (35). Nutshelling is tied to the common expression, "That's it in a nutshell"; meaning, that's it in brief. To apply the strategy of nutshelling to writing, students follow a period of freewriting with a one-sentence summary that captures the most interesting idea(s) found after rereading what was written. This one-sentence summary contains the essence of the freewriting episode—in a nutshell—tight, compact, no filler. We tell our students to try to write a sentence that captures the most interesting item or idea that they came up with in their freewriting. Those who are stuck for what to write can be asked to complete either of these prompts, "I guess what I was trying to say was..." and "What surprised me most in reading what I've written was..." The nutshelling strategy supplies a focus, no matter how chaotic one's writing has become, how far one's thoughts have wandered from the original topic, or how stuck one has become with writer's block. Nutshelling provides an approach for starting over and refocusing a piece of writing. From this one-sentence nutshell summary, students can begin freewriting again, continuing an alternating cycle of freewriting/nutshelling/freewriting until a writer runs out of ideas or runs out of time. The nutshell sentence can later be recycled to act as an opening sentence or a concluding sentence, either for the paragraph, the section, or the entire essay. And writing a final nutshell sentence even helps put closure on the session.

Writer's Notebooks

The most frightening thing to many writers is the blank page. Knowing where to begin, what to write about, and putting down that first gripping sentence is daunting. We've talked about freewriting as one technique, but another way writers can prepare to write is by keeping a writer's notebook. Unlike exercises like freewriting that can be accomplished in class, a writer's notebook is a place to write about life—things that happen or that the writer notices or hears or sees on an everyday basis. Topics for writing come from life, often life experiences, yet we do little to help developing writers find ways to notice and generate authentic topics.

Writer's notebooks are not diaries. When we first tried asking students to write every night about anything they wanted to, we didn't exactly know how the students would actually use what they wrote. We had a general sense that these nightly writings possessed the possibility of being "turned into something"; however, we didn't actually help our students discover what writers notice and write about. Most of our students wrote diary entries, such as, "Today was pretty boring. We had gym and I hate field hockey. I wore my new jeans and my Christmas sweater to school. Heather said she liked it. After school I did homework and then watched some TV." Obviously, there wasn't much in these notebooks to generate a meaningful piece of writing or to give a writer inspiration or a place to begin.

So, if writer's notebooks aren't journals or diaries, what are they? They are notebooks, or folders with paper, that a writer can carry around and write in when ideas appear. In a paradoxical sense, they are a place for writers to write when they aren't writing. Some writers use a "steno" notebook, others prefer the classic black-and-white marble composition notebook. What's important is that a writer's notebook can go places with the writer. A sturdy notebook stays with a writer most of the day, fits in a backpack, goes on car trips, and waits before and after team practices and dentist appointments. In this digital age, some writer's notebooks can even be kept on a laptop computer. Writer's notebooks help writers record possibilities, those moments in time that are lost if not written down immediately. How many wonderful things have been written in one's head but lost when the writer tries to write them later? A writer's notebook is always at one's fingertips and will become a writer's friend once he or she is familiar with their use.

Like any type of writing, the kind of writing we generate in a writer's notebook grows with experience, but novice writers find some direction helpful as they begin to use their notebooks. Ralph Fletcher (1996), nationally known teacher and writer, has demonstrated the power of writer's notebooks in numerous books for teachers and students, including *A Writer's Notebook: Unlocking the Writer Within You*. Although written for intermediate students, we've used this book with adult writers in our classes. In it, Fletcher gives sound explanations and demonstrates possibilities for the uses of writer's notebooks:

1. *Write about stories.* What are the important stories in your life? Does watching the Olympic Games excite you? How about the Super Bowl? For others, the story might be a visit to the Vietnam Memorial or watching the Rosa Parks story on TV. Events touch our lives, and when they happen, it's important to write them down. Not to share them at this point, but just to record what happened, how we felt, and why it was important to us. We've learned through the years that although we think we'll remember these events, they'll slip out of our minds as the months and years pass. Writer's notebooks are a good record of the important stories in our lives.

2. *What do you wonder about?* Wondering is almost inborn for most of us. Listen to young children. Their first years are peppered with sentences that begin with the word "Why." "Why does the moon sometimes stay in the sky, even in the daytime?" "Why don't cats like birds?" "Why do people hate each other?" When we write down our wonderings, we often ask big questions, and sometimes ones that disturb us or have no answers. After the September 11th tragedy in New York, many people asked the hard questions. We say there are no answers, yet wonderings are also part of dealing and coping.

3. *Write about the small things in life.* This is perhaps one of our favorite suggestions from Ralph Fletcher. Most writers think that writing has to be about big, important ideas, but if we look at good writing, writing that has spoken to us over time, we find that writers write about the little things in life. The details of the world are important. We need to teach ourselves to notice what's around us, using all our senses and really describing. For example, "When I got home this evening, it was almost dark and I was exhausted. Patty, my Westie, slowly got up from her cozy position in the corner of the couch, stretched, yawned, and jumped down to greet me. I was just getting home, and her day was just beginning. It's humbling to think that this little creature revolves her life around when I come home. That's true love or at least complete loyalty."

4. *Nurture ideas in progress,* "seed ideas," as Fletcher calls them (30–34). Many writers put down ideas that later germinate and grow into the big idea or the story. Sometimes ideas for stories, poems, memoirs, or investigative reports pop into our heads. The writer's notebook is the place to record these ideas. We've written some ideas about life in the city when we were quite young. We keep returning to this topic in our notebook and now have many ideas for a memoir we want to write for ourselves and our grandchildren. Now it's time to take these seed ideas and turn them into something.

5. *Write about the pictures in your mind.* If we open our eyes, there's so much to see. We need to stop to smell the roses. As writers we need to stop and write about the pictures we see in our minds. We need to notice things and write them down. For example, "Today I watched with our grandchildren the butterflies flit around the butterfly bush in our backyard. It was such a brief moment in time, but the picture in my mind is of Ryan and Brooke flitting up and down, much like butterflies themselves as they pirouetted around with sheer joy and excitement. The little children and monarch butterflies seemed to be flying about together, a summer dance of beauty and innocence. I need to work on taking this picture in my mind, now that I've recorded it and maybe someday returning to turn the picture into a poem. We'll see."

Other ideas in Fletcher's book include recording talk, making lists, writing memories, using writing to inspire, and recording secrets.

Organizing Thoughts

As writers continue to list and generate seed ideas and memories, ideas emerge as possible topics, and writers can arrange these thoughts by drawing trees, cluster maps, webs, and diagrams. Topics generated for a writing can be represented hierarchically as a tree with one large trunk, dividing off into two, three, or four major branches, each of these breaking out as smaller limbs. Cluster mapping involves a nonhierarchical grouping of ideas. As ideas are brainstormed (see Figure 4–3), they are grouped with the ideas that are similar (see Figure 4–4). Webs are similar to trees in that they explicitly make the connection between ideas, yet they differ from trees because there is no implied linear progression from major to minor ideas (see Figure 4–5, see p. 90). Diagrams, such as Venn diagrams, use a series of interlocking circles to indicate where ideas have areas of shared concerns. Students who seem to prefer the physicality of ideas can be directed to write each item on an index card and then arrange the cards in piles or patterns on a table, shuffling and rearranging as often as seems worthwhile (Boon 2000). In fact, a brainstormed list of items can be organized in any variety of ways. The actual drawing of the web or cluster is not as important as the activity of grouping and linking, which acts as a stimulus for further thought and better writing.

Writers can also arrange their ideas in a more traditional form, as an outline, and see what sort of order is suggested. One student might notice that the list seems to involve a time sequence, things happening in a "first, then, and finally..." pattern. Another student might sense that some items are the causes of a group of other items. The items might divide into categories such as "part of the problem"

Married Names

take husband's

keep maiden name

hypenate

children's names

choose a different name

husband takes wife's

foreign names mispronounced

woman's right to choose

husband's right to choose

parents' right to impose choice

society's right to impose choice

government's right to impose choice

tradition

ownership

unity as couple

credit problems

self-perception

already established socially

already established financially

Figure 4–3. Original brainstormed list

and "part of the solution." Sometimes writers prefer to reorganize the list before beginning to write the draft, numbering the ideas in the order they are to be dealt with. As writers move to drafting, they can cross off ideas, just as items are crossed off a grocery list as they are found on the shelf in the store.

A workshop approach also encourages students to work collaboratively on their own separate topics. One student might generate a cluster map such as the one in Figure 4–6. A second student could examine the prewriting cluster and describe what she thought about what had been written and what the situation reminds her of, responding in another list or a freewriting, such as the one found in Figure 4–7. The original writer could then respond to the response, clarifying what was true to his original intention and what was a development of it.

The second response obviously piggybacks on the first, but both students respond by looking for a commonality in their two situations. The first student might come up with a nutshell-type sentence, "everyone loses when someone tries to climb over someone else or delights in someone else's misfortune." The second writer might come up with a little different insight, "reporting 'the truth' and

Married Names
Options a woman has when choosing a married name:
    wife takes the husband's last name
    wife keeps maiden name
    wife hypenates her last name with her husband's
        maiden name-husband's name
        husband's name-maiden name
    husband takes the wife's last name
    wife and husband together choose a different name

Reasons why women choose the last name that they use:
    tradition
    name well-established in the community
    taking the husband's last name denotes ownership
    to show unity between husband and wife
    husband has bad credit/wife has better credit
    foreign names are often mispronounced

Who has the right to choose the woman's last name:
    the woman
    the husband
    his parents
    her parents
    society
    government

What difference will it make:
    How does last name affect the children?
    If a woman is well-established socially/financially by a certain name,
        what impact will the name change have on her?
    How does a woman's last name change her self-perception?
    What name does the children use if the woman chooses a name other
        than that of her husband?

Figure 4–4. Organized list by suggested categories

knowing the facts is not always as welcome as we thought." The collaborators could trade observations back and forth, amplifying their comments and synthesizing their observations about what the other has written until they reach a new understanding. At this point, they are free to continue their writing using any or all of the collaborative prewriting ideas they coauthored.

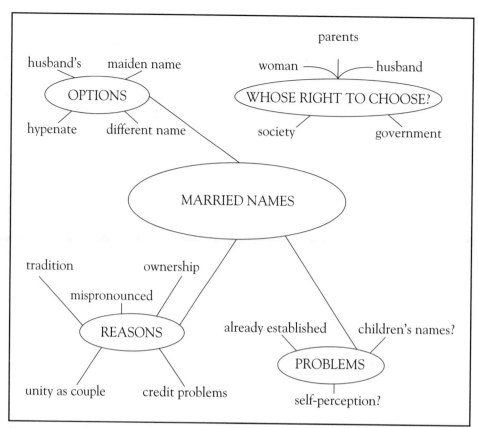

Figure 4–5. Brainstormed list as a web

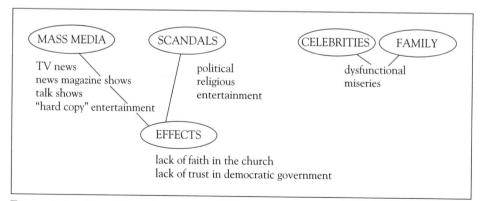

Figure 4–6. Prewriting as brainstormed clusters

This looks like it's about how families and famous people are screwed up and so the media has to do stories about them, some real news, some trash news. The Big Stories seem to be the ones about politicians, priests, and celebs. Nobody minds when celebs mess up but the other scandals cause more serious and lasting effects. This sort of reminds me of when brothers and sisters tattle on each other, reporting the least transgression, hoping to win their parents' favor. Sometimes it backfires because the parents don't like the "snitch" any better; they lose faith in both kids, the informer and the guilty one alike.

Figure 4–7. Prewriting interpretation of the clusters

Writers' workshop acknowledges that there are times when freewriting and clustering won't produce the needed ideas. Sometimes writers need to actively look for ideas, doing some reading and research. Writers' workshop allows time for students to pursue these expeditions by visiting the library, browsing CD-ROM disks, or surfing the Internet. Writers who know very little about a subject can boot up a CD-ROM encyclopedia or use a search engine, click and read the research, and then return to the prewriting list. Workshop teachers might sometimes need to warn writers about the temptations of simply importing material from another source, calling it plagiarism or simply poor research, but this can be a natural springboard to a minilesson on using summarizing, synthesizing, and paraphrasing skills.

Drafting and Responding to Writing

At some point, much like a parent running alongside his or her child's bike and holding on as she learns to ride, teachers have to let go and watch their students fly, drafting from their prewriting notes, ideas, and sketches. As Anne Lamott (1994) writes in *Bird by Bird: Some Instructions on Writing and Life*, "My father . . . taught us to be bold and original and to let ourselves make mistakes . . . [but] we all ended up just the tiniest bit resentful when we found the one fly in the ointment: that at some point we had to actually sit down and write" (xiii). Of course, writing is by its nature a solitary act, but even as writers are writing, they do not have to be alone. The writing workshop approach endorses the communal aspect of writing. If knowledge is socially constructed, then the expression of that knowledge is to some extent created in a social setting. Writers' workshop teachers believe that it is important not only to get students to write about topics that they care about, but it is equally important to provide response to their writings in a timely fashion, ideally during the process.

Melanie Bills, now a secondary English teacher, remembers her first encounter with this type of response:

> As the papers were handed back, it took me several minutes to get the nerve to turn my paper over to see the dreaded grade. Staring at the paper on my desk, I could see the red ink bleeding through. I thought right then that she had crucified me—me and my writing. To my complete amazement, when I turned my paper over, the blood I had seen through the paper was not error corrections, it was simply comments. My teacher had marked where words and ideas had struck her as strong or interesting. She made notes about how words, sentences, and ideas made her feel as she read. At the end of the piece she had left me a note saying what she thought, how she felt, and how she interpreted my thoughts... my teacher's feedback was one of her ways of individualizing instruction for all of us. She responded to each of us as people—not just with a grade. (Siebert et al. 1997, 110)

Students need response, but all feedback is not same. Teresa Savin (2002), a Florida teacher, says that

> generic comments, like "good" and "awkward," don't point out exactly what is great, or what could be better and why, in a student's work. To be useful, the feedback must be specific. By that I mean a comment should contain specific references, such as "I like the part in the introduction about your first doctor's visit very much. You did a good job showing how scared you were." This comment tells a student of strengths and weaknesses. Specific feedback can go a long way to encourage a student to work. (8)

Workshop teachers know the value of having a real audience for writing, one including students and adults outside the classroom. Professional writers have a network of trusted friends and colleagues with whom they share their drafts. Many teachers try to simulate these writers' circles by having their students write to each other during the drafting, revising, and editing of papers. Workshop teachers often go out of their way to find ways for students to exchange papers-in-progress with students in another English class or in another subject, such as social studies or history, in another geographical area or socioeconomic area, or in another grade level. Good teachers have been doing paper exchanges for years, but technological advances have taken care of the most obvious problem with these exchanges—the time they take. With email, exchanges can be accomplished as quickly as if the two groups were in the same building.

But no matter how much care teachers take in having writers who share similar interests or assignments offer their reactions to each other's writings, its success depends on the response received. Nothing is more disheartening or empty than a response that simply says, "I liked it" or "It was good." It doesn't stimulate further writing. A favorable comment is always welcome (it could have been the opposite reaction), yet students realize that "It was good" hardly says anything about the meaning that the reader constructed and is less than helpful to a writer trying to decide whether the reading was what was intended. Frustrated for their students, teachers react by advocating constructive criticism, an oxymoron if there ever was one. Criticism translates into fault finding and even well-meaning remarks in this vein are seen as negative. As authors ourselves, we have always been bothered by the oxymoron of "constructive criticism." We agree that response from concerned readers is helpful. Questioning, suggesting, collaborating is not "criticism" and we hold the same standard for responding to student writing as we do for responding to each other's professional writing (articles for professional journals, letters to parents or administrators, and literary writing such as stories or poems): as an interested reader, offering suggestions for revision without taking over control of the writing. The decisions for revision should always belong to the writer.

Students make generic comments because they have seen little in the way of models of collaborative, generative response. Workshop teachers know how important it is to spend time modeling ways to respond to writing because success depends on writers learning how to help each other, how to act in a community of writers. Teachers and students can generate a list of questions that writers would like their readers to answer. For example, "What did you like the best (and why)?" gives a place to begin because this tells a writer what a reader would like to see more of. A second question could be, "How did you relate to it? What similar experiences or thoughts have you had?" because a writer might find it helpful to know if a reader has had corresponding experiences. And often retelling what was read is a way of letting the writer know whether you as a reader brought the author's desired meaning to the text. A follow-up question might be, "Was there any place where you had trouble following it or making sense? Is there anything you wonder about or want to know more about?" Sometimes it's helpful to know where a reader had trouble maneuvering through the text. These are usually places writers can elaborate and clarify.

Keeping Track of Writers

If we are to teach to students' needs, it is essential to keep track of conferences and student progress, though it can be sometimes daunting. To help with management and organization, we find using modified versions of Nancie Atwell's (1998) Status of the Class concept helpful. It is a matrix listing the names of the students down one side and the days of the week across the top, with each of their plans for the day. Atwell says:

> When I call the role,...I record topic, genre, and what the writer intends to do...who [is] starting a new piece, continuing a work in progress or concluding one, editing, conferring with me or another student about...content or craft,...brainstorming titles, proofreading, typing,...reading published models...collaborating with another writer [or] abandoning a topic or genre that isn't working. (107)

Instead of having the teacher fill out the progress report form, as Atwell does, some teachers let the students complete the information by circulating the form at the beginning of each class. The teacher can then quickly collect the form and use it to enter notes while circulating around the room, conferencing with those who request it, noting who is at what stage on which project. The notations serve as management tools as well as assessment because it is easy to tell with what regularity a student has been on task. Part of the risk of a student-centered classroom is trusting students with the responsibility of deciding what they wish to work on each day. By keeping an updated form, the teacher can look back at the end of the week to see the effectiveness of the conferences (with a simple check, check plus, or check minus) and the development of the writer's progress over time.

Some teachers make the students completely responsible for maintaining the record of their activities by having an individual status of the class form kept along with their writings. The form, which might look like an appointment calendar, includes in each box the name of the project worked on for that date and what was done each day. An alternative is a works-in-progress list containing the title of each piece, date started, and date completed. This way, the students are responsible for demonstrating what they've been engaged in, giving them freedom with accountability. As Atwell says, "I've come to understand how personal a decision it is when a teacher settles on a system of record keeping. We need to ask ourselves: What's useful to me as a teacher? What's manageable and convenient? What won't eat up my teaching time? What will help me know my students and be accountable to them? *What do I really need to know?*" (110).

Conferencing

In a transactional classroom, the conversation surrounding writing must be supportive rather than directive; "by suggesting thought processes the writer can use, rather than prescriptions for words on the page, the teacher can give help and yet still leave it to the student to solve the problem" (Zemelman and Daniels 1988, 167). When talking about writing, both about the process and the product, the discussion can be an intimate conversation; that is, a discussion can take place between a writer and a reader, a student and another student or teacher. These intimate conversations are referred to as *writing conferences*. They are scheduled opportunities to discuss students' writing with them individually and usually help them verbalize their purpose for writing, iron out their plan for the piece under discussion, and clarify their feelings about what they are writing.

There is no one ideal time to conference, but if teachers wait too long to talk with students about pieces they are writing, the intervention will seem punitive. In other words, such a conference will be perceived as a discussion in which the teacher will "correct" what is wrong with a piece of writing (Atwell 1998). Responding to writing in conferences should be seen as an opportunity to listen to what the student has to say about the writing and to respond to what the student perceives as his or her needs as a writer, not as an opportunity to do copyediting in front of the student. Our goal is to help students make decisions about their writing during conferences rather than directing them on how to proceed or how to "fix" their writing. In a writing conference, much is said without words. For example, inexperienced teachers tend to look at the paper and rarely at the student. For this reason, transactional teachers ask the student to identify portions of the paper or problems to focus on and be the one to make any marks, changes, or corrections on the paper.

If we are serious about listening to what a student has to say and interacting during the writing process, then the discussion requires that we be near the student and the writing. This means sitting next to the student, on the same side of a table or desk. This arrangement makes it unnecessary to take the paper away from the student. If a student must hand the paper across the table in order for the teacher to read it, the student gives up the paper, in a very real sense. By sitting *beside* the student, the student may read the paper aloud to the teacher, place the paper on the desk between them, or hold the paper while the teacher reads it. If the conference is held in a computer lab, a teacher is able to read the text on-screen while sitting next to the student at the keyboard. Either way, the student retains control of the paper and control of the discussion; the teacher is sitting in as an advocate, not as an adversary.

It is equally important to remember that a conference involves talking, not merely reading over a paper and giving verbal red marks. To help start the conference, teachers should ask questions that give students a chance to talk about the process and their paper. For example, asking Melissa, "What's your paper about?" gives Melissa a chance to verbalize the purpose of her writing and affords the teacher the opportunity to respond as someone interested in the premise of the paper, not someone making judgments. If Melissa explains that she is writing about her desire to attend an out-of-state college and her discussion of this situation with her parents, her teacher might respond by saying, "I see that attending this school is very important to you. I don't know much about that school. How did you find out about it?" Follow-up questions like this signal to the student that her teacher is interested first in what she has to say, rather than worried about how she will go about saying it. When students realize that teachers are interested in their ideas, they are more likely to be open about their needs as writers. Melissa might just say in the course of the conference, "It's not enough for me to write about how great this school is and how much I want to go; I have to find a way to convince my mom and dad to send me there."

As a conference proceeds, process questions help students assess where they are in their writing and help them decide how they might want to proceed. A teacher might review the thoughts Melissa has expressed: "Okay, Melissa. You said that you don't think you are being convincing enough. Explain to me first what you are trying to say." Giving students a chance to explain what they see as the purpose of their writing allows the teacher to ask questions that help to focus, such as "Of all the things you'd like to tell your parents, what's the most convincing point you're making?" When students answer questions such as these, they are more likely to make their own discoveries about what is needed to improve their writing.

When asking questions in a conference, teachers should ask questions that students can answer, rather than questions that put students on the spot. (Remember, the teacher's responsibility is to facilitate, not to show who is smarter.) The point of conferencing conversation is to encourage a writer—to direct and guide as well as support. If the student thinks a paper is finished, the teacher might ask questions about what the student likes best or how the student thinks a reader will respond to certain parts. At this point, a teacher helps the writer read the paper as a reader would.

One of the most difficult listening skills for a teacher to practice is being quiet. Teachers know the importance of "wait time" when asking questions in whole class discussions, but sometimes they forget that wait time is valuable during individual conferences. Students need time to think about what they are trying to say. When a student is silent, teachers must resist the impulse to jump in and manage the situation. Thoughtful reflection should be respected.

Teachers in a constructivist class are constantly challenged about the appropriateness of marking errors in standard edited English and lapses in stylistic etiquette. Writing involves conforming to convention; however, the traditional overemphasis on usage and correctness holds adherence to convention as an end in itself. Regardless of how desirable conforming to the accepted way of doing things is, no matter how revered or socially ordained, writing is more than that. There is a time for teaching editing conventions, and that time happens to be late in the process. When teachers respond first as someone interested in a writer's ideas, then the writer will be more open to suggestions about ways to best communicate those ideas in an editing conference that focuses on form. Even then, what the student learns about conventions should be what he or she is ready to learn. In a conference, teachers should limit their focus to one skill at a time, something the student sees a need to learn. It hardly makes sense to use the conference time to explain the varieties of *their/there/they're* if the student has simply misspelled the word or to teach the subtleties of the semicolon if the student has no need to use one. There is not enough time to try to do everything in one piece of writing.

Amy Johnson's (2002) students were writing expository essays in which they answered the question "What is love?" Amy explains:

When I first read Nicole's draft of her essay, I noticed she was scattered. She had some interesting ideas about love, but the piece read like freewriting, not an organized essay. I wanted her to find a focus. If she could do that, I was confident she could use many of her ideas to back it up. We sat down to talk after school.

TEACHER: What are you trying to say with this piece?
NICOLE: It's just what I think about love.
TEACHER: What do you think?
NICOLE: I don't know.
TEACHER: What do you want people who read your piece to realize about love?
NICOLE: It's hard. It can be happy. I guess there are different ways to look at it. Love can be difficult and good. It is kind of an oxymoron.
TEACHER: Maybe that is your focus. That love is an oxymoron.
NICOLE: Yeah.
TEACHER: How would you organize your paper then?
NICOLE: I'm not sure.
TEACHER: What could your body paragraphs be about?
NICOLE: I guess I could do one on how love is difficult, and one on how great it is.
TEACHER: That's a good idea. Then in your introduction and conclusion, you could introduce the idea that love is an oxymoron.
NICOLE: Okay. I know what to do now. I'm going to go home and work on this.

I was surprised at how well this conference went. When I first sat down with Nicole, I was concerned that it would take awhile for her to find a focus. Instead, by just giving her a few prompts, she was able to determine that love was good and difficult. I was pleasantly surprised when she used the word oxymoron and when I told her she had found her focus, she was pleasantly surprised (and relieved)! And, this happened in the span of just a few minutes.

Recently, I have made it my personal goal to conference more with my students. Sometimes I collect drafts and make comments, but that takes a great

Interesting first statement

It is amazing how quickly how two people can meet and fall in love. My grandparents, Don and Ruth Baret, are an excellent example. They encountered each other for the first time at a youth group meeting at Church. Although they did not talk to each other, they did see each other and Grandpa said to himself that Grandma was the girl that he was going to marry. Shortly afterward, there was a dance at the Mesonic Temple. Grandma and Grandpa were each with their own dates when they started talking to each other. The two couples and a few friends rode home on a streetcar. Thankfully, Grandma left her phone number so Grandpa could call her back. They then went to the New Year's Eve dance at the Mesonic Temple. Both attended classes at Pitt, and liked to eat together at the Tuck Shop restaurant. They got to know each other better and found that they were both from similar backgrounds. The two families got along well, and Grandma and Grandpa eventually got married.

Break into par.?

He wasn't home? Not clear

What kind of dance? school?

What kind of restaurant? (if it matters...)

How?

Grandma and Grandpa both told me that it was probably love at first sight, and they got married at a small Presbyterian church in Moundsville, West Virginia on April 29, 1949. They got married quickly because Grandpa had to go to the ROTC after graduation. Grandma and Grandpa also decided that it was a good idea to get married, as all the veterans were doing it and they loved each other.

It is commonly said that opposites attract. This may be true in physics, but it is not true with Grandma and Grandpa. Both are Republican Presbyterians from Pitt who grew up with the same values.

Did he go away?

Strong statement

After 53 years together, their marriage is still going strong. They have weathered through disagreements and settled their differences, and have been through two children, three wars, and five television sets. Grandpa fought in the Korean War, leaving Grandma with her two-year old son Donnie. They got through their two years of seperation by sending by sending many letters and pictures back and forth.

Order? maybe this should be in par #2

I love this sentence. The contrast b/w 2 important things (war + children) with something everyday is striking. This would be a great last statement

Despite an ever-increasing divorce rate, Don and Ruth are a couple who met, fell in love, married and survived many trials and tribulations. Their love for each other is a strong today as the day they met!

Great start! Consider reorganizing some parts + adding more detail!

Figure 4–8. Example of student paper with teacher response

deal of time and it doesn't seem very effective at times [see Figure 4–8]. Often, students ignore my comments or don't understand what my comments mean. Plus, instead of putting the focus on the student, the responsibility falls mainly on the teacher's shoulders. And that really doesn't help kids be better writers.

Instead, I try to meet individually with my students. To keep the conference student-centered, I try to ask very general questions like:

> What are you doing with this piece now?
> What is your next step?
> What are you trying to say?
> What do you mean here?
> I am confused by this. Can you explain it to me more?

By having a one-on-one conversation about the writing, the student is forced to vocalize what it is he or she is trying to say. I usually find that this helps students figure out for themselves what they need to do, just like the example above. Sure, I could tell students how they can improve their papers, but I want them to work through the problems themselves and think about their writing.

I've found that conferences like this are vital to improving student writing. Unfortunately, it is often difficult to meet with students one-on-one during class time, especially when the class size is large. I usually meet with students before or after school, or during lunch. (6–7)

Even if there were enough time to do everything, conferences should still be relatively brief. A student needn't read every word written; it is more important that the student talk about the writing and identify for him- or herself what needs attention. Students have been trained to wait for their teacher to solve all their problems and work on the entire piece. We once heard Donald Graves call this "writer's welfare"—students sit back and let someone else take care of their writing, instead of taking responsibility for the writing themselves. This dependence on the teacher is slow to disappear, but if a teacher takes a risk and trusts that as students write more, make more choices, and respond to risk-taking encouragement, then independence will surface in the classroom.

What to Ask and How to Ask It

Having said so much about the importance of speaking and listening to students, teachers may feel tongue-tied when holding one-on-one conferences. As mentioned earlier, the teacher might ask some opening questions at the beginning of the conference: "What's your paper about?" or "How is the writing going?" The teacher might ask the student to read the paper, if its short enough, or to read a section that seems to work particularly well or is particularly troublesome. After the reading, the teacher can offer a comment, saying something that the student will regard as helpful rather than critical. Teachers who are nervous or hesitant about this might remember some of the suggestions offered by Nancie Atwell (1998), who says "kids usually write as well as they can. As you help them move forward, their best will get better" (225).

Teachers should "work the room," moving randomly around the classroom, stopping briefly at students' desks, keeping an eye on what's going on while giving the writer individual attention. Going to the student makes the conference seem like a "visit" with the author, rather than a summons to the teacher's desk.

A conference isn't an editing session; the teacher can't become perceived as the "fixer." The goal is make the student independent. Atwell says, "ask kids to tell you about the writing—what it's about and what's happening. Ask them to read or talk to you about the lead, a section that's working well, or a part they need help with" (224). Students will want teachers to read every word, but teachers can read brief sections or skim drafts to look for problems with Higher Order Concerns (HOCs), those pertaining to focus, development, structure and organization, and voice (McAndrew and Reigstad 2001).

In conferencing, teachers should be specific and positive, offering comments directly linked to what the writer's done that is praiseworthy. The verbal equivalent of rubberstamped *excellents* or *very goods* rarely make anyone feel warm and fuzzy. Talk about the writing as a piece of writing, saying for example, "I like the image you chose here . . . " or "Your conclusion seemed to pull both ideas together." Atwell says, "A piece of writing that isn't working yet, isn't working yet; it's not bad" (225).

If the piece seems to have too many ideas and tries to cover them all in a scattergun approach, the teacher might respond, "I can see that you are interested in many different ideas," naming some of them to be more specific. Then the teacher could ask, "Which idea strikes you as the most important?" or "What's your favorite part?"

Most likely, by suggesting that the student concentrate on one part or idea, the next draft will suffer from a narrowness of focus. At this point, the teacher might respond simply by saying, "I don't understand" or "Could you tell me more about this?" Another approach would be to say, "I get the feeling that you've had to leave out other things you know about your topic, but I'm interested in hearing more about it." If the student counters that he or she is out of ammunition, the teacher could ask, "Where could you go to find out more about your topic?" or "Who could you ask so that you can build on what you have? Sometimes students overwrite; that is, they put too much information in a piece of writing, perhaps overgeneralizing a rule from a earlier conference—tell the reader more, more, more. A teacher might ask, "What point are you trying to get across to your reader? What parts of this are most important to what you're trying to say?" The teacher might then ask the student to consider what parts could be trimmed without loss to the piece as a whole.

The phrasing of questions is as important in individual conferences as it is in group discussions, and the way teachers conduct conferences can influence how much responsibility students assume as writers. Atwell tries to suggest phrases for teachers to use until they become comfortable with conferencing (226–229). Her forty-some responses are set up as diagnosis/response; for example: "There isn't enough information; [the teacher might say] What parts need to be explained better so a reader can see or understand them? Mark each with an *" (227).

As teachers talk with each student, they should remember that a workshop classroom needs minimal distractions. Speak softly with students; require that they speak softly as well with you and with classmates. "If your volume goes up, the volume in the room will rise to match it" (Atwell 1998, 224). If, huddled in intimate conversation, speaking in hushed voices, the students find the consultation encouraging and special, they will come to believe, as Anne Lamott (1994) did, that "I could do what other writers were doing. I came to believe that I might be able to put a pencil in my hand and make something magical happen" (xx).

Many pieces of writing begin as narratives. This is well and good, since we organize our literate lives around stories. However, students sometimes make their writing little more than a list of events—first this and then, and then, and then. Often, a sense of reflection upon the events is missing. A teacher might simply ask the student to consider, "What do you think this means?" or "How did you feel when this happened?" The teacher might respond, "I can tell that this event is significant to you. Why do you think this is? Have you changed in any way because of it?" Students have important stories to tell about episodes in their lives that were life-changing and teachers can encourage them to share such events in time in their writing. One of Amy Johnson's students, Nicole, remembers how the cruel actions of peers cost her the loss of a dear friend. In her writing, Nicole not only shares the experience but finds the chance to share her sadness and regret. That's the power that writing has when students write about something meaningful to them. (See Figure 4–9.)

Sometimes writers take forever beginning a piece, taking time to set the scene, introducing the major characters or elements, going on about contextual details rather than introducing their thesis. A teacher might feel that the piece really begins on the second page but avoids explicitly pointing this out. Instead the teacher might say, "As a reader, when I read your introduction, I'm not sure where this is going" or ask, "What is the purpose of your introduction?" If the students seem unsure where to begin, the teacher might even suggest that students use their hands or a piece of paper to cover up paragraphs or sentences to see how the piece would sound without them.

Endings are difficult; some people have trouble saying goodbye. In timed situations, from classrooms to live television shows, endings are sometimes rushed, "Well, that's all we have time for today." Other times they're padded because we've ended too soon—television producers give the sign to stretch out the ending, resulting in the "happy talk" at the end of shows such as the eleven o'clock news, and

When the elementary schools merged together for the Middle School, I was mostly separated from my fifth-grade buddies, and I had to make new friends. Well, that was the situation I was in. I wanted to "fit in."

During fourth and fifth grade I became friends with this girl named Maria. She and I did everything together, but one day while I was sitting in study hall and she was sitting at the table in front of me, this girl named Lindsay came up and sat down next to me. She seemed really nice and she wanted to be my friend.

After we swapped phone numbers, she pointed at Maria and said, "Do you know her?"

I said, "Yes, her name is Maria."

She said, "I cannot believe you know her. She is such a dork!" Then she took a piece of paper, rolled it up in a ball, put it in her mouth and spit it at her. It hit her right in the back of the head.

Lindsay burst out laughing and Maria turned around and pushed her big round glasses higher up on her nose and said, "What was that for?"

Lindsay said to her "you're such a dork!" Maria looked at me really confused. Silence overcame me. I was so amazed. I couldn't believe I just let that whole thing happen without saying a word. Maria moved a couple tables up and I thought that was the end of it, until lunchtime.

I was wrong. When we all went in the cafeteria for lunch I sat by Lindsay and her friends there. We were all talking about our homework assignments when Maria came over and asked if she could sit with us. Lindsay stood up and got in her face and said, "There is no more room at this table." With that Maria sat down right behind me at the other table by herself. Unfortunately, it was taco day. Lindsay sat beside me and signaled for everybody to watch. She took some cheese from her taco and put it in Maria's hair. They all started laughing, and I started too. Then, when Maria was going to her throw away her trash, my foot was out in the aisle and she tripped over it. We all burst out laughing. Maria gave me that "I thought you were better than that" look. That did it. I knew Maria was mad at me. I felt terrible. I felt like someone had just pulled the perfect cloud that I was floating on out from underneath me, and I was plummeting towards the ground as my heart fell to my stomach.

When the end of eighth period bell rang Lindsay, her friends, and I crowded around Maria's locker. Lindsay knocked Maria's books out of her hands and threw her backpack down the hall. After she gathered her things and walked down the hallway, we got our things and left too. Maria called me after school and asked me why I did that.

I said, "I don't know." Then she asked for her "best friend" necklace back. I said, "Fine, have it your way!"

I know it was stupid to do all those things to one of my good friends, but with Lindsay there, I felt like I had to do it. I lost my best friend because of something someone else thought I should do. I'm never going to do that ever again. I regret doing that to Maria. She moved away to Colorado, and I never got to apologize for my actions. If I could do it all over, I know I would have realized what I was doing and how it was wrong.

Figure 4–9. Maria

teachers fill the time with personal anecdotes or a review of what was just discussed. Writers have the same problem—sometimes the conclusion to a piece feels either too rushed or else it seems to repeat itself over and over. During a conference, the teacher might ask some or all of these questions: "How do you want your reader to feel at the end of your piece? What would you like the reader to walk away knowing after finishing? How does your conclusion do it?" In the case of an overly wordy conclusion, the teacher might ask, "Are there any other places where your piece could end?" and encourage students to use their hands or a piece of paper, as they did with the introduction, to get a visual sense of alternative endings.

Ending the conference may be as difficult as ending a piece of writing. Instead of shouting "Next!" or reviewing what was discussed, a teacher might better see what the student gained from the conference by asking, "What do you think you'll do next?" This approach reinforces the notion that writing is continuous, recursive, and directed. If the conference closes with the students having a plan for revision or for a new project, they will leave with a sense of themselves as writers rather than as students who have been examined. Conferencing at the students' desks makes it easier for the teacher to end the session by getting up and moving to another part of the room.

Peer Response in Writing Conferences

Some teachers see the problem with unproductive peer conferencing as a matter of students not knowing how to give advice; however, conferencing is not about "fixing up" a classmate's paper. Conferencing is an opportunity to share pieces of writing with a reader, who reacts as a real audience, asking questions, sharing perceptions, and offering suggestions when asked. Effective teacher-student conferencing will model for students how to respond to each other as readers and as writers in peer conferences. Peer conferences will be productive when they are perceived by students as chances for writers and readers to share ideas and reactions.

As with any new activity, peer conferencing must be learned. By the time students are in secondary school, many are uncomfortable sharing ideas in peer groups. This is not to say that students are shy or reticent. Much of the discomfort felt working in groups can be traced to the competitive pressure for grades, compounded by a belief that sharing is cheating, a form of "not doing one's own work." Successful conferencing depends on students working together collaboratively and noncompetitively, students who believe that real writers aren't graded, they're evaluated by readers reacting to what they say and how they say it. Thus, members of a class need time to get to know one another. (See Chapter 2 concerning establishing community.) Groups can be established according to interest (students sharing concerns or curiosities), personality (students simply enjoying working with each other), convenience (students working on the same piece of literature or at similar places in their writing), and need (students whom their teacher feels may learn from each other). Working together necessitates moving desks around or using a table, but more importantly, group work necessitates knowing what each person's role is in the peer conference.

Each person in a group conference is primarily a listener, constituting an audience of one. As the writer reads aloud, students need to learn to listen in order to discuss the subject of the piece, focus on its ideas, ask real questions about what they are interested in knowing, indicate what parts of the piece "work" and what parts are vague or confusing, and let writers know what they, as listeners, want to know more about. By *listening* to the writer rather than reading the piece, peer responders avoid assuming the role of proofreader. (A listener cannot hear comma faults and misspelled words.) Editing can be dealt with later at conferences set aside specifically for that purpose.

In the beginning, and often long into the semester, students tend to give shallow and unhelpful responses. Frequently, the responses go in either of two directions: "This is wonderful, great; I can't think of a thing to tell you to make it any better" and "This piece is lousy; It's not what she wants, but I don't know what to tell you to make it any better." Obviously, neither response is of much help, but the second is definitely the more demoralizing. A key rule in conferencing, then, is to be supportive. Students should be encouraged to look for what is good and then to continue beyond merely congratulating the writer, "this is great . . . ."

In the beginning, students appreciate some helpful hints from the teacher for peer conferences. They might be simply presented with a formula at first. For instance, "Retell what the writer is saying, so that the writer can determine if the piece of writing says what the writer thinks it does." A procedure technique might be suggested: "Identify for the writer what you consider to be the strongest part of the piece, explaining why you feel this way, and then ask one question of the writer which you feel would clarify for you any part that seemed vague or unclear." Some teachers and students find guidesheets useful. We add one caution here: guidesheets can easily become extensions of teacher control. Guidesheets in a constructivist classroom are not prescriptive; instead, they are open-ended enough to allow for genuine response and questioning. Even teachers who understand this distinction must make clear to their students, who have had years of experience with worksheets and dittoed directions, that guidesheets are meant to help them structure their conferences, and if at any point they feel other concerns are more important or they enter into a productive discussion of any one area, it is not necessary to address all the questions on the guidesheet. A peer conference guidesheet can be constructed to suit the class and the topic, and modeled after one used by

1. Make a positive, rapport-creating statement to the writer.
2. Make two positive comments about the paper. What are its strengths?
3. Describe any weakness you find in the areas listed below. Suggest a strategy to eliminate each weakness. Record your comments below.
   a. thesis or focus
   b. voice or tone
   c. organization
   d. development
4. List any weaknesses you see in sentence structure, punctuation, usage, and spelling. Suggest a strategy to eliminate each weakness. Record your comments below.

Figure 4–10. Tutor critique sheet

Donald McAndrew and Thomas Reigstad (2001) (see Figure 4–10) or another used by Steven Zemelman and Harvey Daniels (1988) (see Figure 4–11).

Because techniques for peer conferences must be learned, many teachers abandon them before giving students adequate time to feel comfortable with them. Since teachers often have little patience and want everything to work immediately, when

Be as specific as you can in answering these questions. Your comments will help the writer improve his or her paper. Share your responses orally with the writer after he or she has read the piece through at least once.

1. What event did the writer focus on?
2. Why do you think the writer chose this topic?
3. How did the writer feel about the incident when it happened? How do you know?
4. How does the writer feel about the incident now? How do you know?
5. What part of the paper did you like best? What part impressed you the most? Why?
6. What, if anything, confuses you about the narrative as written?
7. What would you like to know more about?
8. What would you change about the content or arrangement of this paper?

Figure 4–11. Peer critique sheet: Personal narrative

a group has difficulties and seems to be floundering, teachers need to give students the chance to solve their problems themselves. Peer conferences need teachers to support them rather than to solve all their problems. If the time comes when it is to the students' advantage for the teacher to intervene, it should be done strategically. For example, there are times when regrouping intervention is needed—one student is dominating, personalities are in conflict or simply not meshing, or the students do not seem interested in each other's topics. Teachers will only know these things, however, if they are acting as facilitators and careful observers of the conferences. Changing partners can be done positively, letting students see that their teacher is supporting the process, by suggesting for instance, "Darren, I see that you wrote a paper about the news media. Would you please change partners with Sally, so that you can respond to Eric's paper about reporting in the presidential campaign." The students involved will see the intervention as helpful and none will feel singled out as failures in the conferencing process.

Positive peer conferences depend on the climate in the classroom and the expectations for writing and responding set up in the class. If students are given opportunities for responsibility and feel that the purpose of writing is to communicate their thoughts and feelings about a topic to a real audience, they will react accordingly in a peer conference. If students get the impression that the purpose of writing is to receive a good grade, to write in a way that their teacher feels is best, or to exhibit a knowledge of form and structure, then the conferences will proceed accordingly. It is really up to the teacher to define and establish such goals.

Parading and Modeling for Students

Rick Chambers (1996), a former secondary teacher in Ontario, Canada, believes his role as a teacher is to be "part of the writing environment;...writing when the students write,...sharing problems and rough drafts with the students. He is learning with them, and modeling the process for them. He shares his work in progress, and throws his rough drafts in with the students' for peer reading and assessment. He takes the same risks as he asks the students to take, and in so doing, demonstrates his vulnerability, which almost always forges an easy rapport with the class" (13).

Similarly, Jim Mahoney (2002), formerly of Miller Place High School in New York, decided to try writing spontaneously in front of his students, after hearing Nancie Atwell explain how she composed some pieces of writing on an overhead transparency. He explained to his students that he wanted to write individual thank-you notes to each of eighteen girls on the J.V. soccer team in appreciation for a gift for being their coach. "I began by writing some of these notes on a transparency," Jim said, "to show my students how I would solve the problem of what to say after I said, 'Thank you very much for the wonderful gift.' I also wanted to show them how to avoid sending a form letter by using some of the same words, but then personalizing the message with a few comments about the person receiving the note" (101).

Sometimes the students suggest what to write, and the teacher records their words on a transparency and overhead or at the computer with a projector. The important part is the modeling that goes on as the teacher does the typing and the students do the thinking. Thus, students learn, "So that's how writers think!"

Writers' workshop teachers need to be comfortable with the notion of modeling, performing their craft in front of their students. An interesting twist on this idea is the notion of *parading*—joining in and marching along with someone doing something interesting (Gray 2001). In parading, there are no predetermined models or patterns of behavior to be reproduced or standards to be met. As the parade moves along, onlookers get caught up in the experience, join in the activity, and participate as long as their interest holds or the parade continues. In this light, modeling alone isn't enough; teachers need to get students excited about being writers (and readers, for that matter). Only then will students become engaged in their learning. And when they do, they'll be learning the way most people do, marching behind or alongside others—teachers, mentors, peers—who are knowledgeable or more proficient in the craft. We once heard David Sanborn, the Grammy-winning saxophone player, confide to the audience as he was introducing his band that whenever he goes out on tour or books a studio for recording, he tries to find players who are better than he is. That's how you grow as a musician, he said. David Sanborn might have been speaking of Lev Vygotsky's (1978) Zone of Proximal Development; to learn, we need to be challenged to tomorrow's development, ushered by more experienced paraders whose enthusiasm and expert expression sets the tone and guides the way. As Anne Lamott (1994) in *Bird by Bird* says, "Writing taught my father to pay attention; my father in turn taught other people to pay attention and then to write down their thoughts and observations. . . . He taught . . . me to put a little bit down on paper every day, and to read all the great books and plays we could get our hands on. He taught us to read poetry. . . . [and] I began to believe that I could do what other writers were doing" (xii, xx).

Revision: Imagining the Better Text

Substantive revision is tedious and is hard work. Revision means to envision another version; *re*-vision: to imagine what is not—to imagine the better text. Revision means being able to recast sentences, alter diction, and rethink these considerations as Higher Order Concerns. Workshop teachers help students reflect on their writing as it takes shape and facilitate revision by modeling, demonstrating, suggesting, and encouraging revision. To know how to do those things requires vision.

When our daughter (who is now a K–3 reading teacher, we're proud to say) was in tenth grade, we asked her how she made her papers better. Laura told us that when she got a chance to work on a paper again, she fixed the words that jumped out at her. She added sentences and changed a few words (if she could think of better ones). She remembered adding a sentence to the end of a paper she had recently turned in. When we asked her friend Leah the same question, she said that she waits for the teacher to tell her where to "add some details." If the teacher wasn't available or didn't actually tell her, then her strategy was to find someone "who is really smart" to read it. Otherwise, she didn't really know what to do. As ineffective as these revision strategies seem, writers become fixated with the way they approach revision—good or bad. Mike Rose (1980) referred to this dilemma as writers having rigid rules and inflexible strategies; writers revise in a particular way because that's the way they've always done it. Unaided, students develop idiosyncratic strategies for revising their papers: they make it longer, adding more to the end of the text; they substitute words; they correct punctuation, grammar, and spelling; but to learn more substantive revision, they must see a need for revision and be open to suggestions of possibilities.

Unfortunately, just as with prewriting and drafting, there is no one way to teach writers to revise by following a certain sequence of steps. The essence of revision involves moving away from one's drafts to look at them from different perspectives, a talent that takes time and practice to develop. Different strategies will appeal to different writers, and some techniques are more helpful than others in developing productive strategies to "re-see" one's writing. In a workshop setting, teachers can model developing a "reader's eye" and students can practice until they find their own rhythm.

Students are often told to revise by developing their ideas, adding more details, or being more specific. Too often they are just told these revision truisms and never get to see revision done firsthand. Writers' workshop teachers can model the moves, and students can then practice on their own or on a partner's writing. All of these moves are tentative and must be judged by how they look and how they sound when read.

Revision is easier in response to readers' true questions rather than in response to directions or commands. What does the reader understand, want to know, like, or react to? One doesn't learn to revise by being told what to do; one learns to revise by listening to the reader—whether that reader is oneself or someone else.

Minilessons

It is most often during the revision stage of writing that the teacher has the most opportunities for direct teaching. The lessons teachers teach in a writing workshop classroom are a result of the needs expressed in their students' writing. Minilessons are short, to the point, and demonstrate a strategy, skill, or technique a writer can use immediately—minilessons address writers' needs.

The length of minilessons varies according to the depth of the issue being addressed. Minilessons dealing with word choice, mechanics, and form can be taught in five to fifteen minutes. Other minilessons require more time, usually in the form of writing demonstrations. Jim Mahoney's (2002) students call his minilessons "maxi-lessons," a dig at his tendency to talk beyond the ten to twelve minute limit he tries to adhere to. "In my classes, students felt that . . . any lesson I gave, long or short, was time taken away from things they needed to accomplish" (66).

Many of these minilessons have to do with style and characteristics of different genres. For example, minilessons can tackle action verbs, intensifiers, verb tense, and first- or third-person narration. Nancie Atwell (1998) offers lists of possibilities for minilessons and actual scripts of minilessons she uses to support student writers by addressing their writing needs. These scripts take teachers into the classroom of an expert teacher of writing and allows them to listen in during minilessons. For example, "You could describe a physical state in your writing with adjectives or adverbs: 'I was really very hot.' Or you could show it: 'Sweat dripped off my glasses. . . . You may want to read through your draft and mark in the margin anywhere you find yourself describing to the reader something that you could be showing instead" (165).

Dealing with Verbs

For years, writing teachers have been saying: nothing puts more life into writing than *action* verbs and conversely, nothing robs life from writing more than *to be* verbs, textual equivalents of mathematical equations: X is Y; Y is Z; thus, X is Z. Students remain unconvinced, but a workshop setting gives the opportunity for students and teachers to work on recasting sentences with *to be* verbs. We give students a list of the variable forms of *to be* (*is, was, were, will be, are,* and the negative forms, *is not, was not,* etc.), and ask them to simply circle them in a completed draft. For example, a student might turn up the following sequence: "The cost of most cars today is over twenty thousand dollars; I think cars that cost over twenty thousand are too expensive. As you can see, cars are too expensive." One or two statements of fact are acceptable, but these verbs hide the action in nouns. "The cost of most cars today is over twenty thousand dollars" can be rewritten as "Cars today cost over twenty thousand dollars."

We suggest to students who have an abundance of *to be* verbs that they look at the words that precede and follow the verb, searching for a word that might make a better verb. For example, "Spending federal money on nuclear power plants is a waste of our limited tax dollars" can be improved by looking at the words before and after *is*. The phrase *a waste* can be used as a verb, *wastes*, transforming the sentence into, "Spending federal money on nuclear power plants wastes our limited tax dollars." Students might object that this change is nothing major; the two sentences mean the same thing, but a playful demonstration of stylistic changes may be enough for students to join the parade.

Editing

Editing is different from revising. If revising involves Higher Order Concerns (HOCs), then editing involves Lower Order Concerns (LOCs)—"matters related to surface appearance, correctness, and standard rules of written English" (McAndrew and Reigstad 2001, 56). In editing, our focus shifts from concerns that emphasize the draft as a whole to those looking at sentence structure, punctuation, usage, and spelling. Editing involves getting text ready for final publishing. For the most part, students know how to write complete sentences and punctuate them correctly, but grammar and usage errors buried in the text often escape detection.

Some teachers believe that their job is to teach writers to be editors; however, most of us know there is much more to the writing process. It makes more sense to support writers while they are writing, while they are making meaning, and to leave editing as a polishing activity that writers engage in when they are ready to display their work. If we want to help students become better and more confident writers, the time to help is during the process when writers are shaping thoughts and ideas. However, editing can and should be taught, since a correctly edited piece of writing helps a writer express thoughts clearly and in a way that is "reader friendly." So, the question is when and how to teach editing.

No matter when it is discussed, editing is more difficult than it seems. For one thing, it is hard to be one's own editor. An author is aware of the complexities and premises for a piece of writing and is not in a good position to judge where a text's mechanics might cause a reader to be confused. Students who have trouble with incomplete and run-on sentences have trouble spotting these problems when reading text for meaning. The same is true of problems with subject/verb agreement and pronoun/antecedent agreement. Instead of using workbook exercises, writers need strategies to help them look at their own sentences the way that an editor does. To edit, one needs to step back from the writing and read with a fresh eye.

Someone else, a peer, a teacher, can help give editing advice. Writers can work in pairs with teachers, tutors, or other students, checking each other's work for run-on sentences, incomplete sentences, agreement errors, and sentence variety. However, most students would prefer to have their teacher tell them what to do instead of relying on the other people in class. The students feel that the teacher will know what each writer should do to correct the piece (to get a good grade), while the other students in the class will be equally confused about what to do and give advice of dubious worth (in terms of bettering a grade). Perhaps the students are right; they have had little training as editors, other than reading something and saying, "That's nice." The students in each writing group need to be shown editing and evaluating strategies so they can offer each other valuable advice—strategies for acting in a community of writers.

Anyone who has purchased a DVD player so that they can be treated to the restoration of deleted scenes from their favorite movies soon learns that there is probably a good reason for the "cutting room floor." Much of the art of filmmaking comes in knowing what to cut out and what to leave in. For example, this paragraph originally began in one of the draft versions, "Mathematically, the inverse of addition is subtraction, and so it is true of revision." After the DVD analogy was added, the point was made and the math connection seemed unnecessary and redundant. Too often, students rarely think of cutting anything; after all, it might be good. They honestly don't know. Workshop teachers spend time showing them how they go about deciding what to cut and what to keep; they spend time giving practice in cutting and judging the effect. We begin by focusing on repeated words, asking students to look for places where the same phrase, expression, or words turn up. Cutting and trimming are important editing techniques.

Often writings tend to collect problematic "fuzzy" words that are either overused or virtually meaningless, such as *very, really, quite,* and *rather.* For example, directions for changing a lighting fixture in the house might warn, "Removing the old fixture may be very dangerous if you neglect to turn off power at the fuse box." The word *very* adds little to the information and it can be deleted. Other problematic words include words that begin with *th-: this, these,* and *there,* which are frequently little more than placeholders, dummy subjects of sentences. For example, "*There* is a section provided to teachers..." can have the dummy subject deleted and replaced with the real subject, "A section is provided..." or "There is such pressure to cover so much material that teachers feel..." will benefit from a stronger verb, "The amount of material to be covered pressures teachers to feel...." Allowing students to see teachers reworking their own writing is part of getting them to engage with their writing, to join the parade.

We also show students how to look for nominalizations, words that end in *-ion,* and suggest turning the nominalizations back into active verbs. For example, "The confusion is the result of unstructured lesson plans . . ." could be rewritten as, "Unstructured lesson plans confuse . . . ."

As with many of the editing strategies, students may object that they don't perceive any difference in the reconstructed sentences, regarding the changes as further instances of the arbitrary behavior of English teachers. It is worth a little time to frame the difference. For example, many people enjoy watching the winter Olympics but are baffled by the scoring. The downhill skiers are awarded the gold, silver, and bronze according to the fastest times down the mountain. The skating competition is another matter; other than applauding when the television commentator prompts them, few understand what distinguishes one skating performance from another. Many believe the points are awarded according to the subjective nature of the judges. However, the performances differ in terms of style, grace, difficulty of execution, economy of movement, preciseness of movement, control—much the way alternative versions of sentences differ from one another. Judgment has to do with experience and therefore expertise. More experienced writers are able to see stylistic differences in execution.

Using Spell Checkers, the Thesaurus, and Style Checkers

Computers now come with three standard features that, used properly, can make the editing tasks a writer faces a little less tedious: spell checkers, the thesaurus, and style checkers. Teaching students to edit using a spell checker and a thesaurus is mainly a matter of teaching them to be careful in adopting the computer's suggestions. Teaching students to edit using style checkers is trickier. We discuss these tools in greater detail in Chapter 5, "Computers, Websites, and Technology."

Sharing: Writing That Goes Somewhere

Many people consider publishing as the last stage of the process of writing, but we like to think of it as sharing. Sometimes simply sharing writing with classmates is enough satisfaction, but if writing is meant to be read, then writers have to finally hit the metaphorical "send" button. Teachers can nurture this stage of writing by locating others who would like to read the students' writing. This can include school venues, such as literary magazines, student newspapers, poetry collections, club newsletters, and school websites. Student writing can be shared in the community in local newspapers, church newsletters, or sport and civic club publications. The sharing can extend even wider through writing contests, such as the National Council of Teachers of English Writing Achievement awards, and publications that feature student writing, such as *Merlyn's Pen*. A more complete exploration of all the possibilities can be found in Chris Weber's *Publishing with Students: A*

Comprehensive Guide (2002). Another way of sharing writing is to give it as a gift.

Bob Dandoy, a teacher from Karns City in Pennsylvania, tells of one of his eleventh graders who brought a piece of writing to him for a conference; it was about her dad and what he meant to her. The emotions she felt were revealed through a series of prose snapshots of her dad, watching him work around the house, vacations shared, and private personal moments. As Bob read the piece, tears began to well in his eyes. He was thinking of his own daughter. He told his student there were a few details to clean up, but in general it was ready for the "real test." Bob promised to show her some fancy fonts on the computer if she'd like to give it to her dad for Christmas. She said, "No. His birthday's in November; that's when I want to give it to him." She printed out a good copy, wrapped it up in a box, and took it home. The following day in class, Bob asked the student what her dad thought of the writing. The student said, "He cried."

Jim Mahoney (2002) says most of us share a memory of a child

who runs off the school bus or who comes racing in the door, waving a drawing from school. The child is full of glee and races up to the person, presenting the work as a present. It may be a crude drawing, a picture with some text, even a greeting card for a special occasion. The person receiving the work will usually hug the child first, accept the gift, . . . hold it out for admiration, . . . [hang it] in a place of prominence, perhaps on a bulletin board or on a refrigerator, . . . [and finally save it where] treasured gifts of love are kept: a scrap book, a special folder, a drawer, a box. This work has been real enough to go somewhere special. Usually a grade never appears on it. Such a mark would be entirely irrelevant to the receiver.

Why does such real writing stop when students get into upper elementary school or into secondary school? Why has authentic writing been replaced in the curriculum by school writing? Is it any wonder that the energy the artist had as a child disappears when all the writing is assigned and it is meant almost entirely for the teacher. (94)

Teresa Savin (2002) says that,

As a rule, every piece of work done in my classroom has the opportunity to be seen or heard by other students. It is not enough that the teacher has read it; to complete a piece of work, turn it in to the teacher, and not see it again until it comes back with a grade does not incorporate audience. A wider audience can be achieved by inviting peers to enjoy the work as well. This may be done by showcasing work on the walls of the classroom, inviting students to volunteer to read their own work aloud, or simply asking them to find a partner and read each other's work. Last year when the issue of attending school year-round was introduced for debate in Chicago, my classes wrote letters to the Local School Council (LSC) expressing their opinions. Several of my students cite receiving a response from the LSC as the highlight of the year. Students are more likely to find purpose in an activity if they know others besides the teacher will be seeing what they are doing. (6)

One of our students, Christa, remembered feeling that lack of purpose in writing that was going nowhere.

As the years went on [in school], things began to change though. . . . I was no longer able to connect through writing because I was being forced to write essays and research papers on topics that did not interest me in the least. I wasn't having fun anymore and my writing showed that, at least to me. My grades never fell but my passion for writing was lost. It wasn't until my freshman year of high school that the joy I found in writing returned. Everyone talks about that one teacher who influenced them beyond all others. My freshman English teacher truly changed the course of my life by helping me find myself though writing once more.

Another student, Melissa, remembers discovering the power of writing when she wrote an editorial for the school paper in her junior year of high school. She says, "I wrote a satirical piece about popularity and stereotypes. . . . and a giant controversy ensued. The cool part was that the people who understood the article thought I was a god. I had groupies for one day in my life." Students won't soon forget writing that goes someplace. As Jim Mahoney says, "If we can take the kids as they mature and still allow them to write for those genuine purposes, they will have drunk at a well that will sustain them through some of the other kinds of writing they will be asked to do in the secondary schools" (94).

And still the debate continues—Is writing a talent? A skill? One philosophy of writing says you must be born a writer. This is the romantic notion that the gift is within us. In order to discover writing talent, a student must delve inside, seeking inner truth, insight, and creativity. Writing on this level is very much outside of what is teachable. Writing can be nurtured, coached, and enabled, but not taught. Another philosophy sees writing as a communication skill that can be learned much the way other communication skills are learned—talking, facial expression, vocal nuance, and body language. Some things can be directly taught: holding a pen, the shapes of letters in cursive writing, and the need for punctuation of some sort. Other skills can be modeled, such as wit, metaphor, and the periodic sentence. Some skills can be nurtured the way talent must be, such as experiencing the way writing is used in the past and learning a set of heuristic rules or devices that can prompt the next thought or idea. So writing, whether conceived of as talent or skill, can be developed in humans to an extent largely dependent on the evolving writer.

For Further Exploration

1. Visit a classroom in which students are engaged in a writing workshop. What is the teacher doing? What are the students doing? How is the work-shop structured? How are the elements of a writing workshop (community, choice, time, structure, and response) evident to an observer?

2. Keep a writer's notebook for yourself for a week or two. What did you learn as a writer from the experience? What did you learn as a teacher of writing?

3. Conference with someone about their draft of a piece of writing. How did you respond to the writer? What questions did you ask? How did the writer respond to you? To your questions? What was difficult? What would you change or what would you need to learn to do better?

4. Look at a set of student papers. What minilesson or lessons emerge from these papers? Design a minilesson based on what you see.

5

Computers, Websites, and Technology

Politicians, bureaucrats, administrators, and even parents will press for the expanded use of computers in education; they will continue to confuse economy with efficiency. Uncertain or lazy teachers who cannot think of more productive ways of using computers will open the classroom doors to the programs. They will admit the agent of their own destruction.

—Frank Smith

Teachers, parents, administrators, school board members, and community leaders want the best for their schools and the students in those schools. They are absolutely convinced that students need to be computer literate now that we are in the twenty-first century, even if they're unsure exactly what that means. Unfortunately, the push for computers in the classroom is often symptomatic of organizing a curriculum without having a theoretical understanding as the guide.

Let's not kid ourselves. In much the way that using a hammer will not make me a good carpenter, computers are merely tools that can extend our abilities, not substitute for ability. Computers and technology aren't going to make our students better writers, more knowledgeable adolescents, more insightful consumers, or any of the other promises we've been believing since the dawn of the digital age in the early 1980s. Spell checkers on computers will help writers spell more words accurately, but they will not catch every problem or provide the correct variation. Truthfully, they will help those who already know how to spell. The ability to compose in word processing, revise, edit, and print clean copy will benefit those who know how to write, but the computer's potential benefits will not magically transform a writer beyond what he or she is already able to do.

Having a house stocked with books, magazines, and newspapers will not make one more knowledgeable unless the person takes advantage of the personal library and reads the information at his or her fingertips. So too, the computer, with its

CD-Rom disks and Internet capabilities, will only extend the house of books, delivering more and more raw information that must be digested and assimilated to become knowledge. If literature doesn't become a "poem" (to use Louise Rosenblatt's distinction) until a reader transacts with the text, the information that is available in cyberspace doesn't become knowledge until a person interacts with the data. We suggest teachers invoke a mantra Donald Graves once suggested for examining the point of our educational endeavors (Strickland 1990), and ask, "What's it for?"

At one time, computers were used for drill-and-skill programs, online versions of five-paragraph essays, and focusing attention on error detection. Now it seems computers are for making web pages and surfing the Internet. What happens when computers are introduced in a classroom depends on teaching style, student writing activities, and classroom climate. In a transactional classroom that fosters learning communities and student-centered activities, the computer can advance an alien environment in which students are focused on solitary activities, transfixed by the computer screen, and gazing into cyberspace. It is important that teachers make the effort to use computers to support the curriculum they have already designed. This won't be easy, since computers are not a single entity; the computer ads don't hype "multitasking" for nothing.

On one hand, the computer, specifically its word processing software, is a tool to help writers write—yet it's much more than a writing instrument. On the other hand, the computer, with all its attendant technology, is a porthole to sites of information, much of which can be brought home, that is, downloaded off the Internet. It is a tool to find things out. With CD-Rom disks and PowerPoint presentations, the computer is a tool to deliver instruction as well as raw information. The computer also connects itself to other computers and allows data to flow in both directions. This ability allows people to share mail (email) and conversation (communication in chat rooms). With email and web cameras, it's a communications tool a bit like a telephone. So, the computer is a tool that is able to foster community, while it enables writers to write and researchers to find information. And, with writeable CD-RWs, zip drives, and hard drives, it's a storage device like a book. If our analysis of computer technology is to be multidimensional, we need to examine these four aspects of computers to see how they are used for writing, instruction, communications, and storage.

Writers Writing

The most obvious application of the computer to the world of English language arts is its ability to help writers write. Again, we mustn't kid ourselves. There is no program that will transform poor writers into expert ones, poor spellers into great

117

spellers, or poor revisers and editors into thoughtful, careful crafters of prose. Since the early 1980s when we first began looking at the effect of personal computers on writing, we believed (and hoped) the computer would make a difference; it didn't (Strickland 1984). Writing prompts, invention strategies, and electronic typing on the computer had no greater influence than the same good teaching performed in a noncomputer environment. Nothing one needs to be "hooked on" or drilled with will be any more effective on the computer. Thus, teachers should abandon the search for the perfect software or perfect website, and they should concentrate on figuring out what the computer can do for writers that cannot be done with simple paper and pen. If reluctant writers become writers by writing, word processing on the computer will support and even encourage these students once they realize that word processing makes it much simpler to change things around and make adjustments without retyping their whole paper.

Most will admit that the computer provides a much neater rendering of what writers would otherwise put down on paper. Depending on a person's keyboarding skills, it may be easier or harder to draft on the computer. People who went through school with paper and pen report that they have difficulty composing with keyboard and screen. Some of these writers would die without yellow legal pads and number two pencils. Our students, however, have grown up with computers. The personal computer—Apple's Macintosh or the IBM PC—is older than they are. In fact, for them, there have always been iMacs, Windows, PalmPilots, digital wireless phones, and the Internet. For them, writing by hand in school, especially for tests, is arduous without technology. So, our students are comfortable with computers; more than likely, they're not as comfortable writing.

We need to begin with drafting. Everything suggested for writing workshop works equally well with word processing: freewriting, focused free writes, quick writes, and so on. Freewriting with a computer encourages a free flow of words on the screen—words easily correctable, easily expendable, and easily rearranged if not in quite the right order.

The procedure for freewriting with a computer is pretty much the same as it is without computers. Students are directed to begin to write whatever comes to mind about their subject (or even their lack of a subject). The same restrictions apply when using the computer—do not go back with the backspace key, the delete key, or even the left arrow key; writers are directed simply to keep writing. We ask them to write until the screen is completely full. That might take five to ten minutes, just as freewriting by hand. Once they fill the screen, ask them to stop at the end of the sentence and get a printout, if feasible. This will allow students to see what they've written.

In the case of freewriting, when great stock is put on the spontaneous generation of ideas, the computer might work against some writers. Less experienced writers want the perfectly clean words to be just right on screen; they go back to fix typos and to rephrase ideas. The built-in careless abandon that works so well on paper isn't possible when working on screen; there are no cross-outs, circled words, or arrows drawn to indicate changing order. Freewriting on screen is different, so we must allow for this. We need to encourage delaying surface error corrections and fussing with syntax until later in the process, but allow for writers who can't stand the mess.

For those who are severely distracted by the look of the text on screen, we advocate a technique that the late Stephen Marcus (1991) called "invisible writing." For those who can't help looking back at what they've produced, rethinking what they just wrote, Marcus suggested simply turning down the brightness of the screen, so students cannot see what they've written, to "temporarily 'hide' text while students brainstorm" (9). Marcus warns students that their fingers will strike the wrong keys, words will be horribly misspelled, sentences won't make sense, and grammar will be nonstandard. But he promises his students that the frustration will be worth it; their creativity will be heightened. Computers with separate minitowers have monitors with separate on/off switches that will accomplish the same thing, the feeling of writing with one's eyes closed or while blindfolded.

When students complain that they just have to look, Marcus suggests alternating visible and invisible writing in bursts of two to five minutes. After an invisible freewriting session, the screen could be brightened to write a one-sentence summary, one capturing the most interesting idea(s) found after rereading what was written. Tell students to try to write a sentence that captures the most interesting item or idea that they came up with in their freewriting. Actually, the looking back may not only be necessary but also instructive, showing students how much writers rely on rereading what has been written so far to stimulate thought and coordinate cohesive writing. Of course, this technique comes with a warning. Since writers naturally rely on what they've written so far as a stimulus to what they'll write next, invisible writing is offered not as a way to teach writing, but as a creativity booster, to be used when students feel their internal editor stifling their creativity.

Revision on the Computer

When students begin to revise their drafts, the computer's real benefits show as it allows writers to do what is impossible or unlikely with a handwritten revision. For one thing, the computer can change a writer's conception of revision as separate from editing; revising is much more than simply conforming to standard edited English (spelling, usage, grammar, and punctuation). Additionally, revision activities that involve moving words, phrases, sentences, and even whole paragraphs can be done much more easily when using the computer's copy/move sequence on selected text. Yet, merely having students work with computers will not automatically make them better revisers; students need strategies for revision that help them reflect on their writing as it takes shape. It is the teachers, not the computers, whose responsibility it is to demonstrate, using sample papers displayed by overhead-type "gizmos" (as one teacher called them—devices that take the computer screen and project it like a transparency), how writers actually work through a paper, experimenting and thinking aloud, the way Jim Mahoney does with his students (see Chapter 4).

Students ask what they need to do to make their writing better. Advice to "look at their writing though the reader's eye, noticing gaps in the information, precarious inductive leaps, and missing links" (Guth 1988) isn't as helpful as it seems. Knowing how to do those things requires modeling and demonstrating. Experienced writers reexamine and revise their texts in various intuitive ways; less experienced student writers need to be taught to look at their drafts from different perspectives, a talent that takes time and practice to develop. Students need alternatives to the idiosyncratic strategies for revising their papers that we've already discussed: making them longer by adding more to the end of the text, substituting words with the thesaurus, fixing punctuation, grammar, and spelling. Revising isn't simply revisiting a text; it means envisioning another version. The success of the revision depends on the seriousness of the writer's investment in a writing weighed against the cost of "redoing" the piece. And the charm of teaching revision with the computer, as any writer will attest, is that after every change, the alteration is undetectable; it has visual integrity—every draft looks original, alleviating the recopying aggravation of revision. When teachers help students see the possibilities that computers offer through electronic manipulation of texts, they will facilitate more substantive revision.

The three strategies we offer for use in classrooms—outlining, paragraphing, and cumulative sentences—aren't necessarily strategies that experienced writers use; however, less experienced writers may find these strategies help develop a reader's eye. These and many other strategies can be found in *From Disk to Hard Copy* (Strickland 1997).

Outlines

One standard writing instruction strategy is to compose an outline; however, we find creating outlines more helpful at the revision stage than at the generating stage. To make a revision outline, direct students to save the original and create a copy by renaming the file. With the original safely stored, the writer creates a sentence outline by identifying one sentence within each paragraph that contains the major idea and deletes everything else from the paragraph. For students who have difficulty with the "major idea" concept, have them work backwards, deleting sentences in a paragraph until they find the one sentence that absolutely cannot be sacrificed. Once writers have reduced each paragraph, all the original paragraphs will be represented in an outline by an equal number of sentences.

Students can examine the sentence outline to find one sentence that seems to express a thesis (what the writer wants a reader to think or be shown by the paper as a whole) and duplicate that at the top of the outline to act as the controlling statement. The remaining sentences can be sequenced, if so desired, by capital and lowercase letters and Roman and Arabic numbers. But more importantly, the outline serves as a way to check coherence and spot gaps, leaps in logic, and missing connections.

Paragraphing as a Revision Activity

The paragraph convention, indenting four or five spaces as a section begins, is a typesetting custom that some writers still finding puzzling. Handbooks skirt the issue with tautological advice telling writers that paragraphs contain one main idea and a new paragraph should begin when a new idea is begun. Any draft completed with long paragraphs, maybe even as one long paragraph, can be restructured as several shorter paragraphs. But until we began writing with computers, this decision meant rewriting or retyping the entire paper, a task most hope to avoid. With a computer, deciding to make long paragraphs into shorter ones is easily done.

Admittedly, worrying about when to begin and end paragraphs can be a distraction during the drafting process of writing, but paragraphing can become a generative process, one helpful to revision. We ask writers to read their completed draft, paying attention to any paragraph that is over 100 words, telling them that the average paragraph is approximately 95 words. When they reach a section that feels like a new paragraph may be about to begin, a new aspect is introduced, the subject begins to change, or the words give that "and another thing . . ." feeling, the writer simply presses the enter key, moving text after the cursor to the next line, and indents the text with the tab key to form a possible new paragraph. Moreover, if the new paragraph isn't quite right, the original paragraph can be restored by moving the cursor to the concluding period and pressing the delete key until the paragraph is rejoined.

Cumulative Sentences

When creating new paragraphs, the white space makes a paper easier to read—a courtesy to one's readers. But even more important than courtesy, the split paragraphs are primed for the development of cumulative sentences, a strategy based on Francis Christensen's (1978) generative rhetoric. Cumulative sentences add right-branch modifiers to sentences, elaborating on the basic premise, explaining a term, or completing a thought, the way this sentence does. Students can be taught developing, adding, and specifying by learning to write noun phrases, verb phrases, and absolutes—a concrete revision strategy. Too often, the revision rule students have learned is "say more" when asked to elaborate or add detail, and details tend to get added to the end of their drafts when writing longhand because adding them anywhere else means copying the paper over. Of course, when writing with a computer, details can be added anywhere in the paper—within a draft, within a paragraph, even within a sentence—while retaining visual integrity. For example, a student could be directed to return to any sentence in their essay, one such as this: "When separated from her, my thoughts constantly focus on Rita." [and add information:] "When separated from her, my thoughts constantly focus on Rita, *making me feel tingly inside, giving me a goofy look on the outside, one that others might characterize as the look of a lovesick fool.*"

Or another example might be: "Although he is shy and self-conscious, he is also obsessive and controlling." When information is added, the sentence can become: "Although he seems shy and self-conscious, he also acts obsessive and controlling, *waiting for me to return home, calling me thirty minutes after I leave him, asking me questions that make me somewhat nervous, and interrogating me like he's a male Judge Judy or something.*"

Students who have been shown Christensen's principle may return to any point in their text to add information, generating more ideas that, in turn, spark more thoughts. This type of strategy works best with sentences from the students' own writing rather than sentence-combining exercises. To be effective, the strategy must help writers reenvision their own drafts.

Editing

When students get to the editing phases of writing, the computer offers many conveniences. Most classrooms and even many homes have copies of dictionaries, style handbooks, and Roget's *Thesaurus*. Unfortunately, few writers interrupt their work to consult these books. Computers offer all three as a part of the standard word-processing package.

The most popular convenience is the spell checker that highlights possible misspellings, normally flagging the words by underlining them in red. Spell checkers employ a master list of words taken from a dictionary to see if a given string of letters constitutes a pattern-match with any of the words on its list. Spell checker inquiries do not bother with meaning, pronunciation, or linguistic history. A spell checker is not infallible and teachers need to make students aware of the feature's

122

limitations. Spell checkers are like seat belts: they have to be used to be useful. If you use the wrong form of a word, but spell it correctly, the spell checker doesn't tell you of your error. Similarly, spell checkers are not case sensitive; they won't catch uncapitalized initial words in a sentence, provided they are spelled correctly in the first place. Proper nouns are particularly troublesome. Sometimes the spell checker picks up on a word that is not in its dictionary, so the computer automatically assumes the word is misspelled. Spell checkers will also pass over words that are correctly spelled but not actually the word intended. If I wrote ". . . unchecked to this *pint*," and meant *point*, the spell checker would respond, "remaining words okay." Homonyms are also worrisome: *weather* for *whether*, for example. A student would be better off typing *wether* because the spell checker would suggest both alternate spellings, *weather* and *whether* (and four others), asking the student to make the choice. When it does flag a word not in its dictionary, then writers have the choice of dealing with the problem at the moment, often by simply right clicking the mouse, or waiting until the document is finished and running the spell checker on the entire file.

The thesaurus tool works the way Roget's renowned reference work does: when students choose the thesaurus option from the tools menu, the computer offers synonyms (and some include antonyms as well). The thesaurus suggests options; the student must make the choice, and therein lies the problem. Teachers will want to caution students against wholesale replacement of words for variety's sake. The word-processing program we used several years ago provided a definition for each word its thesaurus suggested, along with its part of speech, but many do not. Our current word-processing program gives lists of comparable words. For example, for *experienced*, it offers *accomplished* as one of its substitutes, and for *accomplished*, it offers *brilliant*. An experienced writer may or may not be brilliant. More experienced writers know that each word has its own nuance or shade of meaning (in England, almost everything is *brilliant*); less experienced writers must learn this by broadening their reading, not by clicking on a thesaurus list. Spell checkers and the thesaurus make the writer responsible for the replacements of flagged words, and we want our writers to learn to be responsible for their text.

Style checkers or grammar checkers, as they are also called, give additional advice that the student must make sense of: missing marks of punctuation, subject/verb agreement, sentences marked as too lengthy, missing modifiers, adverb problems, missing objects of verbs, passive voice, redundant phrases, run-on sentences, and fragments. The "document properties" feature also offers information about average sentence length, word length, and paragraph length. Many students lack grammar sophistication and find the advice understandably confusing; some go along with whatever is suggested; others decide to avoid the grammar checker entirely.

There seems to be no way to predict what information will be given by the style checkers and what percentage of the information will be accurate and valuable. In a workshop setting, students could use the style checkers in groups of two or more, so they have someone to ask about the wisdom of following the advice given. Teachers might also submit a piece of their own writing, to be analyzed before the class, to demonstrate how the statistical information and the advice given by style checkers must be filtered by the writer according to the writer's intentions.

Web Publishing

If we contend that writing is meant to be read, then the computer's network file server and the Internet's web pages offer natural places for students to publish. Teachers can create spaces on the school's network server dedicated as reserved for student writing. The files would then be readable by anyone authorized to be on the network. Teachers can create web pages for each class period so that postings are available to anyone with access to the Internet. There are many sites and programs that make creating web pages almost as easy as filling out a job application. One website address we've found is *www.edu-cyberpg.com/internet/ interestingsites/developing_a_web_site.html* (and it needs to written as one line in the URL box). In any case, the software supporting the creation of web pages is developing so quickly that any teacher interested in web publishing can count on the fact that at least two students in any given room will be able to make this happen quicker than you can say, "check with the principal." The usual caveats apply here: check that it's okay with parents, the school board, the school administration, and caution students about writing anything too personal or that they wouldn't be proud of seeing on the evening newscast.

Technology for Delivery of Information

A new information age is said to have been brought about by the computer. Information, in the form of raw data or as organized instruction, can be delivered in multiple formats to individuals and to classes of individuals. If the increased amount of writing promoted by the computer is not in itself enough to improve writing, some teachers feel that software provides the help needed. It is important, however, to look at how software technology views language learning, remembering that, in a transactional context, students learn to read while they are writing, and they learn about writing by reading. Some software programs offer to analyze and check writing conventions with computerized spell checkers, style checkers, sentence parsers, and online handbooks. These programs put undue emphasis on correctness rather than on meaning, and considering the dubious accuracy of the programs, give students either a false sense of security or a heightened anxiety about their abilities. Online handbooks, although more convenient than book versions, sometimes give confusing advice, often of value only to someone who already understands the rule being alluded to.

Integrated software, now available on diskette or CD-Rom disks, addresses the whole writing process. Software packages such as *Academic English* and *Daedalus Integrated Writing Environment* are usually theoretically sound, but they can be misused by being applied in a lockstep fashion. Some packages force a student to complete its prewriting exercise before allowing the writer to start on a draft. Some programs turn the prewriting exercise into a five-paragraph theme. Such applications take the fire out of writing. Even if the technology allows a student to move around at will, the student might not be aware of the options and react to the sequence as just another algorithm—first this, then that. A transactional teacher must present the integrated exercises as demonstrations of possibilities and encourage experimentation and risk taking.

When the computer was first introduced in the writing classroom, many teachers worked on creating computer programs that would respond meaningfully to text (Schwartz 1984; Selfe and Wahlstrom 1983; Strickland 1984). Dawn and Ray Rodrigues (1986) suggested using word-processing files to give short lessons on writing, lessons that were interactive in the sense that students entered information in appropriate places within the files. These guidance files, which they called *lesson files*, dealt with separate rhetorical activities. Guidance files are a planned sequence of activities, presented screen-by-screen, having the advantage of allowing students to return to previous screens to revise or modify answers. The guidance files contain prompts to writing, offering a myriad of writing activities—focusing on paragraphing, prewriting, editing, and more—and suggesting a variety of writing tasks. Rodrigues' guidance files operated as word-processing text files, so they could be created by a teacher with a basic knowledge of word processing, making it much more realistic than creating programs written in computer languages. For example, one guidance file might be named FIVE-Ws. A student who retrieved that file onto the screen would receive an explanation of the five *ws*—*who*, *what*, *where*, *when*, and *why*, and could interact by answering the five *ws* concerning a topic of their own choosing. When the student finished and saved the file on their disk, the student had both the questions and the answers, any or all of which could be copied to another file for drafting. Any teacher can create these customized guidance files.

Today we recommend using a sophisticated presentation tool such as PowerPoint to create these guidance files. For example, many teachers assign some form of an autobiographical essay. We have created PowerPoint slides called

Autobiography, based on a guidance file originally created for word processing by Rebecca Laubach, a ninth- and tenth-grade teacher at Mars Area High School (Strickland and Strickland 1993). The PowerPoint slides can be shown to the class as a whole, with an overhead projector, or given to the students to access individually from a server or floppy disk (see Figure 5–1).

Another example is a character development guidance file, Family Gems (see Figure 5–2), based on Laurie Morrison's earlier file, called Pirate. She created it to help her New Wilmington, Pennsylvania students with creative writing, and it's detailed in *From Disk to Hard Copy* (Strickland 1997).

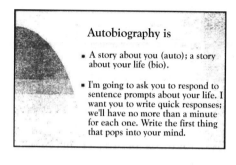
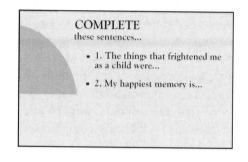

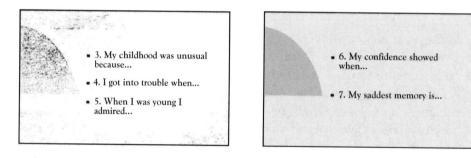

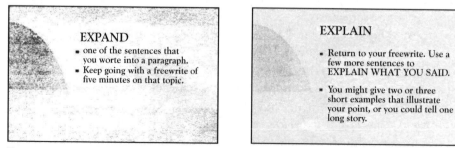

Figure 5–1. Autobiography PowerPoint slides

Completing guidance files such as Family Gems sparks ideas for variations of the character sketch. Not only can teachers create guidance files to generate characters, but they can be used to analyze characters in a class reading. The guidance file might be a suitable way to ask readers to place the character in a new situation, applying both the author's description with each reader's unique interpretation of the character. For example, a teacher might ask students reading *The Giver* (Lowry 1993) how Jonas would react if he

a. saw his sister break a rule?
b. were chosen to be a nurturer?
c. hadn't escaped with Gabriel?
d. could return to his original home ten years later?

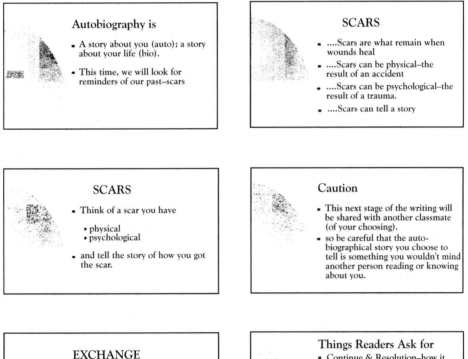

Figure 5–1. Continued

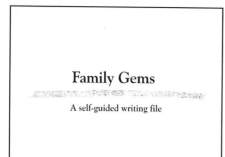

Family Gems

A self-guided writing file

A mental picture

≈ When a writer thinks of each of the characters that will be a part of a story, the writer creates a mental picture of the character.

≈ The writer then decides what personality traits that character will have. For example, will the character be friendly? sensitive? aggressive? successful? or selfish?

You have the power

≈ As a writer, you have the power to develop your own characters, letting the reader know what type of person your character really is and how your character acts.

≈ In this lesson you will answer questions about your character and write about him or her, using that information.

≈ This is what we call a character sketch.

Imagine a Member of Your Family

≈ Close your eyes and imagine a member of your family–Mom, Dad, Sister, Brother, Cousin, Aunt, Uncle, Grandparent...

≈ Look closely at the one you picked and notice all of the details that may give you clues about the type of person that he or she is and how he or she may act.

Answer the following questions about your family member

≈ a. What is your family member's name?

≈ b. Is there a story about when he or she joined the family? Wedding? Adoption? Birth?

≈ c. How does your family member talk? What's his/her favorite expression to say?

≈ d. How does he/she laugh? Use comparison.

≈ e. How does he/she move? Use comparison.

≈ f. Are there any other unique features about his /her appearance?

Concentrate on how your family member feels

≈ a. What would make your family member happy?

≈ b. What would make your family member sad?

≈ c. What would make your family member frustrated?

≈ d. What would confuse your family member?

Figure 5–2. Family Gems PowerPoint slides

How would your family member react:

  a. if he/she won the Powerball lottery?

  b. if someone gave him/her a gift?

  c. to a child who was crying?

  d. if he/she was hurt?

  e. if he/she saw a beggar?

  f. when meeting an old friend?

Write a story...

  try to work in your family member's appearance, using your previous answers.

  try to work in your family member's personality, using your previous answers.

  try to work in how your family member reacts in different situations, using your previous answers.

Well done!

  You have just completed the rough draft for your character sketch.

  Review each paragraph, adding information if needed, removing nonessential details.

  You might also check your spelling and punctuation.

  When you are satisfied, save your character sketch file and print out a hard copy.

Figure 5–2. Continued

Students could react to each other's answers to the prompts, deciding as a class who responded to the situation the way the character would and mark places in the book that support their ideas.

Of course, the computer as a presentational device could be used in minilessons, individualized instruction, and even whole class direct instruction. But what about information delivery that doesn't originate in the classroom, either with the teacher or the students? The computer can also present information from CD-Rom disks, such as *Encarta*-like encyclopedia programs, and the Internet's websites, which house various sorts of information.

Borrowing from Electronic Sources

The temptation to engage in unrestricted or unregulated borrowing from electronic sources is a problem that exists with information found on CD-Rom disks and the Web. When we used to spend an inordinate amount of time teaching "note cards," we were trying to stress the importance of good record keeping skills, tying information presented in the research papers back to their sources, with footnotes, endnotes, and in-text citations, all to avoid unintentional plagiarism. Now the technology allows users to copy and paste right from the original source into their document. It's one thing to read to gain information to help generate material for a written composition, it's another thing to simply import material. Students today need more time discussing the importance of acknowledging sources and intellectual property rights instead of the mechanics of note cards. But if even those who should know better can carelessly forget quotation marks or a parenthetical citation, should inadvertent appropriation in a student paper surprise us?

One experience with CD-Roms involved a student turning in a seven page paper for a one- to two-page assignment on a topic of personal interest. This student, whose interest was gambling, had produced a concise "history of gambling," but he had authored it only in the sense that he used his CD-Rom disk to locate the encyclopedia entry on gambling and downloaded the information to his paper. He had no sense that it was plagiarism or bad research; he was quite proud of the paper.

Another student recently handed in an assignment that contained these two paragraphs (here labeled A and B) within the same paper:

(A.) In the 1930s and 1940s, the jukebox craze swept America. It was the single most loved—and sometimes hated—symbol of its era. Once a feature of thousands of bars and diners throughout the United States, its familiarity made it a friend. It was the jukebox into which the lonely trucker at the coffee shop dropped his nickel to inspire dreams of his baby back home. It was the jukebox that the kids made for in Chuck Berry's song when they wanted to hear something really hot, and the jukebox that linked communities whose local operator stocked it with songs and dances from the old country.

(B.) When my mother was a child she would have dinner every Friday night with her brother and grandmother. She loved to play the jukebox. The diner she attended had miniature jukeboxes right on the table. She and her brother would always fight over the jukebox, but they never left until everyone had heard what they had wanted to. Playing the jukebox brought her family together. They always looked forward to Friday nights. According to my mother, every kid that she knew loved to play the jukebox. The jukebox was a great part of the popular culture of the time.

The student admitted that he freely used material from various websites to complete his assignment. Never mind that the A paragraph seems quoted word for word from another source and that the B paragraph is clearly in the student's voice; the A paragraph is much more sophisticated and stylistically complex. It has an average of twenty words per sentence, the other only twelve; it has a forty-word sentence, almost double the length of any of the other paragraphs. And what does a teenager know about a trucker's lonely dreams or the 45 rpm Chuck Berry tune referred to (it wasn't "Johnny B. Goode")? What worries us is that the student was proud of his initiative of gaining material and had no sense that the inappropriate borrowing was wrong or that the material had another person's voice.

More than ever before, the technology will require teachers to demonstrate that generating material for a writing involves digesting material from other sources, using summarizing, and honing paraphrasing skills. This is much easier to do when students have a choice of topic and are interested in making the knowledge theirs. Believing that nothing is learned if a student is simply punished for plagiarism, we asked both the "gambling" and the "jukebox" students to read the information they had downloaded from the CD-Rom disk and the Internet and "say it in their own words." Even then, teachers will still need to give feedback so that students don't get the impression that changing a few words or rearranging sentences does the trick. Both students found that doing real research required synthesizing information from a variety of sources (including personal observations and personal interviews).

Electronic Reading

If writing with the computer presents new challenges, then reading text on a computer screen can be said to be trying as well. Computers can make reading a more interactive process. For example, teachers can ask classmates to read each other's papers, and instead of responding to question prompts, students can be directed to write a comment in places where they had difficulty reading the drafts. In most word-processing programs, there is an option in the Insert menu of the main toolbar that allows comments to be linked to a place in the text, embedded, and clickable to read or even convert to text. The inserted comment will often appear in a different color, for example, in yellow, or in a text box, clickable with the mouse.

In addition to supporting interactive reading practices, computers can deliver e-books—complete books, novels, short stories, and poetry are now available on-line, on PDA readers and CD-Rom disks. Yet, a caution must be advised when using a technology that takes advantage of digitized sound, data-driven animation, and full-motion video interface delivering text, graphics, and images for enhanced reading. For example, if students read Martin Luther King Jr.'s "I Have a Dream" speech or "Letter from Birmingham Jail," on a website, they might be able to actually hear it read by King or a professional actor. The site might offer linked files—a brief biography of King, a newspaper account of his most famous march, or perhaps a television special covering the events surrounding his death—that could be selected from highlighted text or pop-up/pull-down menus, offering a truly multimedia-enhanced interactive reading. For another example, a CD-Rom disk might offer a more sense-oriented experience of a literary classic, such as Homer's *Odyssey*. It might be presented in an eye-pleasing large font in one portion of the computer screen, with a boxed portion for an appropriate illustration, a drawing of Homer, one of the characters in the epic, or a map of Greek islands, with overlays providing other points of interest to sample. The illustration box might also have a link to a full-motion video segment corresponding to the text—something from a PBS production or even a made-for-TV-movie. A link on the screen could take one to a clip from the movie *O Brother, Where Art Thou*, loosely based on Homer's tale, or to a reading of the text by a professional narrator, an option that would allow struggling readers to hear the text as their eyes follow along. Finally, all the important concepts, allusions, and references would have footnote-type links, locations that could be clicked on to retrieve an explanation or corresponding information that the author of the interactive software thought would be helpful. The linked documents would themselves have links, ad infinitum. As a student reads the classic, the CD-Rom offers a plethora of footnotes and a variety of experiences.

Yet, we know that there is a ghost in the machine, as they say, and it's an anonymous programmer working for a software corporation. If our theory of reading holds that linguistic or visual cues in the text trigger responses and activate associations that create meaning, what happens when the trigger is pulled by the software programmer responsible for creating the links and supplying the content at the other end of the link? From a transactional perspective on technology, the computer could pose a danger by usurping the meaning-making function of the reader because the software has been constructed in such a way as to embed the meaning of the text in the program with links rather than encouraging a reader to bring meaning to the text. To give an example, a student might respond to a reading of Edgar Allan Poe's "Annabel Lee" in a journal or a class discussion that the poem's line "my darling, my life and my bride" triggered an association with a movie seen recently, such as *Sweet November*. How much different would the personal interaction with text be if the association was a programmer's, who embedded it in the CD-ROM version? A link at that line could play a video clip of the movie's tragic climax. In fact, it wouldn't matter if the video clip was a brief lecture by a college professor, explaining the line as a reference to Poe's first sweetheart, Sarah Royster Shelton, a presentation more seductive than an ordinary classroom lecture. The point is that the technology has, in effect, forced a "reading" on the student by encoding an association—one given added weight because of its presentation. The interactive reading privileges one "reading" of the text over another, and since the linked possibilities are already there for the student reader to sample, the finite number of links supplants the infinite associations of imagination.

Again, we must ask, "What's it for?" If the purpose is to give the student information, then the computer has made great advances. If the purpose is to provide opportunities and situations where students may discover and experiment in order to create knowledge or meaning, then the computer may thwart our desires. The interpretation by one reader—the programmer—sets the parameters for inquiry as codified by the very creation of the links; the preexistence of established readings, validated as "correct" or possibly correct, makes the reader simply a follower of paths and eliminates any active role in construction. In this sense, the technology creates an electronic counterpart of the teacher's manual, the magic book that has the answers in the back. Although the computer is just a tool, it is not value neutral.

Networking for Communication

Not only does the computer present information, the computer networks with other computers. Its *connectivity*, as this aspect is called, means data flows in both directions, allowing text-based and sometimes voice communication. The most common applications are email messaging and chat room conversation. For us, our interest is in the way the computer fosters community, supporting writers and researchers.

Inasmuch as learning is a social construct and knowledge is negotiated and validated in a community (see earlier discussion in Chapter 2), it becomes clearer that the value of computers in a transactional context depends, to a great degree, on how the teacher approaches their use. We believe computers should be used in collaborative situations; however, this will require conscious effort, since computers and technology are not designed for social interaction, except on their own terms. Computer classroom/labs can heighten isolation; the "terminal" draws a student into itself, not out. Students stare at a monitor, receiving, even completing, assignments online, and develop a task-oriented mentality that says work at your own pace at your own time. Students feel more comfortable helping each other with computer operating questions and problems. Unless it is encouraged as appropriate, students will probably not talk with one another about their learning, behavior that might be considered "cheating" in other situations. Teachers must encourage helping others with their learning and problems with written expression. In a transactional classroom, the teacher is only one more voice within a community of learners, not the arbiter of meaning—the meaning of a poem, the value of an essay, and even the causes of the fall of the Soviet Union are arrived at and agreed upon by those present in the discussion. Learning is organic, shaped by contradictions, growing with the viewpoints and arguments being offered.

Some teachers use the connectivity of the computer to supplement their conferencing. Networking allows teachers to continue student/teacher and peer conferencing begun in the classroom while adding email, listservs, and public posting areas for response outside the classroom. Some schools support connectivity by providing email accounts for students and facilitating listserv discussion groups, but teachers can get their students enrolled on commercial sites for email and discussion groups. Many students have email accounts with *hotmail.com* and discussion groups can be organized through *groups.yahoo.com*, and most people don't seem to mind the presence of commerical banners enticing them to purchase various essential items. Chat rooms can be found through sites that are open to teachers and their classes, such as *tappedin.org* and *blackboard.com*. Teachers will also want to spend some time discussing safety and etiquette when writing email or participating in chat room conversations. For example, although email can be easily forwarded to others unknown to the original author, students should refrain from doing so without permission, remembering that others might not be as scrupulous.

Our colleague at Slippery Rock University, Danette DiMarco, believes connectivity helps her students broaden their sense of writing as a private enterprise. For her students, she says that writing includes not only face-to-face sharing with a small group of classmates but also public discussion of their writing in "an online writing environment, where they are able to provide and receive feedback from a wider writing community" (Strickland 1997, 43). Typically her students engage in peer response in class and then post "online responses to a designated number of works" to the interactive environment, the electronic bulletin board. Then the students read and post their own written comments about their classmates' posted works and the responses written by others. Danette reminds her students that "everyone deserves to receive an equal response." Danette feels that integrating traditional strategies with technology-based responses helps her students understand peer response as a special type of writing that, in and of itself, "necessitates oral as well as written response." Her students complete the cycle when they return to the classroom to discuss and evaluate the post-and-respond process.

Learning in a computer environment is fostered when there is time in class to give and receive feedback from other learners, to make immediate changes to work in progress, to risk trying new things, and to ask advice of a teacher who is also a learner. The computer lab is a special workspace where classmates, though working at terminals, are accessible and their work is shareable. At its best, networking on a computer offers a choice distinct from the teacher-centered traditional classroom. The computer affords teachers a place for two or more people to hold writers' conferences, using the same screen or conversing over a network. For example, Laura might post a draft of her paper on developmental learning delays, a file named AUTISM.DOC for others in her class or writing group to access on a local network or over the Internet (email, listserv, or bulletin board). After downloading and changing the file name to something else, such as AUTISM .TWO or AUTISM RESPONSE.DOC, her friend, Erin, could read Laura's text and alter the original, insert notes to Laura within the text, or write a response to Laura. Once finished, Erin would post the new file (AUTISM.TWO) to Laura, providing her with the feedback that all learners desire while allowing Laura to maintain responsibility for and authority over her writing, since she still has her original document intact (AUTISM.DOC).

Some think computer communications level the playing field because it strips external clues about identity that color our perceptions—gender, age, and race. Computer communications are less restrictive because students needn't compete for attention of the teacher in order to be recognized in academic discussions and needn't follow formal rules of classroom behavior. Computer communications promote the activity of learning rather than the passivity of "being taught." Teachers who encourage using a computer in this type of community teach that time spent in a collaborative effort—learning by interaction with other learners—is as valuable, maybe even more valuable, as getting individual work done or getting the assignment finished.

Technology for Storage

Computers are not only tools for writing, presenting information and instruction, and networking conversations, they are also a means of storage, a radically different medium than any other device teachers or students have previously considered. When students are finished with a draft, the computer files can be stored in digital code on a magnetic disk—a hard drive, a "floppy" diskette (now encased in hard plastic), a zip-drive disk, or even a writeable CD-RW disk. While stored on a disk, the file is safe but unreadable. To become text again, it must either be called up on-screen again or printed. However, the printed version no longer resembles a typewritten paper. Most computer labs have access to laser printers, and some students even have desktop publishing at their fingertips. We have seen students reprint their essays five or six times to get it to look right on the paper. Transactional teachers have to convince students to relax their concern for the look of the material and concentrate more on the meaning, encouraging them to fiddle with text on-screen at various levels—word, sentence, paragraph, printing it to read again, and going back to write more. Unless transactional teachers model the process, students will continue to be seduced by appearance.

Some teachers promote computers as writer's notebooks—places to store memories, notes, and ideas to be recovered later for writing. Just as storytellers rehearse ideas in their mind or replay memories, students are taught that storing information in a computer file eliminates the burden of having to remember everything they wanted to write or ideas that might not be useful at the moment but are worth preserving. The stored ideas are, of course, retrievable for use in another document or as a printed version.

Some teachers encourage their students to create websites on which to post their own writings and links to subjects that they're interested in. Teachers should remind students that websites aren't read in the way that other texts are—books, newspapers, magazines, textbooks—and so writing that is posted on websites should reflect this different way of reading. Websites are sampled; that is, readers' eyes move quickly up, down, and across text, pausing briefly to take in what jumps out at them—pulsating graphics, highlighted words, items with bullets drawing attention, text in larger font size or a different typeface. Writers need to remember how their readers will be expecting to read and organize accordingly. Three characteristics have been found to improve writing for readers using websites: it should be concise in style, quickly scannable, and objective in content. Specifically, certain formatting features, ones that would not be valued in a traditional piece of student writing, are beneficial to websites: highlighting keywords with font size, typeface, and color variations (hypertext links often appear in blue lettering on-screen); breaking sections with objective headings that are more meaningful than witty, humorous, or punny; arranging information in a list with bullets; presenting compact, tight paragraphs organized in a front-loaded, newpaper-style inverted pyramid (working from most important details to least important); and trimming the word count to spartan prose that might be less acceptable or elegant in more traditional writings (Morkes and Nielsen 1997).

The Future with Technology

Distance learning, which generally includes any situation where the learner doesn't have to be physically present on the campus, will not change education significantly until it delivers something quite different from lectures on a screen. Distance learning will have to take into account interactivity; successful learning depends on interaction within an environment that can respond, giving direction and assessment. Web-based classes taught on computers and featuring education software, which present text, video, graphics, and audio, must engage the learner to compete with traditional delivery of education.

Transactional teachers would hardly consider configuring a classroom where the learner receives information from an authority figure, manipulates the information according to a predetermined set of directions, and then receives feedback as to how adroitly the information was assimilated and returned. Yet this context for using computers to teach continues because that is what a computer does; it is an information delivery system. There needs to be an understanding of using computers that moves out of the entertainment mode, in which computers are used to play games, solving dilemmas according to the rules of conduct, and into the constructive learning mode, in which problems are solved by finding creative solutions. "The value of the computer is that it allows kids to learn by doing," says Roger Schrank, pioneer artificial intelligence theorist and former professor at Stanford and Yale universities. "People don't learn by being talked at. They learn when they attempt to do something and fail. Learning happens when they try to figure out why." Schank believes technology will transform education. "The computer is our Trojan mouse," he said. "It allows us to get our foot in the door to do something radical and difficult" (Green 2000). If anything, technology makes it clear that education is no longer about learning what is and what was—the material that shows up on standardized tests. Education is about preparing to make connections, seeing new associations, and creating in a world where information is available and accessible at the end of a computer keyboard. These are the same skills that writing employs. If Chomsky was right that human language is too complex to be explained as mimicry, that every child possesses the ability to create utterances that have never before been uttered in their presence, then every essay, every poem, every journal entry, every freewriting makes new connections from old information, sees new associations between disparate notions, and is, all and all, an act of creativity.

Of course, others add that information is not understanding; information is not education; information is not learning. Transactional classrooms are concerned with understanding, with learning, and with making meaning rather than the retrieval of information. Computers need to be interpersonal as well as interactive; "Education depends on relationships between people," counters online learning critic David Noble, a York University professor (Green 2000). The computer as a writing tutor will need to have a human component, which the artificial intelligence programmers have yet to develop. Teachers, human teachers, will continue to be necessary for real education. This aspect is missing from many current approaches using computers to teach language, reading, and writing; teachers offer questions, artifacts, problems, and situations, and students must do something with the information. Students have to discover new information and formulate interpretations. The teacher can then validate those interpretations or offer other information to modify them (and the teacher's interpretation can be modified and validated as well). Instead of performing activities that are by their nature predetermined, whether delivered by educational software or web-based environments, and expecting learning to take place, language-rich classrooms with computers will engage learners, bring groups together, and foster collaborative learning and communication between and among discourse communities.

For Further Exploration

1. Visit a classroom that uses a computer lab as part of the writing workshop. How is a sense of community among writers supported? How does the teacher use technology to teach prewriting? Revision? Editing? Do students seem comfortable using the computer as a writing tool? How?

2. Try some of the suggestions for prewriting mentioned in this chapter. As a writer, what did you discover?

3. Design a self-guided writing file. Why would this be helpful to students? How would it be used? If possible, have a group of students work with your file. What was their reaction to this experience?

4. Visit some online writing labs (OWLs) listed below. What are some advantages of using such centers? What are some drawbacks?

Colorado State University	*http://writing.colostate.edu*
Michigan Technological University Writing Center	*www.hu.mtu.edu/wc/ welcome.html*
Purdue University Online Writing Lab	*http://owl.english.purdue.edu*
University of Maine Writing Center Online	*www.ume.maine.edu/ ~wcenter/*
University of Michigan Online Writing Lab	*www.lsa.umich.edu/ecb/OWL/ owl.html*
University of Oregon Writing Online	*http://darkwing.uoregon.edu/ ~uocomp/word.html*
University of Missouri Online Writery	*www.missouri.edu/~wleric/ writery.html*

6

Assessment and Evaluation—
Codependent but Different

*The central function of assessment, therefore, is not to prove
whether or not teaching or learning have taken place, but to improve
the quality of teaching and learning, and to increase the likelihood
that all members of society will acquire a full and critical literacy.*
—NCTE/IRA Standards for the
Assessment of Reading and Writing

The terms *assessment* and *evaluation* have been used synonymously and even used interchangeably with other terms such as *grading* and *marking,* each referring to the mysterious scores imposed on learners, as determined quantitatively by their teachers or by testing companies. More importantly, these scores are usually terminal marks, signaling the end product of a course, a unit, or a school career. Actually, each of these terms—*assessment, evaluation, grading, reporting*—means something quite different (see Figure 6–1).

Assessment, Evaluation, and Reporting

Assessment refers to a collection of data, information that enlightens the teacher and the learner, information that drives instruction. Good teachers assess constantly, initiating the first stage of a recursive process. They observe what is happening in their classrooms, kidwatching as Yetta Goodman (1978) would say, and then they talk to students, asking them questions about their learning (conferencing as writing teachers do or interviewing their subjects as naturalistic researchers do). Good teachers devise ways to record their observations, and they assess and adjust their teaching based on these assessments. They also share assessments with their students, so students can adjust their performances to meet criteria for personal expectations or those standards imposed on them by their teachers or by others.

Assessment $\longrightarrow$	Evaluation $\longrightarrow$	Reporting
teacher must gather data, collect work samples, we observe, we talk with, we gather evidence that learning is happening	teacher and student assign a value to what has been collected and use the evidence to formulate a determination of progress	teacher and student share the evaluation in some summary format, traditionally a grade on a report card, but reporting can also include celebrations, presentations, and portfolios

Figure 6–1. Continuum of observing/understanding learning

Teachers assess informally and almost routinely. For instance, when they say at the end of class, "That went well today," or "Whew, they just don't seem to get this; what should I do next to clear this up?" they are assessing. In much the same way that good teachers assess their own performance, they constantly look for indications of student progress or understanding, either as individuals or as a group. Although this type of assessment takes many forms and is managed in a variety of ways, two features are important: assessment is ongoing and assessment is a collection of information—data in the form of facts that help teachers put the pieces together, much the way students collect data when looking for an answer to their problems. Teachers investigate learning, gathering evidence to illustrate not only that their students are learning, but what it is that they are learning. Many teachers act as researchers in their own classrooms, using analysis of their evidence to help all concerned understand the learning process—students, parents, administrators, and themselves as teachers.

Evaluation is the product of assessment, a step further toward understanding and drawing conclusions. Although sometimes used in much the same terms as assessment, evaluation is the next step in a recursive process. After gathering data—information and evidence—teachers, like any other group of researchers, must put the pieces together, evaluating the products of their efforts and the progress of their students. This evaluation is neither subjective—an opinion based on what the teacher instinctively feels—nor simply an average of scores. Rather, evaluation uses a variety of assessment techniques and validates its conclusions by investigating relationships in the data, triangulating the data, and analyzing what is gathered from a number of perspectives. In this sense, evaluation is helpful to learners rather than simply judgmental of them, understandable to them rather than mysterious, and anticipated by them when they have been involved in the assessment process.

Our values guide our evaluation—what we value as teachers shapes what we evaluate, what goals we set, and what instruction we offer. Similarly, what students value shapes their evaluation, their goals, and their learning (Hansen 1998). "Our evaluation practices operationally define what really matters for students and teachers," says Elliot Eisner, critic of the standardized testing industry. "If our evaluation practices do not reflect our most cherished values, they will undermine the values we cherish. We need, in other words, to approach educational evaluation not simply as a way of scoring students, but as a way in which to find out how well we and our students are doing in order to do better what we do. Evaluation should be regarded as an educational medium, an important source for school improvement. And what it addresses should reflect the educational values we believe important" (Strickland and Strickland 1998, 20).

Reporting is the third step of this recursive process. After assessing and evaluating, teachers have the responsibility of sharing their evaluations with the interested parties, primarily the students but also their parents, administrators, other teachers, and, of course, the general public. Reporting is valuable to those outside the classroom who haven't been involved in the assessment and evaluation process. Traditionally such reporting has been limited to report card grades and standardized test scores, but some teachers are using a number of nontraditional ways to report progress and success. For example, students present what they learned and record it on videotape to be played for various audiences, such as parents at open house night. The videotape helps parents understand a transactional/constructivist approach to learning, while allowing them to "see" learning happen. Another way to report what students have learned is to find a repository for their productions. For example, when students complete a research project of their own choosing, the finished reports could be housed in the library by subject, along with other reference material, so other students could learn from their research. This provides not only an authentic audience for the students' work, but it gives teachers a way to report what has been learned.

Some teachers, like Jane Blystone of North East High School, Pennsylvania (1997a), hold a "coffee house" night, an exclusive gathering of students and a limited number of guests, in which students read from their writings and share their experiences with those gathered. Another sort of report would be a night of celebration, similar to athletes' sports banquets. As a celebration of accomplishment, a writers' banquet can be held, with an awards ceremony to honor selected pieces of student work. As much as possible, students should be included in the process of selecting work to be honored, with multiple categories and a variety of highlighted entries. We would further suggest that all entries be reproduced and celebrated in a class book, so all the writings are valued. The reproduced entries could be distributed to those attending in much the same way that conference proceedings are published, tangible evidence of celebration.

Traditionally, the standard way to report to learners how well they have met the expectations for an assignment or course is with a report card grade—the numerical score, letter, or percentage assigned to a product, much the way eggs and cuts of meat are graded. However, teachers are not obliged to follow the traditional forms. For example, some teachers give papers a plus (+), a check ($\sqrt{}$), or a minus (−). Some use letters, such as S for satisfactory or I for improving. Whatever symbols are used, grading is a way to assign a symbol to represent achievement. Grades are difficult and often tell little or nothing about what a learner knows or has accomplished. (Grading is discussed later in greater detail.)

Definitions Are Important

With all the various terms used to describe assessments, some can be quite confusing. For example, *alternative assessment, authentic assessment,* and *performance assessment* are frequently (and mistakenly) used interchangeably. Teachers who are working to provide their student-centered classrooms with authentic learning tasks have moved away from testing—for some very good reasons. For too many of us, our educational preparation preached the virtues of writing test questions with answers that were "accurate, relevant, and of the most appropriate scope in relation to the other answer choices" (Popham 1988, 142)—in other words, multiple-choice questions satisfied by only one right answer.

Alternative assessment is a broad term, popularized by Grant Wiggins (1989), referring to any type of assessment that deviates from the traditional model exemplified by locally-created tests and standardized examinations with their multiple-choice, one-answer format. Although the traditional model of assessment is still validated by professional test makers who assemble state and nationally mandated examinations that sacrifice validity for reliability, many teachers use alternative methods to assess student learning.

Authentic assessment refers to tasks that are real and meaningful to the learner in today's world. Assessment is authentic when it is part of instruction and learning. Such assessment is a tool for learners as well as for teachers and involves multiple tools that look at learning processes and product from a variety of vantage points. Researchers look for understandings by triangulating their data (see Figure 6–2); that is, looking at things in a variety of ways. Authentic assessment tools, such as anecdotal records and checklists, use observations, conferences, surveys, and samples of student work to make the assessment real. This refers not only to tools

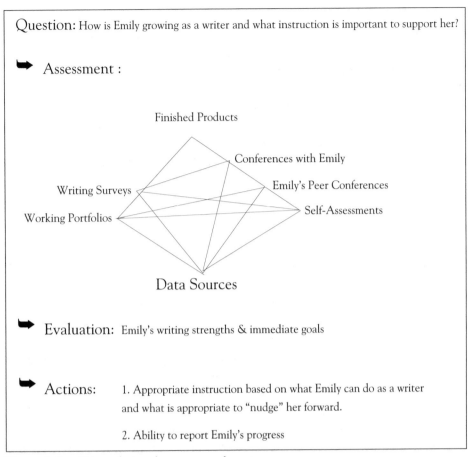

Question: How is Emily growing as a writer and what instruction is important to support her?

➡ Assessment :

Finished Products

Conferences with Emily

Writing Surveys

Emily's Peer Conferences

Working Portfolios

Self-Assessments

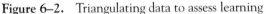

Data Sources

➡ Evaluation: Emily's writing strengths & immediate goals

➡ Actions: 1. Appropriate instruction based on what Emily can do as a writer and what is appropriate to "nudge" her forward.

2. Ability to report Emily's progress

Figure 6–2. Triangulating data to assess learning

but to what is being assessed. In authentic assessment, *real* also refers to context and is a part of authentic (or real-life) learning.

Before we use any assessment tool, we should revisit our definition of *learning*. If learning is accumulating discrete bits of information, then known-answer testing and one-answer worksheets make sense. However, if our goal in education is to help students become more than passive receptors of info-bites and to become meaning makers who construct knowledge in a context that is useful in their own world, then the assessments should be "either replicas of or analogous to the kinds of problems faced by adult citizens and consumers or professionals in the field" (Wiggins 1993, 206). Wiggins maintains that skills and knowledge need to be assessed in school the same way as they are in the real world.

Performance assessment, which may be alternative and/or authentic, refers to any type of assessment that provides opportunities for students to put what they have learned into a meaningful context and demonstrate what they know. Performance assessment may include demonstrations, portfolio exhibitions, presentations, murals, stories or books, and dioramas, but it can be even broader than this. Even testing can be a form of performance assessment if the tests are designed in a way to afford the learners opportunities to connect, explain, and demonstrate how knowledge they have learned is now part of a larger context that makes it their own (Wiggins 1993). Performance assessment offers students ways to demonstrate what they have learned by putting the knowledge and skills acquired through classroom activities together with their prior and distinct knowledge of the world.

To use knowledge to some end, to produce something, gives students an opportunity to demonstrate what they know and involves issues such as choice, research, creativity, and time. Teachers must remove artificial constraints to whatever degree possible in an educational setting and combine both the authentic with the performance aspects of assessment. For example, a performance assessment similar to a science fair is a literacy fair. At a literacy fair, like a dancer's recital, an artist's show, or a musician's concert, students present their work, talking about the process of a work's creation, giving a performance of a dramatic work or a reading of a poem or a passage, or showing an artifact in another medium that represents or interprets a piece of literature or an original work. Parents, interested members of the community, administrators, civic leaders, and other students are invited to see the presentations of various projects. With a variety of different things going on in different classrooms, the audience roams around and sees the different presentations, performances, and projects. Attendees are often amazed to see how involved students get when they choose what they want to do and when they have a real audience. Such "performances" provide opportunities for students to engage in learning and for teachers to assess reading, writing, listening, and speaking as these language arts were used to make meaning.

Knowing students as individuals means being able to talk with an individual student or parent or administrator about that student's progress and growth and to use specifics, not just vague numbers or percentages. What are the student's strengths? How are they best exhibited? What are their needs? Their goals? How will they work toward these goals? Questions such as these aren't answered by a grade. They are outgrowths of the process of learning—a process that is organic, unique to the individuals involved, and collaborative between teacher and students. However, to find answers, teachers need to know how to gather the data and then how to analyze the information, much the way anthropologists and sociologists conduct research. Such gathering and analysis requires a knowledge of qualitative assessment techniques, such as keeping anecdotal records, conducting interviews, compiling checklists, and carrying on dialogue discussions.

Checklists—Simple, Fast, Succinct

When students, their teacher, and the curriculum have identified the traits that are desirable for a specific subject or task, these can be listed on teacher-created instruments called *checklists*. In addition to assessing products or artifacts of learning, checklists can record observable student behaviors that both teacher and students have determined as desirable. The teacher, acting as observer, looks for evidence of such traits as he or she works with students in the community of the classroom. Teachers need to be able to quickly record observations while working with students if the checklists are to be helpful, especially during cooperative learning projects, group presentations, and class discussions. The purpose of these assessment instruments is to keep the teacher focused on what is important and provide a record of student growth from information gathered over a period of time, much the way that the Status of the Class reports do. They need to be simple and to the point, requiring a minimum of writing on the teacher's part. This is a particularly efficient method, especially for teachers who are responsible for large numbers of students, as many secondary teachers are. As we all know, some students get noticed naturally—the students who are bright and articulate, the leaders of discussions, and the students who are having academic or personal difficulties. Not only will this system help a teacher identify the needs and strengths of those students, it will also help the teacher identify those students who are between either extreme, the students who haven't been noticed lately, the ones who fall through the cracks.

Some teachers keep the checklist in a notebook or log, marking in it at different times of the day. Some use a three-ring binder of checklist forms with a tab for each student. Some keep electronic observations the way nurses in some hospitals now chart their patient's information, entering data into a notebook computer. Other teachers like to keep checklists on a clipboard, jotting down quick observations during the day on a sheet of peel-off blank address labels, making them easily portable from group to group or from student to student. These notes can be removed at the end of the day and transferred to a notebook divided according to classes, a page for each student.

Checklist assessment techniques can only be used in classrooms where teachers have opportunities to observe and students have opportunities to assume responsibility for their learning. For example, a teacher in an English classroom may want to keep track of writing behaviors that are important for development in composition. As students are working on drafts, conferencing, revising, or editing, the teacher may be watching for evidence of the students' understanding of the writing process. If so, a checklist like that found in Figure 6–3 may be helpful.

By using this type of checklist, the teacher and student can easily pick up where they left off at the next conference. For example, after the conference on

Figure 6–3. Writing conference checklist

Student Name (Title of Work)	Conf date	Focus Thesis	Opening	Organization	Development	Transitions	Sentence structure	Conclusion	Usage Issues	Comments
Ashley (mod art)	3/21	+	+	✓	✓	−	−	−	✓	strong intro. needs an ending, work on trans.
Laura (soap opera)	3/21	✓	−	−	−	NA	NA	NA	NA	first draft. discussed voice. biggest concerns.
Benjamin (acting)	3/23	+	+	+	✓	+	✓	✓	−	almost ready. needs to clean up some loc's; edit
Jason (security)	3/23	+	−	+	+	+	+	✓	✓	still needs a catchy opening to draw reader
Kim untitled	3/23	−	−	−	NA	NA	NA	NA	NA	struggling to find a topic or focus
Alicia (reporting)	3/23	+	+	✓	✓	✓	+	−	NA	have needs but done potential. suggest prewriting
Kelly (health care)	3/25	+	+	+	+	+	−	+	+	could work on variety of sentences, a beginning new

Symbol Key:

+ well developed
✓ satisfactory
− needs attention
NA not applicable at this time

3/21, the teacher and Ashley know that she needs to work on the conclusion of her piece and to check for ways to make transitions and sentence structure clearer. At the next conference, her teacher will be able to immediately identify which areas Ashley was working on.

Checklists devised by teachers, or by teachers and students together, can foster better organization and communication. Students can be furnished with editing checklists that can be kept in their writing folders and used as a reference when their writing is ready to be edited (see Figure 6–4). Such a checklist helps students doublecheck their assignments before handing them in. There are no gradations of quality on such a list, its purpose being one of organization rather than one of evaluation. However, gradations of quality could be added to the checklist, making it similar to a rubric and appropriate for use as an evaluative tool.

DEVELOPMENT
—1. Addresses the topic
—2. Has sufficient amount of writing
—3. Has sufficient support and details relating to the topic (reasons, comparisons, incidents, examples)
ORGANIZATION
—1. Has a beginning, middle, and end
—2. Has unified paragraphing
—3. Has sufficient transitional words
—4. Has focus and is easy to follow
SENTENCE FORMATION
—1. Has sentence variety
—2. Has complete and correctly formed sentences
—3. Avoids run-on sentences
WORD USAGE
—1. Is vivid and to the point
—2. Uses correct grammar
—3. Has subject/verb agreement
—4. Has clear word choice
MECHANICS
—1. Has correct capitalization
—2. Has correct punctuation
—3. Has correct spelling

Figure 6–4. Editing checklist

Checklists may be used for assessment or for evaluative purposes—that is, they may be *formative* or *summative*. Although formative and summative checklists can look similar, formative checklists are used to record data during assessment and summative checklists are used to make evaluations, based on collected data. A summative checklist can be rather formal, as in the case of one used in place of or along with report cards; or it can be informal and even filled out by the student and teacher together in order for the student to self-evaluate. Students can also use checklists. Criteria listed on a checklist guide can be marked off by students as they work toward the completion of a project, writing piece, or even a portfolio. When both the students and the teacher generate and maintain checklists, students begin to understand what's important.

Rubrics

A *rubric* is an instrument that makes explicit the criteria of a given task—what is expected—and the various levels of expression—what an exemplary response for each component would look like. In other words, a rubric articulates in a grid design the definition of a task as well as the gradations of the quality for each of the separate elements. Rubrics sometimes simply label the degrees of quality, either with text such as *good, adequate, not satisfactory*, or as numbers, such as a scale of 1–4. Rubrics are helpful for both teachers and students because articulating criteria for any assignment, project, or task helps teachers and students communicate. For the teacher, a rubric can help define a task for students by making criteria and components explicit, and in doing so, provides many teachable opportunities. Rubrics for evaluation are not new, but if they are to be used to authentically assess student achievement, teachers should make them clear and explicit so students can determine the quality of their own work. For example, the rubric in Figure 6–5 lists the criteria and gradations of quality for oral presentation. The columns to the right of the criteria describe the varying degrees of quality for each criteria.

As students and teacher create rubrics for writing assignments, they have to work together to define the criteria for the piece of writing—what should be included, what should be demonstrated, and what format it should be. They also have to decide on the gradations of quality. How do we define "good" writing? Neil Cosgrove, a colleague of ours, does this by creating the rubric with his students. He asks each of them to bring in an example of what they feel is good writing and they bring in everything from published works to advertising copy to newspaper stories to music lyrics. His students then work collaboratively in groups to try to articulate what traits made each piece of writing "good." Neil then collects the individual groups' contributions, copies them, and distributes them to the class. Once more in groups, his students construct descriptions of the traits of good writing. Neil

CRITERIA	EXCELLENT 3	COMPETENT 2	LIMITED 1
TOPIC	student addresses the topic clearly and provides examples to illustrate the point	student addresses the topic but provides few examples	student does not address the topic
ORGANIZATION	presentation includes a strong introduction that gains audience attention, followed sequential/ organized progression of ideas	presentation includes an introduction and follows a relatively organized progression of ideas	presentation has a weak introduction and ideas are difficult to follow
VISUAL EFFECTS	student uses visuals in unique and interesting ways	student uses visuals to support the point	few visuals are used or visuals are used ineffectively
EYE CONTACT	student establishes good eye contact with audience and makes audience feel as if they are being spoken to	during most of the presentation, student maintains eye contact with audience	student establishes minimum eye contact with audience
VOCAL PROJECTION	student enunciates clearly, uses expression, and is clearly heard by the audience	student speaks clearly, but with little expression, and is heard most of the time by the audience	student does not enunciate and is difficult to hear
BODY LANGUAGE	student uses gestures and mannerisms to enhance the delivery and does so naturally and effectively	student uses some gestures and mannerisms to enhance the delivery	student uses few or inappropriate mannerisms that distract from the delivery

Figure 6–5. Oral presentation rubric

considers this an *inductive rubric* because the students work from the specific instances of good writing to the general categories. The rubric that is generated becomes a guideline for his student writers and the evaluation grid is used for grading their papers. Neil, as well as other teachers, have found that rubrics can actually improve student performance by making expectations clear to them and demonstrating to students how to meet these expectations (see Figure 6–6).

Rubrics such as that in Figure 6–6 are also helpful to students during the process of learning. When criteria is clearly stated in gradations of quality and defined in explicit terms, students can begin to look at their own as well as another student's work with a more critical eye, increasing their sense of responsibility for their own work and their own progress. Rubrics can prompt students who find it difficult to give peer response and those who have trouble giving valuable feedback other than comments that concentrate mostly on lower-order concerns, such as spelling, usage conventions, and handwriting.

Although rubrics reduce the amount of time teachers spend actually evaluating or grading work, teachers must be prepared to spend time up front, constructing the rubrics or explaining them to the class. As we've mentioned, students are engaged in learning during the conception of the rubric, and by the time the rubric is constructed, or at least explained, quality time has been spent talking about the task itself and the process, time redirected away from worrying about grades and the teacher's reaction. By using the explanations of quality described on a rubric, teachers find that they can be much more specific about students' strengths and areas in need of improvement. As Jennifer Abrams (2002), an educational consultant for the Palo Alto Unified School District in California, reminds us, "The key element in delivering appropriate feedback is specificity" (9). A rubric that directs a student's attention to a conclusion that failed to pull the threads of the argument together is more helpful than a *vague* or *needs work* scribbled in the margin.

Rubrics are appropriate and extremely helpful in classes that are heterogeneously grouped. They can be set up to accommodate learners at all levels of development, identifying what students can do, instead of what they can't do, and helping students set individual goals. They also help students get a more accurate and complete picture of what is expected of them and lets them see areas in which they need to develop.

Creating Rubrics

As with anything else, we learned to develop rubrics through experimentation. There are many commercially produced rubrics that some teachers are required to use, but the most useful ones are those generated by the individual teacher or by the teacher and the class. We have adapted "Understanding Rubrics" by Heidi

CRITERIA	EXCELLENT 5	COMPETENT 3	LIMITED 1
INTERESTING STORY STRUCTURE	good beginning; catches interest; suspense; middle holds it; good ending resolves everything, satisfies, touches reader; is memorable	beginning/ending are interesting but not ones that grab you as a reader; okay middle story part; maybe not a prizewinner but it has promise	unsatisfying beginning and/or ending; wonder why you told it
ORGANIZATION	story is focused, understandable, and suspenseful; good structure, flows well, flashbacks, and foreshadowing	story is standard, straightforward, but sometimes confusing in its telling; sometimes goes on with extraneous details	bounces around; lacks focus; story is sometimes unclear or difficult to follow
STORY FORMAT	story is told with dialogue and action; we care about the narrator and characters	story is simply told—first I did this, then I did this, and they said this; doesn't really get involved with characters	inconsistently told; not sure who's speaking, jumps points of view
SHOW, NOT TELL DETAILS	story is rich in details and description; there is an attempt to show details and emotions rather than telling, not just details to make it boring	details are present but mostly it's the reader filling in the fine points; descriptions are told not shown	pretty generic—little or no visual details to help reader; characters are flat, not people we care about
FORMAT	story is told in correct English, using paragraphs and punctuation, good sentence structure	story generally correct, using standard edited English; some problems with short sentences, repetition, or punctuation	story is hindered by lack of attention to standard edited English
PRESENTATION	typed/word processed 12 point font; title; handed in on time; revision of draft done in class	presentable but not carefully attended to; maybe late; odd font or size	sloppy presentation

Figure 6–6. Writing rubric

Goodrich (1996/1997) to present suggestions to keep in mind when designing a rubric and ways to engage students in the rubric's creation (see Figure 6–7).

In our experience with rubrics, we found that defining the criteria seems to be easier than defining the gradations of quality. Gradations of quality are unclear when the terms are not adequately defined. If terms such as *excellent, good, satisfactory,* and *poor* are to be used, such labels should be defined through models. The teacher should demonstrate for students what *good* means by showing the students examples of what is considered *good,* or better yet, by giving students an opportunity to define such terms through their own reading and discussion. If a rubric is to be used that does employ numbers or grades as gradations of quality, it is essential that students be shown models with explanations that clearly define the gradations. It's possible, however, that the gradations of quality can be clearly explained on the rubric itself, so students have a clear understanding of quality. For example, in Figure 6–8, which is a rubric used district-wide for portfolio evaluations, the gradations of quality are clearly explained by the use of terms such as *exemplary, commendable, adequate,* and *in progress,* and the definition of the terms are supplied so the rubric can be used while the portfolio is in progress, not just as a final product evaluation. Terminology such as *in progress* encourages the student to continue work, instead of marking the student's portfolio with a terminal low score. Teachers should remember that the primary purpose of evaluation is to help students know what they have accomplished, so they can move forward, setting clear goals for future learning. Many things that teachers look for are subjective, such as imagination and creativity; they are difficult to quantify, yet are the most important criteria when producing or demonstrating what we know. Although teachers should be careful to avoid unclear language, it is possible to include criteria such as *creativity* if the term is defined through concrete examples. By looking at examples, students and teachers can actually arrive at an operational definition of what the term *creative* means for an individual assignment or task. Teachers should be careful to look at what's important, not what's easiest to score (Wiggins 1993). This is true for all forms of evaluation, including testing.

Test Is Not Necessarily a Four-Letter Word

There was a time when we would have thought that *authentic testing* was an oxymoron. Traditionally, testing deals with known-answer questions, even when asked in essay form. Whether questions ask students to explain the symbolism in *Moby Dick,* describe the causes of the feud between families in *Romeo and Juliet,* or discuss the reason Hester Prynne wears a scarlet letter, they are still known-answer questions, ones asking students to display their powers of memory and retention.

1. *List criteria.* Begin by listing specific criteria. What elements should a finished product have? What components of the finished product are normally taken into consideration during its evaluation? In addition to essential elements, consider listing optional attributes that might be exhibited in "better" versions of the product.

2. *Articulate gradations of quality.* Some find it easiest to begin with extremes, the *good* and *poor* ends of the spectrum and then fill in the middle. Words like *good, satisfactory,* and *poor* need to be defined operationally through example. What makes a piece or writing or a project "good"? Students recognize when a product is good, but they need to be able to define what makes that piece "good." Using models, discuss what makes a product "good."

3. *Avoid ABC conversions.* Try to avoid scales that are easy to turn into an A, B, C grade (otherwise you might as well just use ABC gradations). Instead, concentrate on articulation of quality only as far as it can go without becoming "hair-splitting." There is no set number of gradations, but it typically averages between three and five.

4. *Allow class time for the development and use of assessment tools such as rubrics.* This process takes time. Although the final grading or evaluation may go quickly (or more quickly) when using rubrics, the process of creating rubrics should not be rushed or short-changed in the interest of "time." Assessment is a part of the learning process and is therefore worth class time and valuable for those involved in the process.

5. *Try trial runs with the rubric.* The teacher and students can practice using the rubric on student samples, to get a sense of what works and what might be unclear. This is similar to using anchor papers to train readers when doing using holistic scoring.

6. *Be willing to revise the rubric.* The rubric should help students revise their work, but the rubric itself may need revision throughout the process. If the practice runs with the rubric indicate a need for revision, make sure all students are clear about the revisions and why the revisions were needed.

7. *Use the rubric for self- and peer-assessment.* Since the same rubric can be used for both assessment and evaluation purposes, the rubric should be used as often as possible during the process for self- and peer-assessment.

Figure 6–7. Suggestions for creating rubrics

Categories	Exemplary	Commendable	Adequate	In Progress
Focus	Purpose of individual portfolio extended	Purpose of individual portfolio illustrated	Purpose of individual portfolio stated	Purpose of individual portfolio confused/no focus
	Entries connect to a central idea/concept.	Entries exceed requirements.	Required entries present	Entries missing
	Reflections are in-depth and applicable in other areas.	Reflections are supported and vali-dated by analysis.	Student reflects an acquired understanding of skills.	Minimal or invalid reflections
Organization	Cohesive plan Creative	Logical plan	Attempted plan	No plan
Format	Pride in detail is apparent.	Attention to detail	Neat	Sloppy
	No mechanical or usage errors	Minimal mechanical and usage errors	Mechanics and usage errors do not interfere with over-all presentation	Mechanical and usage errors impede overall presentation
Content	Quality pieces that demonstrate inte-gration of skills: communication problem solving life skills technology citizenship	Demonstrates improvement of skills: communication problem solving life skills technology citizenship	Demonstrates a basic understanding of skills: communication problem solving life skills technology citizenship	Lacks evidence of understanding of skills: communication problem solving life skills technology citizenship
Interview	Presentation is carefully and pur-posefully developed with detail, reasons, and facts.	Presentation is developed with details, reasons, and facts.	Information is adequate.	Information is inaccurate.
	Thoughtful planning	Planning is evident.	Presentation shows evidence of some planning.	Little evidence of planning.
	Good voice level, no hesitation, good eye contact	Frequent eye contact; few nervous gestures or movements	Voice can be heard and understood. Occasional eye contact; some nervous gestures or movements	Awkward pauses; voice level too low; distracting gestures.

Figure 6–8. Fully articulated rubric

Before we design tests, we need to reconsider what learning is. If learning is accumulating discrete bits of information, then multiple-choice testing makes sense. Grant Wiggins (1993), however, suggests that our goal in education is to help students become more than passive receptors of info-bites and become "intellectual performers" who make the knowledge their own in a context that is useful in the world. Aimee Buckner (2002) agrees, "My goal [as a teacher] is to nurture my students into becoming lifelong learners. It is not to nurture my students into becoming lifelong test takers. . . . I have to make good instructional decisions that will not only get them through this test, but will last a lifetime" (215).

Tests are one way for students to perform with knowledge, but we need to offer them other ways to demonstrate what they have learned by putting the skills and knowledge acquired through course content together with their prior and distinct knowledge of the world. To do this, teachers must provide opportunities in test situations in which students "do" literacy or language-based transactions. Portfolio exhibitions, presentations, demonstrations, or artistic models come to mind, but it can be even broader than this. Wiggins (1993) explains that tests can be designed in a way to afford the learners opportunities to connect, explain, and demonstrate how content knowledge they have learned is now in a larger context that makes it their own.

When constructing tests, the phrasing of test items gives insights into how students are being asked to demonstrate what they know. The verbs used to direct the students tell not only what is being asked of the students, but how much is being asked of them. Bellanca and Fogarty (1991) categorized these verbs into three classes. The first is made up of verbs such as *describe, count, match, name, recite, select,* and *tell.* This class of verbs involves little more than recall and students are simply asked to collect what they know and regurgitate it. In the next category, test questions make use of words like *compare, sort, reason, construct, solve, distinguish, explain, classify, analyze,* and *inform.* This moves beyond the collection of facts for the sake of facts to the use of facts to connect, deduce, and generalize. The third category of test questions uses verbs like *evaluate, imagine, judge, predict, speculate, apply, estimate,* and *forecast.* This asks students to idealize, envision, and predict.

Bellanca and Fogarty borrowed from the wisdom of Oliver Wendell Holmes, who represented the thinking process as a three-story building: "There are one-story intellects, two-story intellects, and three-story intellects with skylights. All fact collectors who have no aim beyond their facts are one-story men. Two-story men compare, reason, generalize, using the labors of fact collectors as well as their own. Three-story men idealize, imagine, predict—their best illumination come from above, through the skylight." Bellanca and Fogarty imposed their three categories of gathering, processing, and applying onto Holmes three-story intellects and created a house whose floors were decorated with the appropriate verbs and with stairs leading up to higher levels, featuring a skylight for good measure.

Jennifer Abrams (2002) says that, "If we want to make sure students are learning, . . . our assessments can't be a guess or a student's facial expression" (9). Yet, we don't want to revert to an end-of-the-unit test to hold students accountable. If we want to know if students actually did the readings and the work assigned, there are other ways to obtain this information. "We need to elicit [congruent] behavior that can be seen or heard. . . . a piece of writing, an oral response, a drawing, . . . a demonstration, or some other measurable action" (9).

Some teachers award credit when nongraded work is completed, demonstrating that actual learning took place. Jeff Golub (2000) calls this the "proofs of purchase" system, students offering tangible evidence that they completed the assigned task. Just as the cereal makers required us to send in four box-tops as "proofs of purchase" in order to get the secret power ring, these "proof of purchase" activities "engage the students in reflecting on some aspect of the text [written or read in class] or [classroom] experience" and "help the students connect . . . [and] see them as relevant to their own lives" (105). These activities ask the students to do something along the lines of what Grant Wiggins calls for—applying what was learned to what was already known. These "proof of purchase" activities help the teacher to see to what degree their students are engaged in learning. Some teachers even allow the students to decide how they might prove the learning took place.

Xinia Foster (2000), a young teacher in Florida, explains,

> The real trick . . . is that you provide so much opportunity for hands-on experience and learning in the classroom that by the time the "proof of purchase" comes along students understand what needs to be done. If you have had a variety of activities that have created an engaging environment for your students they too will buy into this idea. As a matter of fact, I would say most prefer it to the "end of week quizzes." . . . When grading using a proof of purchase project, you are basically saying that the learning process is important, not the letter grade. . . . As for those reluctant learners, oftentimes you win them over in the process. Since I usually had the students work in groups, those who did not originally want to work found themselves involved. The other students made sure that they contributed, since many times the project was a group effort and affected everyone's grade.

One Bradenton, Florida teacher, Brittanny Lemieux, remembers having to give quizzes during student teaching because her cooperating teacher "didn't believe in the possibilities of the 'proof of purchase' system." Since getting her own classroom, she says, "my students have not yet taken a . . . multiple-choice test. In fact, since they know ahead of time what their proof of purchase assignment will be, many start on theirs ahead of time, when they feel individually that they have the hang of the material." Another Florida teacher, Jennifer Parker (2000) agrees, "Parents actually loved this system once they understood the rationale behind it and . . . I found that students took more pride in the grades earned—their sense of ownership was stronger!"

If learning is to be authentic, teachers will need to give students opportunities to use authentic means of demonstrating what they have learned. Rather than having students pick answers or do a quick "dumping" of all they know about a topic in forty-four minutes, we need to "ask the student to *justify* answers or choices" (Wiggins 1993, 206). When constructing tests to act as performance assessment, teachers should be careful to ask students to use their knowledge to some tangible end, to produce something. The questions or problems posed on tests should mirror problems encountered in an authentic experience of the content area. And teachers should remove artificial constraints to whatever degree possible in an educational setting. Rather than requiring tests completed in one seating or papers submitted at one deadline, the problem should be handled organically, developing with feedback. No one solves problems in a vacuum.

For example, in addition to continuous authentic assignments throughout the year, Joette Conger, an English teacher at Downer's Grove High School in Illinois, gives performance-based final exams. Her final exam in Journalistic Writing poses a situation like the ones that journalists face every day working under deadline and asks students to behave like journalists. The students are not always required to write the story; instead they're asked to describe their angle for the story, their focus, interviewees, and some of the questions. In other words, she asks them to apply their knowledge of how a journalist finds a story. When she does ask them to actually write a feature story within an exam period, the students are made aware of the question well before the test date and are allowed to bring a draft with them if they've had the foresight to think ahead. Conger even allows collaboration on parts of the final. Conger's students have practiced these activities in class and in assignments. Her testing situations ask them to perform in ways that they've rehearsed and in ways that mirror authentic situations (Strickland and Strickland 1998, 72–73).

We need to think of testing as a ongoing process, in which students are asked follow-up questions to answers, offering "concurrent feedback and the possibility of self-adjustment during the test" (Wiggins 1993, 206), rather than being grilled in special one-day events. Questions in an organic test situation could be prepared in advance, and students could be asked questions based on their previous answers and be asked to justify answers, as in a job interview. Teachers would be looking for "consistency of student work—the assessment of *habits* of mind in performance" (207).

Time and Resources—The Constraints of Testing

All assessments face constraints, the most common of which are time and resources. How much time should students have to complete a task, and what materials should be available to them? If we believe that the tasks required of students should parallel real-life situations in what's being tested, then the time and resources allowed should be typical of an authentic situation.

Time, one of the more obvious constraints of traditional testing, can be addressed if teachers and students look at tests as processes or performances rather than "brain dumps" of everything they can recall. Formal tests are noticeably constrained. For instance, many standardized tests require a writing "sample" to be completed in a brief block of time, sometimes as little as thirty minutes. Writers know that real writing, writing in which one hopes to demonstrate who one is as a writer, cannot be completed in thirty minutes. Other constraints are tied in to the time restriction: writing about topics that mean little to the writer, those not of the writer's choosing, and those without an opportunity to consider research. Needless to say, writing to such prompts does not demonstrate one's true writing abilities and is therefore neither authentic nor performance assessment.

School districts in some states give student writers time—over class periods, over days—to draft, revise, and edit their pieces, to demonstrate their understanding of the process as well as their ability to write. For example, Barbara King-Shaver (1992) of South Brunswick Schools in New Jersey has developed what she and her colleagues call a process-based examination as an alternative to traditional tests. Process exams allow a longer stretch of time for the exam. For example, on the first day, students might be given a short text to read in class, and they might be allowed to record thoughts or questions they have in a reader response journal. The students would share their responses and questions during a class discussion, during which they may take notes. The next day, a writing assignment would be given that asks them to apply ideas from the previous day's reading to two works read during the year, and they are advised to include in their discussion at least one literary term studied. Their journals and class notes would be available during class, although all their work would be collected at the end of class. On the third day, with their materials returned, they would continue to draft their essays, which would be collected once again at the end of class but returned on the fourth and final day for revision and editing. King-Shaver maintains that a process exam "integrates reading and writing, supports the writing process, supports the reading process, supports collaborative learning, and supports a process approach to learning. In short, the process examination is authentic assessment because it reflects the collaborative reading and writing processes that people use in college, on the job, and in life" (King-Shaver 1992, 7).

Still, we recognize that even process tests are not completely authentic since time isn't under the control of the writer. However, King-Shaver demonstrates how teachers make a round peg fit in a square hole. Somehow we have to take what we know about thinking, writing, and evaluation and apply it to a testing situation. This means teaching students to deal with the constraints of time. King-Shaver gives her students shorter, timed writing tasks, written to prompts not entirely of their own choosing, of the variety found on essay exams in college and the AP exam, because the practice helps make students test-ready.

Testing situations almost always constrain resources, both textual and human, for the convenience of the test makers and supposedly to level the playing field. However, if the task or test is authentic, what would be the purpose of keeping books and materials away from test takers ("clear your desks except for paper and a pen")? If tests are to be more than games of Trivial Pursuit, why not let students bring notes as part of demonstrating their understanding? While undergoing an operation, would anyone want the surgeon to be working from memory? Would anyone want a lawyer who didn't have access at trial to notes prepared researching the case? Wouldn't a mechanic be allowed to consult a manual or discuss a problem with a colleague before tackling a nonroutine problem? Constraints in testing should mirror those constraints a task might have in a typical or real situation. In schools, if tests were unconstrained, students could demonstrate understanding of knowledge and skills in the context of an authentic task by preparing, summarizing, and identifying important topics as they tackle the task at hand.

Teaching to the Test or Teaching for the Test

Tests cannot be set up to test what's in a curriculum because we don't have a national curriculum, something the core knowledge people would like to see. Tests have to outline the world of science knowledge, the world of history knowledge, and the world of English/language arts knowledge and then select from that what is possible to ask about in a multiple-choice format. There are some who believe the questions themselves on standardized tests are biased in favor of males, who read questions for the one correct answer while females read with wider interpretations and see alternative readings. Still others see the tests as prejudiced against African Americans, who have been conditioned to a sort of self-fulfilling test anxiety in which the very high-stakes nature of the test causes them to perform at a lower level. They choke on tests because they know so much is riding on it (Stephanopolis 2000). We can teach to the test because we can sketch out the type of knowledge the test makers are using, and limit the type of knowledge that would fit a multiple-choice format. We can do what the SAT prep people do, teach strategies for handling these questions, and strategies for maximizing time on timed tests, but at what cost? The curriculum is sacrificed to perform well on the tests. We see short-term benefit because the tests are normed to spread out the population in terms of percentages and stanines. If schools across the country begin to teach to the test, the test makers will simply focus on other types of questions or topics moving further away from what is being taught, even if it is taught to enable students to perform well on the test.

For example, a question on a tenth-grade English Language Arts state assessment test (MCAS 1998) asks the following of a given reading passage about a train in the mountain: "This excerpt can best be described as: a. persuasive writing b. descriptive writing c. humorous writing d. technical writing." The passage contains what might be described as technical terms, so the obvious answer (descriptive) might be rejected by a poor test taker, one who is always on the alert for tricks. A later question picks a word from the same passage, gives the dictionary definition, and asks in which language the word originated. Of the three origins given in the definition (Middle English, Old French, and Latin), two are possible answers. Even if someone were to decode this properly, the answer is always the oldest—Latin. But what is the point? Almost no one uses dictionaries on a regular basis and even fewer need to know the origin of words. So the question reveals the point of its asking—not that people who graduate high school need to know dictionary skills, but that a small slice of the population, those who read widely, come from higher socioeconomic backgrounds, and absorb esoteric information, will get this question right and thereby spread out the results for the bell curve. Another question picks a line of the passage, "...has made its slow and sinuous descent around the powerful bends and cork-screws of the shining rails," and asks what the word *sinuous* means. Of the choices given (a. sinister b. cautious c. winding d. long), only the first one doesn't make sense in context. So, the strategy—context—that most good readers use when confronting an unknown word has been disabled by the question. Those who answer correctly are those who knew the answer already, once again benefitting a small portion of the testing population and ensuring that the results are distributed as desired.

The Mixed Messages of Grading

The NCTE/IRA Joint Task Force on Assessment found "When teachers write report cards,...they must...represent a student's literate development in all its complexity, often within severe time, space, and format constraints. They must also accomplish this within the diverse relationships and cultural backgrounds among the parents, students, and administrators who might read the report. Some teachers are faced with reducing extensive and complex knowledge about each student's development to a single word or letter" (1996, 4). So, as teachers around the country try varied and alternative methods of assessment, they're left with the question of grades. Are grades an explanation of product? Progress? Effort? Achievement? Growth? Each of these is a part of what we assess and evaluate in our classes and each has an impact on the learning process and what is learned, but a single grade obviously can't report about all these things.

Perhaps that is why grading generates the litany of laments: "If only we didn't have to give grades"; "I'm worried that someone's going to mention I've given too many As and Bs"; "I don't give grades—my students earn them"; "This kid's parents are going to have a fit, but I'm sorry, this kid just isn't an A student."

Traditionally, assessments consisted of worksheets and tests, made up of mostly objective questions, and awarding grades was mostly a matter of averaging a number of individual test/assignment grades in a grade book—ten or fifteen a marking period for each subject area, for example. But if techniques are to be used that drive instruction according to individual progress, how are teachers supposed to represent all that information with a single letter or number grade that somehow vaguely translates as *superior, good, average, below average*, and *failing?*

Our friend Dave has been going to a therapist lately, and at the beginning of his appointment, he must self-report how well he did the past week on a scale from 1 to 10, a 1 meaning he wouldn't get out of bed (absurd, considering he's in the office) and a 10 meaning he's feeling exuberant (and would've probably skipped the appointment altogether). That seems reasonable enough, until we consider that the remaining eight numbers represent a general high (8–9), middle (4–7), and low (2–3). Dave says his numbers are in the 5, 6, 7 range, which again is not surprising, considering there's really no criteria for the numbers. In statistics, that's known as the tendency toward the middle. From the number given, his therapist believes she can tell if Dave's feeling better or worse than his last appointment, but then she could just as easily have used the rating *good, bad*, or *so-so* or even simply asked, "Feeling better?" The 1–10 scale gives an objective feel to the report, but there is no relationship between the numbers and his state of mental health. Grades in school operate in much the same fashion.

If we think about these qualifiers, *superior* implies a comparison to that which isn't superior (and so forth). These qualifiers require teachers to compare students to something else—each other? Past student performance? Their own or others? National or local standards? District-wide outcomes? If we look at most report cards, there is no explanation of the measurement—*superior, good, average, below average*, and *failing.*

Most teachers, when asked, have a difficult time distinguishing between evaluation and grading. *Evaluation*, the analysis of assessment data, is a judgment about learning or a summation of a learning experience. *Grades* are used more as a form of reward and punishment than as a true evaluation. Teachers evaluate, but so do students, their peers, and a combination of such interested parties. Grading is the responsibility of the teachers alone and when it comes to sharing that evaluation with the world (usually with parents, other teachers, and other institutions of learning), the learners themselves are rarely involved.

The Square Peg in the Round Hole

In the Oscar-winning movie *Apollo 13*, the scientists and engineers in Houston are called upon to make a replacement part for the spacecraft, using only supplies available onboard, parts not designed for the task at hand. When engineers complained that it couldn't be done, they were told to make it work. They didn't have other options; they didn't have other parts; and, they didn't have time. They had to make a square peg fit in a round hole. Grading, whether with letter grades or numbers, is a square peg in a round hole. Grading doesn't exactly fit in a transactional classroom with authentic assessment and evaluation, yet teachers have to grade. No matter how we assess and evaluate, for most of us, there comes a day when the report cards must be filled out and sent home. Like the *Apollo 13* engineers, we must find a way to revise report cards or at least to supplement them with other information that explains grades and gives parents (and other interested parties) more information than just an 85 percent or a grade of B. Sending home supplements, such as rubrics, students' self-evaluations, and narrative comments that address the criteria for learning, will give parents a clearer picture of what their children are learning and what they are accomplishing. Many districts have worked diligently to devise report cards that are more in line with what we believe about learning. Some are trying to move to a more constructivist basis for reporting as they have for teaching, moving along a grading continuum that goes from traditional to constructivist (see Figure 6–9). For example, the more teachers believe students are responsible for their own learning and learn at their own rate, then the more they will want grades and/or the reporting system to be based on clear criteria, reflect that learning and progress, and be the result of joint evaluation. Ultimately, if teachers believe only some can learn, then they must test and grade student learning to determine how each measures up compared to others. However, if teachers believe every student is capable of learning, then they will trust their students and give them adequate time to learn and evaluate their progress individually.

Grades Are Who We Are

Grades are often perceived as a measure of ability. In fact, grades become letters or numbers that define who people are and what they are likely to become (Dreyer 1994). Most teachers have at one time or another been guilty of referring to children as A students or C students, as if such grades define for the world who these people are. Grades not only reflect the teacher's perception of us, but they

---

GRADING CONTINUUM

Teacher-Centered (Traditional)	<————————>	Student-Centered (Constructive)
Curriculum—facts to be mastered		Curriculum—generative/meaningful
Learning is sequential and linear		Learning has no preexisting sequence
Teacher supplies information		Students responsible for their learning
Learners meet grade-level expectations		Learners learn at own rate
Grades are rewards/punishments		Grades reflect learning and progress
Grades are teacher determined		Grades are based on clear criteria
Learning must take place within given time period		Students given adequate time to learn
Teacher solely responsible for evaluation		Teachers and students evaluate jointly
Student learning compared to others		Students evaluated individually
Teachers believe some can learn		Teachers believe all can learn

Figure 6–9. Grading continuum

ultimately become our own perception of ourselves. "I wanted to be a vet, but I wasn't smart enough," confides a character in a novel by Laurence Shames (1995). The man with whom she's speaking responds, "Who told you that?" "The nuns, my father, report cards mostly," she answers. "Ah, report cards," he replies, "they're hard to argue with."

It's difficult to argue with what the report card says about us because many students and their parents believe what grades supposedly tell them, and the students become what schools expect of them or fail to expect of them. This creates a "vicious cycle, an interaction promoted by a numbers-driven culture overly reliant on measures that do not begin to address performance in context," our colleague at Slippery Rock University, Diana Dreyer argues (1994, 9). "Students are all too aware of this grading phenomenon, an awareness leading to dependence . . . on the grade itself, . . . an extrinsic reward—or punishment—so overwhelming that we tend to overlook the intrinsic value of [learning]" (9). Ironically, grades don't define people in the real world outside of school. We could list the famous school failures who became successes—Einstein, Lincoln, Rockefeller—but when asked, everyone can think of someone who wasn't school smart (in other words, didn't get good grades), but who became extremely successful, exhibiting intelligence, even becoming leaders in their field once they left school. We all know "regular" people who were bright and overcame the odds, achieving more than their grades would predict. Unfortunately, not all overcome such odds. Many believe what grades tell them and adjust their lives accordingly, giving up on themselves and their dreams.

Using grades as a reward or punishment is perceived by many as an appropriate way to motivate students rather than by facilitating learning, providing opportunities, helping students see a purpose in school, and finding ways for them to tackle difficult subjects and projects. And grades may even work for a while, but ultimately they are unsatisfying and will rob students of the joy of learning for its own sake. Grading has little purpose and surely no positive effects on learning unless there exists an understanding of what both teacher and learner are responsible for. Grades are usually regarded as something that is *done* to students by teachers. Much of this battle between teachers and students that results from grading also results in hostile interactions between teachers and students and stems from teachers who look at students as lazy, unmotivated, and impossible to teach.

Teresa Savin (2002) flatly declares, "grades don't motivate unmotivated students. . . . Reminding them that failure to work will result in no credit only serves to reinforce the idea that the only reason to work is to receive a particular grade or some other extrinsic reward. This notion places simply getting through the school year ahead of the joy of learning" (1). And giving extra credit to bolster grades only compounds the problem. "It doesn't work. Again, it offers an extrinsic reward, supporting the idea that the final grade is more important than the pursuit of knowledge. Additionally, offering extra credit in large amounts sends the message that students in your class are able to pass or excel without having to do much of the assigned work" (3). And even more mystifying is that students don't respect teachers who give extra credit. As one group of students told Teresa Savin, "[Another teacher] gives us fifty points just for raising our hands. . . . ,[so] what we learn isn't important, . . . All we have to do to get a good grade is act like we want a good grade, and he'll end up giving it to us. We don't even have to really try. It doesn't matter how you answer the questions, either. You could not even hear the question, raise your hand, and say anything, and you still get fifty points. Our grades in that class don't mean anything" (3).

If grades distort the experience of learning, how do students become so grade conscious? By fifth or sixth grade, students learn from the adults who are influential in their lives to covet grades. Parents brag about their child's final grades; the local newspapers print the honor roll from the local schools; grandparents pay a dollar for every A. Parents and teachers make comments along the lines of, "What happened, Megan? You dropped from an A to a B." And how many students have asked teachers what they have to do to move up from a C to a B, only to hear, "Well, I guess you'll just have to work a little harder." Grades also can create a self-fulfilling prophecy, so the end-of-year grades become the predictors of achievement in the next year. Students in gifted programs often do well, in part, because of assumptions made about them and because of the nurturing care they receive from the best teachers (after all, they are the students that teachers aspire to teach). Similarly, the "LD" or "Title" students do poorly, in part, because of the assumptions made about them and because of the lack of support their teachers receive.

What Do Grades Measure?

Many look at grades as a report of achievement, a finite measurement taken at the end of a season, like the baseball standings. Each marking period seems to bring that period of learning to a close with the student expected to start again the next marking period. Grades are usually thought of as an end, not as a step. Since grades are incapable, where and how do we report progress, initiative, growth, and goals for future learning?

Most of the time, achievement grades are used to "sort" students; in fact, we "categorize them so rigidly that they rarely escape" (Silberman 1970, 138). Regardless of whether they're reported as letters, percentages, or numbers, grades measure products, not usually process or progress. Alfie Kohn (1993) maintains that grades fail to provide students with valuable information; instead the process of grading causes students to concentrate on their performance rather than on their learning. He maintains, as do many of us, that the only legitimate reason for wanting to know how well students are doing—the only legitimate purpose for evaluation—should be to help them learn more effectively in the future. Bonita Wilcox (2002), editor of *English Leadership Quarterly*, redirects the question: "Instead of asking, 'What grade does this paper deserve?' the question is 'What can I suggest to help this writer?' Eventually, 'What did I get?' becomes less important to the student than the question, 'Where do I go from here?'" (1).

Grades, according to Kohn, dilute the pleasure that a student gets from working on and completing a task while they encourage cheating and strain the relationship of trust and respect between students and teachers. Evaluating understanding is even more difficult because it requires that teachers consider the purposes and outcomes of a particular course of study when designing evaluation techniques and that they spend the time it takes to help students understand the goals and how to achieve those goals. And if evaluation requires considering purposes and outcomes, then assessment must consider them as well when determining what will be collected and sampled.

The Sabotage of Grading Competitively

Even more detrimental than believing that grades will motivate learning is the myth of the bell curve—the statistically even distribution in which the majority of the population falls in the middle with a smaller number of subjects falling above or below the "norm." Too many teachers, trained in a statistical distribution approach to evaluation, look at grading as a comparison of members within a group. Instead of looking at grading as reporting about students as individuals, they expect that the majority of students' grades will fall somewhere in the middle and their performances will be judged as higher or lower than the norm. For example, a department chairperson once sent a grade distribution report to department members, one showing most students had received grades of As and Bs. The memo asked the question, "Are our students really *this* good?" The implication, of course, was that the teachers had inflated the grades in some way because the students were graded above average. If students are motivated, interested, and want to succeed in learning, doesn't it make sense to grade them according to their demonstrations of learning, meeting the goals and criteria of the course?

And yet, if every student in a class succeeded in meeting the objectives of the curriculum, then each and every one would receive an A, a situation that the public, most teachers, and parents would deem unacceptable. Consequently, the system reinforces methods of assessment and evaluation that ensure that some students won't succeed. In misdirecting student learning, "competitive grading trivializes course content" (Krumboltz and Yehn 1996, 325). It's much easier to ask one-answer questions and fill out worksheets than to set up opportunities for students to make connections and to problem solve. It's much easier to quantify learning by dispensing knowledge and then evaluating the memorization of bits of knowledge. According to the NCTE/IRA Task Force, a major problem that occurs when we try to "align curriculum and assessment [is] that curriculum has reflected assessment rather than the other way around. Thus we have often achieved a trivial curriculum by aligning it with trivial assessments" (1996, 6). "Competitive grading de-emphasizes learning in favor of judging. Learning becomes a secondary goal of education. Clearly then, the need to grade students undermines the motive—to help students learn—that brought most of us into the profession," say Krumboltz and Yehn (326).

The teachers' choice of methods of instruction, their choice of evaluation instruments, and the amount of time and opportunities provided for students to complete tasks allows teachers to subconsciously set up barriers for students, thereby justifying teaching that fails to reach every learner. Competitive grading masks poor teaching because if some students are succeeding, then, the reasoning goes, there probably isn't anything wrong with the teaching or the teacher. Grades that compare students with one another don't encourage students to do the best they can do; rather, they encourage students to do just enough to get by with the grade they have come to believe best describes them. Consequently, many students do little to "stretch" themselves for an A, while others who see themselves as C students feel "why bother, I'll never do as well as the 'smart' students."

Student Involvement in Evaluation

In the traditional model of evaluation, students produce an artifact (a paper or answers on a test), turn it in to their teacher who checks it against some standard of measurement, and the teacher returns the artifact with a score, mark, or grade. Even if this satisfied our desire to know whether our students understood what was taught, it doesn't tell whether they understood the feedback on papers and tests. Ideally, if the feedback is given during the class, the teacher will be able to monitor the student's understanding (Abrams 2002). If that's not always possible, an alternative that Maureen Neal, of Mesa State College in Colorado, tries is having "dialogue discussions" when "corrected" papers are handed back (Strickland and Strickland 1998, 51–53). Neal uses written dialogue to better understand what her students are thinking and doing, an invaluable tool for instruction. When Neal hands back papers, students write back to her, paraphrasing and interpreting her comments and then responding to those comments or questions, including any questions they might have about the grading process or the specific grade. This isn't a formulaic exercise that the students must go through; Neal and her students sometimes send responses back and forth several times before the dialogue is ended. This not only prompts the students to read their teacher's comments, but it cultivates thoughtful consideration of her critical and positive comments, which is necessary to be able to respond. Harvey Daniels (2001) believes schools need to encourage more written dialogue between and among teachers and students. Even if the dialogue contains complaints, using the act of writing to make the comments explicit is valuable in itself, and the back and forth nature of dialogue writing helps teachers and students share responsibility and authority.

Portfolios

While campaigning for testing situations that are unconstrained by time and re-sources, teachers discovered an alternative that addresses the concern for assessing performance over time, the *portfolio*. Generally, a portfolio in education refers to any collection of work, from writing folders to scrapbooks to mandated collections, that represents a student as a learner, showcases their work, demonstrates who they are, what their strengths are, and the range of their ability. The rise in popularity of portfolios in schools is tied to the issue of retention; do students internalize what-ever learning took place or do they forget it as soon as the moment of assessment passes? A portfolio seems to be a multipurpose vehicle for assessment, evaluation, keeping a permanent record of student achievement, teaching, grading, celebrating, and just collecting—perfect for "students and teachers to track the learning experience over a period of time" (Chambers 1996, 1). Portfolios allow an ongoing assessment of active processes ("selecting, comparing, self-evaluation, sharing, goal setting") rather than static products.

Jim Mahoney (2002), author of *Power and Portfolios*, distinguishes

> three types of portfolios: showcase, growth, and limited. . . . I had the best success with showcase portfolios. These contain students' best final products presented in showcase style, using pictures and designer papers as well as paying attention to layout and other design aspects to make them visually appealing. Many students love this type of portfolio and are willing to work hard on the writing that will go into it.
>
> A growth portfolio asks students to show growth in writing over a period of time by including examples of weak early writing along with writing that shows their improvement. The samples might include handwritten drafts of work in various stages. Such portfolios are harder to evaluate than showcase portfolios and are not as attractive to students or outside readers.
>
> Limited portfolios might require all students in a grade to include a particular type of assignment, such as a personal narrative or a literary analysis. These collections might be nothing more than manila file folders that hold the required assignments that students consider their best. Such requirements are generally district- or state-driven and are used to evaluate programs rather than students. They limit student choice and take away much of their incentive to compose their own lives through their portfolios. (27–28)

There are no formulas for using portfolios; however, as with other strategies used in teaching, we believe "how" portfolios are used should grow out of an understanding of "why" we are using them. Again we invoke Donald Graves' touchstone for examining our educational endeavors, "What's it for?"

Ownership/Managing Portfolios

Who decides what is included in portfolios? Unfortunately, the selection is often controlled by teachers and school districts, but sometimes students are allowed to select what is included in their portfolio. We believe work in a portfolio rightfully belongs to the student who created it, and just as teachers show respect for their students in a student-centered classroom, that respect should extend to their productions. "Students own the portfolios"; a portfolio is "a kid's brain on paper," says Jane Blystone (1997b, 4). Jane's concern that students have ownership of their own work flies in the face of an educational system that wants every student to know the same things upon exiting the classroom, the semester, the year, the building. An educational system that rallies behind the concept of every student filling in the same bubble on the same Scantron sheet—having the same core knowledge, some call it—hypocritically castigates the same students for being unable to transfer knowledge (what we consider isolated facts) to real-world situations. Jane regards her students as "works of art in progress, growing and changing as they absorb and integrate knowledge from school and their cultures into their lives, . . . [who] have never been permitted to own what they learn. When the teacher determines what the child has 'learned,' calling it right or wrong, no [real world] thought processes operate. . . . Thinking [in real world situations] requires evaluation, planning, organizing, working in teams, negotiating, and reworking ideas, but students are rarely allowed to do that in school. So how do we think students can connect learning with real life when real life operates differently than our school environment? This is why it is so important for students to *own* portfolios" (4–5).

Jim Mahoney (2002) realizes,

> Some teachers, departments, and even districts want to prescribe the genres that these finished pieces cover. I can see the logic of that from the institution's point of view, but I don't find that students value the same things. It comes back to whose portfolio is it and what is its purpose? Is the portfolio being used to evaluate curriculum success, departmental or district progress, or individual teacher accountability? If so, then the student's portfolio is being used for something else. Perhaps the school or the teacher wants to be assured that every student is proficient in all of the genres. Although I don't think that anyone has to be a jack-of-all-trades, requirements from certain genres can be satisfied in individual marking periods and found in the quarterly portfolios. The final portfolio serves as the culmination of the year, but it is also each student's opportunity to *compose a life*, a phrase I use all the time with students publishing for themselves. They engage in making sense of the big and small issues in their lives. Therefore, students should have a great deal of choice as to which pieces are to be included. (14)

Digital Portfolios

The computer's incredible storage capacity allows teachers and students to create digital portfolios. Computers are capable of storing text (drafts, reports, projects), sound (speeches, in-class reports, readings), and image data (photographs, drawings, handwritten samples) in hypertext stacks. Over and above storing individual files on disk as many of us already do, computers have the ability to store linked files, producing a digital compilation. But instead of simply offering students a way of demonstrating who they are, the computer portfolio can become a virtual transcript, containing artifacts produced each year in addition to courses and grades for each level. In this way, teachers, parents, and the students themselves will have a cumulative portrait of themselves in digital code. Jane Blystone's students keep their working pieces in a big box in the computer lab, rather than in her room, so they don't lose any of their works in progress. Students appreciate the ability to select pieces from everything they've done. If portfolios belong to students, then they are responsible for updating and managing their portfolios.

Teachers' Roles in the Portfolio Classroom

In a classroom where portfolios are used for assessment and evaluation, the teacher's role is varied and oftentimes difficult. There is a fine line between control and support; between choice and lack of guidance. Tierney, Carter, and Desai (1991) suggest that teachers should explain to students what the teacher's role will be in selecting work for student portfolios: helping students articulate reasons for including each piece in their portfolios; and encouraging students to be explicit as to *why* they feel certain pieces should be included and how they reached their decision. "The portfolio's element of choice, as noted above, is a crucial part of the assignment. Students need to have the freedom to make choices about what they think is their best writing, and then to defend those selections in their introduction," says Rick Chambers (1996, 14).

Teachers must also find their role, so students can learn to be responsible for their own learning. Although the portfolios belong to the students, the teacher is their coach, mentor, and facilitator. The teacher sets the practice sessions so that writing in their writer's notebook is a regular event. If students are constantly recording the small moments with as much detail as possible, then they will find material in their portfolios to be shaped into a finished piece. Jane Blystone (1997b) has found ways to support her students in her classes while providing them with the opportunities to learn to make important choices. However, these choices must be based on criteria which is often the teacher's responsibility to help students discover. Jane explains,

> I try to use conferencing to help them avoid being "pack rats" with their work. We do oral negotiation to help them move through some pieces to make them presentable, or as some call them, final form. For example, we do four essays at the beginning of the trimester. I let them sit for three weeks unattended in the working portfolio. Then, the student has a conference with me and I ask nontypical teacher questions, such as, Which one did you like the most? Which was the easiest for you to write? Which do you think you could polish up if you were given time? Then, I suggest they revise the pieces that they selected to include in the showcase portfolio as they need a variety of writing styles in their final portfolio. (2)

Addressing Format Concerns

The look of the portfolio is extremely important to students—they're proud of the format and layout of the portfolio and they want the packaging to present their ideas well. Most students are concerned about format considerations, so it's best to spell out any formal requirements at the beginning of the portfolio process. For example, many teachers ask that portfolios include a table of contents arranged by chronological order, by sections, or by themes. Some teachers stipulate the number of "best" works chosen and some indicate that earlier drafts should be included in the portfolio. Some teachers detail the types of writing that must be included—essay, short story, and poetry. Some teachers, if growth is important, ask that all work be dated. Other teachers ask that students write, on a separate sheet, the strengths that they feel each piece shows and why it was selected. Some teachers ask their students to set reading and writing goals for themselves for each marking period, and then refer to these goals when self-evaluating their work in the portfolio. Some teachers welcome the inclusion of peer responses to student work. And teachers will need to decide whether students are free to remove any writings they wish. Many students are also asked to include a letter of introduction to their portfolio, a retrospective "Dear Reader" essay, in addition to the work done throughout the year.

Jim Mahoney's (2002) requirements for his students are typical; he asks that they include a table of contents and a reflection on themselves as writers and how they used their writer's notebook. His students also reflect upon themselves as readers and how they used their literature logs. None of these activities are new for Jim's students because he's asked them to write a reflection on the work they've done in the previous 10 weeks at the end of each marking period. To help them do this, Jim gives students a handout that details reflective thinking, called "A Backward Glance" (see Figure 6–10). He asks them to find evidence in their writings to support their assessment of their best and their worst reading and writing during the quarter. Completing this reflective review each marking period helps students do trial runs of the type of reflection they'll be asked to do later for the whole year.

Sharing and Celebrating Portfolios

Students need opportunities to appreciate each others' best work by sharing some pieces orally or through some other type of forum. Many teachers see the wisdom in sharing portfolios—with parents, other teachers, administrators, and other students (Tierney, Carter, and Desai 1991). Teachers should encourage students to share their work with their parents and help parents understand the value of a transactional approach to teaching and learning. Tangible evidence such as a portfolio

A Backward Glance
Reflecting on the Writer's Notebook and Literary Log
At the end of the quarter

This is not just an opinion. Give evidence from your notebooks.

Writer's Notebook

- What is your strongest (or most important) entry? Why? What importance does it have for you, the person? For you, the writer?

- What is your weakest entry or one you're least interested in showing or even keeping?

- Where were you when you did most of your writing? Your best writing?

- Are you better off when a topic is given or put on the board or do you write best when you are alone and with your own thoughts and observations?

- What kind of growth or change have you seen in your writer's notebook? How important is this notebook to you?

- If a fire destroyed your things, how upset would you be if your notebook were lost? How useful or tedious has it become to you?

- Did you write anything this quarter because of something you read?

Literary Log

- What is you best literary letter? How do you know? What do you use to rate it?

- Which letter would you like to show to a college recruiter? To your best friend? Someone else?

- Which letter was your poorest? Why? Is this a pattern?

- What were the best responses you received from others? Why? Did anyone give you good feedback or make a good comment or recommendation to you?

- What was your best reading experience? Why? How did you choose or hear about those books?

- What progress did you make regarding your literary letters?

Figure 6–10. Backward glance

will reassure parents that their children are learning everything prescribed by the curriculum and learning it in an atmosphere that encourages responsibility and goal setting.

Rick Chambers (1996) believes, "the students-helping-students paradigm continues to be a marvelous learning tool" (7). He quotes Tom Romano (1987), "To be honest on paper is difficult and risky, quite an accomplishment in itself. To then share those true words with others is a profound act of faith and trust. Such writing and sharing requires a willingness to become vulnerable" (39). Rick says that "writing is so personal, that it takes a great leap in trust and faith to expose oneself to the comments of others. . . . As the course evolved, they learned to appreciate the comments of their peers. . . ." (7).

Teachers who use portfolios for assessment and evaluation soon discover that they must be shared, as all authentic showcase portfolios are, and students who produce their own portfolios are anxious and proud to share them with an audience. Such an audience, however, must be real. Many teachers organize an in-school assembly or an evening social event, such as the coffee house night or writers' banquet mentioned earlier, as an opportunity for students to present their portfolios. In cases where such large events are impossible, resourceful teachers can organize in-class presentations of student's portfolios to classmates, their teacher, and an outside guest, perhaps an administrator invited to attend the class. During these presentations, each student reads selections and reflects on his or her own learning, describing his or her development as a learner. Teachers who have tried these approaches report similar moments of success as students listen to each other and share their portfolios.

What About Grading Portfolios?

Most teachers who have worked with student-owned portfolios would rather not grade them, but the reality of it is, grades are so much of the secondary school culture that they are here to stay. Maureen Neal admits,

> When it's time to actually put a grade on portfolios, for example, I often cringe at what I perceive is the expectation that I should adhere to an implicit (almost ghostly) set of descriptors which represent my department's (unwritten) standard of acceptable writing quality. I find myself caught between my fear that I will be seen by my more conventional colleagues as a "soft" grader and my fear that I will be seen by my students as an untrustworthy, hypocritical demon who springs grading surprises on them after it is too late to do anything about it. I well remember one student . . . who came to me in tears after having received a B⁺ on her semester-end portfolio: "But I learned how to use a colon," she said, "And I never knew how to do that until now. Doesn't that count for anything?"(Strickland and Strickland 1998, 53)

When asked how she graded portfolios, Jane Blystone (1997b) explained,

> When I first started five years ago using "one grade for the portfolio" at the end of a grading period, I was taking a big risk because my school is very traditional, using percentages as the basis of the grading scale. I have never been sure what the difference between a 92 percent (B) on a piece of writing and a 93 percent (A) really meant. It did not tell me if a student could focus scattered ideas into an organized piece, or if the student could use a variety of strategies to formulate opinions, or use supporting details, or find a voice in a piece of writing, or spell correctly, or avoid dangling their participles, or splitting those ominous infinitives, etc. The first marking period I tried this, I had 13 creative students in the class at the time, so we negotiated every detail. After each student had a culminating conference with me, I asked them to put the grade they thought they earned on a Post-It note and place it on the back of the portfolio. I read through the portfolios after class and, on a Post-It note on top of the portfolio, marked a grade that I thought they deserved based on the rubrics inside of the portfolio, my observations, their self-reflections, etc. When they came to class, I asked them to place their Post-It note beside mine on top to see how close we were. Ten of the 13 had selected the same grade I had selected and two thought they deserved half a grade lower and one thought she deserved a half grade higher than I had given. They were thrilled that they [had a sense] what good writing was and that they could come to the same conclusions as a teacher. (3–4)

Jim Mahoney (2002) found that grades become secondary to the pride the student has for the portfolio itself; it showcases what the student *can* do and the students are proud of their accomplishments. He tells of a student who showed his portfolio to Jim's colleague, who was so impressed that he asked to borrow it for a workshop he'd be giving over the summer. The student tentatively said okay while reserving the right to keep it for graduation because he wanted to be able to show his portfolio to his friends and relatives (12).

If portfolios are to find a place in our classrooms, teachers must find ways to grade and to report to parents, without turning these portfolios into competitive products or teacher-pleasing assignments. Teachers should evaluate portfolios based on criteria set up at the beginning of the process, criteria mutually decided upon by the students and by the teacher (Tierney, Carter, and Desai 1991). Neal says she's "tried Edward M. White's (1985) suggestion for a collaboratively-constructed grading scale. Students contribute to it, I contribute to it, and we try it out on sample papers and then revise it through discussion and experimentation. Though this is helpful in many ways, it only seems to postpone the inevitably painful decision-making process, and it is not an acceptable solution to the conflict between process methodology and product-oriented assessment" (Strickland and Strickland 1998, 53).

As part of the assessment process, Jim Mahoney (2002) sets up the requirements for the portfolio, with student choice being central to the actual product, as he explained earlier. The portfolio process helps his students learn to reflect on what they have written or produced. In order to make good choices, however, the students need to learn how to self-evaluate. What makes a piece "good"? Jim has devised strategies to help students begin this reflective process. He asks them to include their five best pieces of writing but to strike a balance between prose and poetry. Depending on which class the portfolio is created in, he sometimes asks that they include a more formal paper, such as a literary analysis. Inevitably someone asks is if it is okay to put in more than five pieces. Jim tells them they can include anything else so long as the required pieces are included. Jim laughs and says his students almost always fill up every page available. And their sense of pride and accomplishment keeps getting replayed. Jim remembers another last day of school, about 3:00 P.M. in the afternoon.

> Grades have been turned in days ago. Most students are gone by 11:00, beginning their summer vacations, but I'm in the computer room with five or six students who still want to make their portfolios perfect. One ninth-grade student is still there with his father, who has come to help him do a few things to his portfolio, such as arranging the papers in plastic folders. They are late, expected home earlier, but still the father works away with his son, saying, "Mom is going to kill us," finally leaving around 5 P.M. (12).

What other activity would get students to stay at school even after their grades have been turned in? Only a writing activity that is authentic and purposeful.

A Final Thought

Remaining authentic in our assessment, evaluation, and reporting comes down to this: "If you teach well, maintain best practices, make instructional decisions based on your students' needs, and make decisions that are reflective of your pedagogy; your students will learn. They will learn well, and they will pass the test. . . . Make a lasting impression—teach your students, not the test" (Buckner 2002, 215).

For Further Exploration

1. Think of an assignment you've given as a teacher or received as a student. Design a rubric that would clarify the criteria of the assignment as well as the gradations of quality. What is the most difficult part of this activity? Why?

2. Looking at a test you have constructed or one you have taken, decide if it is a one-story (fact collecting), two-story (connecting), or three-story (applying) test. If it's a lower-story test, how could it be rewritten to give students a chance to apply what they have learned?

3. Devise a survey you could use in the beginning of the school year. Think of information your students could share with you that would help drive your instruction. Can you devise a survey for the end of the school year that would help assess the curriculum and your effectiveness as a teacher?

4. Visit a classroom or talk with a teacher who uses portfolio assessment. Why did the teacher choose to use portfolios? How are the portfolios used? If possible, speak to a student. What are his or her understandings and attitudes toward portfolios? Are the portfolios graded? How?

7

The Politics of Standardization and Testing

*America's teachers and children don't need national committees to
grade their worth. We need local teachers to reflect on their own
experience, to figure out how the students, the curriculum, and even
the bureaucracy interact in a process we call education. The essence
of being a teacher is knowing who you are, where you are—and
liking what you find. Being a teacher means being able to draw
your own map—instead of relying on mass-produced tourist guides.*
—Susan Ohanian

In recent years, in response to a misperception that school curriculum is weak, our
government has encouraged development of standards in several content areas.
One of the first frameworks for instruction K–12 was published in 1989 by the
National Council of Teachers of Mathematics professional organization. Their
framework was built on a belief that learning mathematics means more than memorizing and repeating. "Learning involves investigating, formulating, representing,
reasoning, and using appropriate strategies to solve problems, and then reflecting
on how mathematics is being used" (Romberg 1993, 36). These standards became
pivotal in the educational reform called for by the National Governor's Association, led by then–Governor Clinton during the senior Bush administration.
Subsequently, during President Clinton's first term in office, several professional
organizations were asked to write the standards for their disciplines.

Not all standards, however, were met with the same excitement that greeted
the math standards a few years earlier. In 1992, the U.S. Department of Education
awarded its Standards Project grant for the English language arts to the Center
for the Study of Reading at the University of Illinois, with the understanding that
the International Reading Association and the National Council of Teachers of
English would work closely with the Center. In 1994, after judging the English

standards to be unsatisfactory and too general, the Federal government ended its involvement, leaving the NCTE and IRA professional organizations to work at their own expense.

The *Standards for the English Language Arts*, which met with both criticism and praise when it was published in 1996, lists twelve standards for English language arts (Figure 7–1).

The *Standards* document supports teachers rather than dictating what and how teachers should teach, announcing that "these standards are intended to serve as

The vision guiding these standards is that all students have the opportunities and resources to develop the language skills they need to pursue life's goals and to participate fully as informed, productive members of society. These standards assume that literacy growth begins before children enter school as they experience and experiment with literacy activities—reading and writing, and associating spoken words with their graphic representations. Recognizing this fact, these standards encourage the development of curriculum and instruction that make productive use of the emerging literacy abilities that children bring to school. Furthermore, the standards provide ample room for the innovation and creativity essential to teaching and learning. They are not prescriptions for particular curriculum or instruction.

Although we present these standards as a list, we want to emphasize that they are not distinct and separable; they are, in fact, interrelated and should be considered as a whole.

1. Students read a wide range of print and nonprint texts to build an understanding of texts, of themselves, and of the cultures of the United States and the world; to acquire new information; to respond to the needs and demands of society and the workplace; and for personal fulfillment. Among these texts are fiction and nonfiction, classic and contemporary works.

2. Students read a wide range of literature from many periods in many genres to build an understanding of the many dimensions (e.g., philosophical, ethical, aesthetic) of human experience.

3. Students apply a wide range of strategies to comprehend, interpret, evaluate, and appreciate texts. They draw on their prior experience, their interactions with other readers and writers, their knowledge of word meaning and of other texts, their word identification strategies, and their understanding of textual features (e.g., sound-letter correspondence, sentence structure, context, graphics).

Figure 7–1. NCTE standards

guidelines that provide ample room for the kinds of innovation and creativity that are essential to teaching and learning. They are not meant to be seen as prescriptions for particular curricular or instructional approaches" (2). Many in English education and in English classrooms see the standards as providing direction for English teachers while providing the openness for teaching in ways that are not prescriptive. James Brewbaker (1997), of Columbus State University in Georgia, finds the absence of specific benchmarks in the *Standards* document a strength, citing Louann Reid of Colorado State University, who praises the generality of the guidelines that "allows districts to set their own proficiencies in ways that . . . best

---

4. Students adjust their use of spoken, written, and visual language (e.g., conventions, style, vocabulary) to communicate effectively with a variety of audiences and for different purposes.

5. Students employ a wide range of strategies as they write and use different writing process elements appropriately to communicate with different audiences for a variety of purposes.

6. Students apply knowledge of language structure, language conventions (e.g., spelling and punctuation), media techniques, figurative language, and genre to create, critique, and discuss print and nonprint texts.

7. Students conduct research on issues and interests by generating ideas and questions, and by posing problems. They gather, evaluate, and synthesize data from a variety of sources (e.g., print and nonprint texts, artifacts, people) to communicate their discoveries in ways that suit their purpose and audience.

8. Students use a variety of technological and informational resources (e.g., libraries, databases, computer networks, video) to gather and synthesize information and to create and communicate knowledge.

9. Students develop an understanding of and respect for diversity in language use, patterns, and dialects across cultures, ethnic groups, geographic regions, and social roles.

10. Students whose first language is not English make use of their first language to develop competency in the English language arts and to develop understanding of content across the curriculum.

11. Students participate as knowledgeable, reflective, creative, and critical members of a variety of literacy communities.

12. Students use spoken, written, and visual language to accomplish their own purposes (e.g., for learning, enjoyment, persuasion, and the exchange of information).

Figure 7–1. Continued

meet the needs of their communities" (78). Critics of these standards maintain that they are too general, abstract, and jargon-ladened. John Leo (1996), of *U.S. News and World Report*, criticized the Standards' child-centeredness and cultural relativism, calling it "bad prose [that] hides bad thinking" (61).

Looking at teachers as decision-making professionals who know their students' needs best has probably been the focus of most of the criticism. Perhaps educators, politicians, and the general public have difficulty agreeing on standards because they all have different agendas, both within and outside the profession, and varied perceptions about what is important in education. If curricular matters must consider students' interests, cultures, development, and needs, it is difficult to agree on much beyond simple generalities.

> As a profession we are currently unable to give the public an assessment of our own schools in ways that reflect what we really care about. Our ability as a profession to assess what matters and to provide a telling picture of the strengths and weaknesses of our institution and the capabilities of our students on dimensions that have educational, not simply statistical significance, is quite short of what we need. This shortfall has been a function, in part, of our history in testing. . . . We have been part of a tradition that has not served us well, and we have not, as a profession, created alternatives." (Eisner 1992, 4)

Media Reporting of Achievement

Our schools and our children are constantly compared to students in foreign countries, especially in the areas of math and science, and the comparisons are seldom favorable. Although these claims are unfair and inaccurate (see Berliner and Biddle 1995), they are what leads to the perception that our schools are in crisis. In fact, the American Education 1996 Report Card showed U.S. students scored near the top on the latest international assessment of reading. American fourth graders outperformed students from all other nations except Finland. American fourth graders placed third in science and above the international average in math, according to the 1997 Third International Math and Science Study. David Berliner contends that, "Public schools still succeed amazingly well for children in neighborhoods where livable wages are earned, decent housing and health care are available, and crime and drug abuse are not everyday problems." In fact, he argues that the use of statistical averages "masks the scores of students from terrific public schools and hides the scores of students attending shamefully inadequate schools. . . . Average scores mislead completely in a country as heterogeneous as ours. We have many excellent public schools, and many that are not nearly as good" (Berliner 2001).

In a recent newspaper interview, Alfie Kohn, former teacher and critic of standardized tests, contends that

> Tests do not improve learning. In fact, many studies show that children learn more and better when not given any grades but are offered constructive comments instead.... Students from primary to college level have greater trouble in understanding new material when they know they will be tested and scored. [And,]... according to the U.S. government's National Assessment of Educational Progress, primary kids who could choose their own books to read, and who never used worksheets and never took quizzes and tests, scored the highest. The children who were constantly tested, used daily worksheets and never chose their own reading material scored the lowest.... "When people talk about school success or achievement, what criteria are they using?" Kohn asked. "If it's temporary retention of facts and low-level skills, then you can achieve it with competition, rewards, drills and tests." You can call that success, Kohn says—but only if you don't care if children ever develop critical thinking, a zest for learning, creativity and a real understanding of ideas.... As for... the naive faith that tests will somehow improve learning, Kohn offers an analogy: Suppose we decide to raise the standards of hospital care by taking patients' temperature on a regular basis. Just before inserting the thermometers, nurses run around—administering huge doses of Aspirin and cold drinks. Voila! The temperatures are down—hospital care is improving! (Landsberg 1999)

We don't place a great deal of faith in national and international comparisons; we only mention these results to argue that the hype of an education crisis sells better than a good report card.

Elliot Eisner (1992) finds "more than a little ambivalence in our own behavior concerning test scores. We have a strong tendency to proclaim the educational poverty of test scores and then turn around and use them as indices of our own success, thus legitimating the validity of the public's concerns about the quality of education. If test scores in their conventional form do not reveal what really matters in schools, we should not use them to judge our 'success.' At the same time, until we have something that is better than what we have been using, I fear we will be obliged to continue to use what we believe does not matter from an educational perspective" (4).

Badmouthing teachers and students is hardly exclusive to American education. When we visited the United Kingdom not long ago, we weren't surprised to read in London newspapers of the poor performance of British children in the areas of reading; that is typical news reporting. The reports reminded us of home. The poorest results were in inner cities and in impoverished school districts. The schools themselves were blamed for the poor results, and of course no mention was made of the different roles literacy plays in the communities where those children live and

181

the communities where children come from homes where parents are university-educated and members of the cultural elite. Nor was any mention made of the accuracy of the measurement that led to such conclusions.

We were surprised, however, by the reports of the university-bound students' proficient performance on their A-level exams, a positive measure of their high school performance and the key to their acceptance into a university. Of course, the news story focused on the fact that because the scores of the seniors were so high this year, many A-level students still were having difficulty finding spots at a university. The conclusion being drawn was that the high number of good grades indicated that the exams must have been easier this year. Such thinking shows that educators and students just can't win. Not one account congratulated the teachers and learners on a job well done because the mind-set is that students are not learning and teachers don't do a good job teaching. The public appears to expect poor test results. "Why, in this country [England], are so many suspicious of success?" writes Kathleen Tattersall (1996), chief executive of the Northern Examinations and Assessment Board. "Let us celebrate schemes of assessment that enable more young people to achieve higher standards of attainment" (28).

A reporter from a Philadelphia-area newspaper recently asked us whether the amount of money spent per pupil in a school district was indicative of student achievement, especially as reported by standardized test scores. We avoided predicting a correlation between funding and test scores, but we did tell the reporter that money isn't the only factor. Common sense tells us that money spent on the tools of education has an impact on the learning that takes place within a school building: money spent on staffing, resulting in smaller class size; consultants, providing support services to teachers; technology, bringing the world into the classroom; facilities, providing a positive, safe, and healthy learning environment; library books, providing not only information, but encouraging reading as a part of life. Although it's risky to equate per-pupil-spending to student achievement, common sense tells us that money *does* provide the tools that help equalize educational opportunity.

Standards: Raising the Bar or Placing the Blame?

When Pennsylvania was working on our state standards, we attended an open meeting in Pittsburgh. The majority of those in attendance were concerned parents, not educators. Though the numbers were small, maybe thirty, they were certainly vocal, committed, and quite sure of what they wanted. And what they wanted was what, we believe, most parents, most citizens, want for their children—a life filled with everything that's possible. Most people would agree that learning provides a way to get there and the ability to read and write is the ticket to this learning. But the agreements begin to break down after this general consensus, especially when we begin to discuss the terms *read, write,* and *learn.* A woman at the meeting, whose homeschooled young son attended the meeting with her, complained about the PA writing assessment test, maintaining that the prompt she had seen was inappropriate (asking the writers to identify a characteristic about themselves that they would like to change). It focused too much on the negative, she charged. Also, unless the scoring of this writing counted only spelling and grammatical mistakes, she doubted it could be objectively scored. Writing is grammar, she maintained. Through it all, we remained silent. After all, we had not asked to speak, and a ten- to fifteen-minute response would have been fruitless, especially at this meeting. And yet, we wondered to ourselves, "Where would we begin?" We had spent our lives reading, researching, thinking, and learning about literacy—what it is, how it's learned, and its place in our culture, so doesn't that make it our responsibility to try to share what we've learned?

Another similar situation happened to us a few years ago at a school board meeting. We had been asked to attend by district teachers to help them explain their workshop approach in the teaching of writing to a group of concerned citizens and to support the adoption of a reading program that focused on literature. While we were explaining the possibilities of such approaches to literacy learning, a parent in the audience slammed his fist angrily on the table and proclaimed, "It's not your job to teach my son how to think; I'll tell him what to think. As a parent that's my job. Your job is to teach him to read and write!" This statement made it clear to us why we could never come to terms with this parent about what a teacher's job was, what school was, or what literacy was. We had completely different ideas about what learning was.

Are learning, knowledge, thinking, or even literacy subjects to be taught? How could one teach anything of substance without facilitating thinking? In *Possible Lives,* Mike Rose (1995) tells stories of schools all over the country in which students from kindergarten through high school are not only literate, but thinkers and doers. These students are fortunate to study with teachers who are not only knowledgeable, but who believe all kids are capable, and consequently, the students in these schools succeed. The strategies these teachers use vary, but the one constant is that the teachers facilitate thinking.

Sharon Davis, a physics teacher from Tupelo, for example, in reflecting on her curriculum, said, "One reason physics is so scary is that students have not been shown that a significant part of physics involves taking a different perspective on the everyday flow of the events around them. For example, could they come to think about the bending of the elbow to eat as a response to electrical impulses from the brain? If students look at life from one perspective only, then much of life will remain baffling. They will be limited in how they function, in what they can do" (Rose 1995, 302). Sharon knows that there is a connection between experience and perception, thought and human growth. Physics isn't about reading the textbook; it's about thinking like a physicist. Until a person thinks physics, it doesn't really exist for them.

And literacy isn't a stable commodity either. Consider the effect that technology has had on literacy; it has, in fact, created a literacy that didn't exist previously, much the way the first printing press did. The way we bank using ATM machines, buy airline tickets online, auction our flea-market, garage-sale items on eBay, all require a literacy that didn't exist ten years ago. Technology is changing the process of writing—how we write and for what purposes. Our students don't need to go to the library to find journal articles; they simply call them up on-screen through library search programs, such as InfoTrack. Yet as much as literacy changes, its purposes remain the same—to make sense of the world around us, to define our culture.

While others may define literacy quite differently, such as the father who didn't believe that "thinking" should be a part of our curriculum, it is our responsibility to look at the literacy that we have the most influence over— school literacy. In Pennsylvania, we find many schools, mostly in poor rural and urban areas that are quite interested in programmed approaches to curriculum, the Core Knowledge movement for example, that wrap up what students need to know in a neat package. Unlike standards, this curriculum outlines the facts that are presented to *all* children in all grades, regardless of development, interest, or need. Instead, all students learn about the Aztec Indians or Mayan civilization before they are eight years old. The students may have never been to Pittsburgh, or seen a subway or an airport, but we'll teach them about ancient civilizations and the history of religion. They may not know that Pittsburgh is in Pennsylvania, which is in the United States, but we'll teach them the names of rivers in Egypt. The curriculum emphasizes "cultural" literacy—history and geography, touts its supporters, and scoffs at the teaching of social studies. Students going through this program will know "stuff." The real question is, how long will they remember the "stuff"? And more importantly, where does this type of learning lead? To us, it's dead-end learning—"a curriculum of death to children not already on the advanced placement track to elite universities" (Ohanian 1999, x). Students need to learn to pose questions, connect, hypothesize, and research to move forward as learners and thinkers. Memorizing "stuff" for teachers and tests doesn't constitute the type of thinking that pushes a learner ahead to the next level of understanding.

Where Does Thinking Come In?

So much time is spent in education deciding what should be taught—the curriculum—and the debate does little to consider literacies—what they are, how they effect learning, and how they are changing as our culture changes. Case in point—a national curriculum. Everyone from the White House to local school boards thinks that students around the country need to all be learning the same things. Unfortunately, we feel that it's too simple an answer for a complicated issue, especially in an age when knowledge is changing at an inexplicable rate. What is it that one needs to know? Do people in Alaska need to know the same things as people in the Outer Banks of North Carolina? In fact, is knowledge the same thing in both places? If we could come up with some standard items, and if they were sensitive to differences and cultures, they might turn out like the standards produced by NCTE and IRA. From our perspective, they might be acceptable and even helpful, but they certainly wouldn't please the government or the writers for *Newsweek* or *The New York Times*. At standards meetings like the ones we've mentioned earlier, we hear citizens demand specific standards, specifying every bit of knowledge that all children should acquire every year of their school life. How could that possibly be accomplished, and more importantly, why would anyone even want to attempt it? Sadly, "without the financing to recruit and retain qualified teachers for all America's children, the most wonderful curriculums, designed to meet the highest standards, will fail. The new president [George W. Bush]'s testing and accountability programs won't change these realities at all" (Berliner 2001). The fact is, literacy in school often has little resemblance to literacy in the world—the literacies of home, of the workplace, of one's personal life. And we think this is one of education's biggest problems—understanding the scope of what literacy is and providing opportunities for students to use literacy to make sense of the world, both inside and outside of the classroom—in fact, bringing the world outside the classroom into the school.

Students, whether in fifth grade, ninth grade, or graduate school, complain that they don't understand why they have to learn certain things, claiming it's of no use to them or they'll never have to use it. The fact is, we've come to believe that, in some ways, the students are right, and furthermore, if they feel so negative and detached from such curriculum, they probably aren't learning it anyway. As parents and teachers, we've found ourselves trying to convince learners that something would be good for them, that it is something educated people need to know, or that it would help them belong to an elite group of people, those known as the "educated and cultured." Susan Ohanian (1999), author of *One Size Fits Few*, echoes Robert Scholes' (1998) criticism of those of us in "education [who] distinguish sharply, and on a bias very close to social class, between those who seek to become like us and those with whom we must deal as lesser breeds. So we decree that we'll get every sixth grader reading Shakespeare and every eighth grader taking algebra, not because it makes any sense for the kids but because these are the kinds of people we want to teach.... You can tell me your third graders read Chaucer... [but] just because you can train children to do something doesn't mean they should be doing it" (52).

In *Hooray for Diffendoofer Day,* a book based on the unpublished sketches and drafts by Dr. Seuss (1998), students in Diffendoofer school have a rather bizarre curriculum (student-centered), taught by eccentric teachers (who encourage all answers and perspectives); in fact, it's one of those schools "that acknowledge and nurture students' different strengths,... [and] is able to come up with oddball plans for oddball students" (Ohanian 1999, 2). When their principal tells the students and teachers, who actually enjoy school and learning, that they must take a standardized test that will determine their fate, as well as the fate of their school, the students are understandably frightened. Their teachers reassure them, saying, "we've taught you what you need to know; we've taught you how to think." Sure enough, the students do well, the school is saved, and they all celebrate. It is a Dr. Seuss tale after all, but the message in this book is no fairy tale. Thinking is the core of learning and that's what must be at the heart of any curriculum. "That's what schools should be about: Teachers and curriculum being flexible enough to meet the needs of each student, not shoving every kid through some distant committee's phantasmic pipe dream of a necessary curriculum for tomorrow's workforce" (Ohanian 1999, 2). Thinking is what prepares all students for standardized tests. Unfortunately, the accuracy and importance of these tests as they are currently constructed has been overstated and the stakes are too high. It's a political, not educational, issue.

Public Opinion Linked to Rhetoric, Not Facts

Public opinion polls, fueled by political rhetoric, continue to show taxpayers dismayed at the state of education in this country. Berliner and Biddle (1995) reported that "only 19 percent of respondents gave the nation's schools a grade of A or B" (112). Paradoxically these same taxpayers seem satisfied with their local schools: "when *parents* were asked about the local school that served their children, a whopping 72 percent gave that school an A or B" (112). One has to wonder what people base their judgments on. One conclusion is that parents have a better knowledge of their own local schools, but must rely on national reports for information about schools across the nation. David Berliner (2001) charges, "Those who want to undermine our public schools often condemn the whole system rather than face the inequities within it. They should focus their attention instead on rescuing the underfunded and ill-equipped schools that are failing children in our poorest neighborhoods.... Are American schools failing or is America failing to educate some of its children? It seems obvious that what needs to be addressed is the wide variation in the achievements of U.S. schools, districts and states."

United States Senator Paul Wellstone of Minnesota, a critic of testing who is suspicious of the motives of politicians, says, "high-stakes testing is the easiest thing in the world to do. You can pump up your chest and say you're all for rigor. And, you know, it sells. But it leaves untouched all of the key variables that explain why students do well or don't do well." Wellstone, the father of a teacher and a former teacher himself, who since his election to the Senate has been "in a school every two weeks for the last 10 years," has sponsored a bill that "would require schools that get federal funds, if they use tests in graduation or promotion decisions, to consider other measures of student achievement as well" ("A Senator Challenges the Test" 2001).

It is odd though that newspapers and political campaigns only report accounts of educational decline, usually based on limited evidence, and most candidates running for public office gravitate to platforms promising to fix public education. News operations and political campaigns rarely tell student and teacher success stories. For example, in an Associated Press story, with the subheading "Education Secretary Emphasizes Quality," there is the obligatory call for much-needed reforms: "A pressing need for more teachers requires a national and local effort to make sure the jobs are filled by people who know their subject and how to run a classroom, former Education Secretary Richard Riley says" (Associated Press 1998, 15). It matters little how educationally sound the reform plan is. For example, Riley is reported to have said, "Teacher colleges must focus more on training instead of theory..." and "...colleges of education should give basic skills tests to students entering teacher education programs..." (1998, 15). Riley himself seems to know little theory of learning, so naturally he thinks teachers need training, rather than an understanding of how people learn. What he was suggesting is already coming true in many states, such as California, in which educational inservice providers are barred from even mentioning any "teaching methods not preapproved by the Board of Education" (Ohanian 1999, 5). And in states like Pennsylvania and New York, students in education programs are required to take standardized tests in reading, writing, and math, like the Praxis, although every graduate has taken courses and other tests that measure their knowledge in these areas. What a coup for ETS when each such test (in a battery of several) costs somewhere around seventy dollars. "Who benefits from new, national tests besides the people selling them?" asks Susan Ohanian (1999, 4).

The current Secretary of Education, Rod Paige, continues to preach the same "sky is falling" message. At his first "Back-to-School Address" to the National Press

Club, Paige (2001) prefaced his agenda with this rhetoric:

> Over the past quarter of a century, the federal government has spent . . . an impressive amount of money to help disadvantaged school districts to succeed. . . . But after all that spending, . . . overall, we have very little progress to show for it. Over the past decade, spending has skyrocketed, but student achievement at every level and in every subject barely budged. In some cases, it went down. While there are excellent schools across America, our system is failing too many children. . . . The numbers show us that what we're doing is not working. I want to stop for a moment and reiterate this point—we know that what we have been doing for the past ten years has not worked. The skills and knowledge of our children are not getting better. It is time for something new. (2)

Of course, other numbers reported by RAND organization researchers (Klein et al. 2000), among other independent sources, show that the so-called Texas Miracle claimed by then Governor George W. Bush and then Superintendent Rod Paige was actually a smoke-and-mirrors trick involving an increased number of dropouts whose withdrawals were underreported (causing improving test results). And the "something new" that Secretary Paige (2001) feels it is time for, isn't very new: high-stakes testing and vouchers for choice in privatized education: "If we want to improve schools, we must give parents information, through testing, and options to use that information by expanding parental choice. School districts are much more responsive to parents who have choices" (5).

But theoretical debate matters little to the television and print media because reports of positive experiences or progress in schools just isn't "sexy." Hard-hitting news stories that delve into manipulation of esoteric statistical data make people reach for the remote control. News industries in this country run by entertainment corporations would rather listen to "spin doctors" than educational researchers. As superintendent of schools, Rod Paige employed a full-time public-relations expert, Terry Abbott, to package his successes and seek high-profile awards (Kirsch 2001). What raises Nielsen ratings and sells newspapers are controversy and calls for reform. "Good-hearted Americans have come to believe that the public schools of their nation are in a crisis state because they have so often been given this false message by supposedly credible sources" (Berliner and Biddle 1995, 3). *Newsweek* and *Time* routinely feature cover stories on crises in education—from ineffective homework to test anxiety, and morning television news programs run weeklong series on dropping test scores, teacher burnout, and illiteracy. The media rarely reports the day-to-day success stories of teachers making a difference because it's not news—no interest, no angle.

But there is a good story to be told. Oklahoma Newspaper Editor Forrest J. "Frosty" Troy (2000) answers the press, the pundits, and the doomsayers with evidence from reliable research published in well-respected sources, indicating that greater achievement is shown than the public would be led to believe. For example:

1. The public is led to believe that public education is so bad that enrollment is dropping at alarming rates because parents are turning to homeschooling and private Christian schools.

> The truth of the matter, according to the U.S. Department of Education, Projection of Education Statistics to 2008, is that "public school enrollment in grades K–12 reached 46,353,000 students in the 1997–98 school year, an all-time high. (2)

2. The public is led to believe that the United States spends more money on public education but receives, in the words of a former secretary of education, "less bang for the buck than any other country in the world."

> The truth of the matter, according to a United Nations Development Survey of Public spending on primary and secondary education (expressed as a percent of GNP, mid–1999s), is that "America [ranks] ninth in the world among industrialized nations" with an "average expenditure per pupil enrolled in public school" of almost six thousand dollars. (2)

3. One right-wing radio talk show host tells the American public that "Our dumbed down public school teachers produce dumbed down students" (Troy 2000, 3).

> According to two sources, The National Center for Education Statistics, 1999; NEA, Status of the American Public School Teacher, 1995–96, "today's public school teachers are better educated and have more classroom experience than their predecessors. Virtually all hold a bachelor's degree and almost half (45 percent) have a master's degree. Half have been educators for at least 15 years, and more than one-third (38 percent) have taught for two decades. They are better educated than private and parochial schoolteachers in America." (3)

4. A former secretary of education, who makes a virtue of hyperbole, claims, "public schools have failed our youth."

> Troy answers with numbers from the US Department of Education Digest of Statistics that, "the dropout rate is at an all-time low (11 percent), the college attendance (67 percent) and graduation rates are at an all-time high. America's graduate schools are the envy of the world" (4). Gerald Bracey comments that the administrations that this same former secretary of education worked for "pushed vouchers and tuition tax credits, with varying degrees of intensity. One of their strategies was never to say anything positive about public schools." So it came as no surprise when this cabinet member admitted he was "alarmed and worried

about the reaction of many parents to the new standards movement; many are retreating. A recent survey showed that when parents are choosing a school for their child, high test scores are one of the least important factors in their decision. The most important in their decision: the child's happiness. . . . Armed with public opinion, we can wear down the unions. But if the parents go soft, we are done." (Bracey 2000)

5. Another right-wing radio talk show host tells the American public that public education is in such a sorry state because the "greedy teachers unions are running the schools."

In fact, "teachers are dedicated professionals who spend an average of more than $400 a year of their own money to meet classroom needs of their students. They work an average of 49.3 hours a week, some 13 hours more than the average school contract requires. They are paid the lowest wages in the industrial world," according to the *Status of the American Public School Teacher, 1995–96*. (Troy 2000, 3)

6. A billionaire businessman touts the virtues of competition by saying that most people are "ready to end the public school monopoly in favor of vouchers."

1997 statistics from the US Department of Education showing "the American public supports public education. . . . and while the quality varies, . . . all but a handful [of the] 87,125 public schools operating in this country . . . are enormously successful. According to the latest Phi Delta Kappa/Gallup Poll, most Americans believe their local schools are doing a good job of preparing children for jobs of the future." (3)

7. The President of the United States, George W. Bush, claims to support vouchers "because too many of our minority students are being cheated of a quality education."

Numbers from the 1998 Digest of Education Statistics, Table 105, "Black children are doing better than ever in public schools. The white public school completion rate is 92 percent, the black rate is at an historic high—87 percent. The Hispanic rate is 75 percent." Troy finds that, "in Wisconsin where vouchers were supposed to rescue Milwaukee's poor ghetto public school children, 40 percent of the students being financed have never been in a public school. Sen. Polly Williams, Afro-American author of the voucher program, now bitterly denounces it as a sham to finance elite private and Catholic schools by taxpayers." (4–5)

8. Private schools claim that they "can do a better job on less money, a $3,200 Catholic school average vs. public school average of $5,800."

The truth is, "if private or parochial schools had to meet public school mandates, the price differential would evaporate instantly. No private school is mandated to provide special education, counseling and dropout prevention, vo-tech education, alternative education, bilingual education, compensatory education, student transportation, health and psychological services, food services or decent salaries and fringe benefits. Public schools are not permitted to pick and choose the students they will educate." (3–4)

Some other cogent facts to bolster the image of American public education are:

- Incidents of public school violence have decreased for nine consecutive years . . . the most common school crime is theft, not violence.
- The curriculum is far tougher today than in 1980, with 50 percent of students taking a core curriculum (four years of English, three years each of social studies, science, and math) at the ACT college entrance level. More than 58 percent of all students are taking advanced math, science, chemistry, and physics courses.
- Student test scores are up, the number of test takers is more diverse, and students are taking more difficult courses. The results of three major tests of educational achievement—SAT, ACT, and National Assessment of Educational Progress (NAEP)—have shown steady gains over the past two decades.
- The math and science portions of the SAT are at a 25-year high; the ACT is up across the board over 10 consecutive years (Troy 2000, 2–5).

More Rebuttals

Parents and the general public seeking positive news might also look to reports such as the "American Education 1996 Report Card," published by the U.S. Department of Education, and they would discover the proportion of high school graduates taking core courses (as recommended in *A Nation At Risk* [1983])—four years of English, three years of social studies, three years of science, three years of math—has increased to 52 percent by 1994, up from 14 percent in 1982. In the same period, the percentage of graduates taking biology, chemistry, and physics has doubled from 18 percent to 36 percent. Students scoring a three or above in advanced placement (AP) courses tripled since 1982. The number of AP examinations receiving a passing score rose from 132,000 in 1982 to 476,000 in 1995. Combined verbal and math scores on the SAT rose seventeen points from 1982 to 1995, an improvement occurring at the same time as the numbers and ethnic diversity of test takers are increasing. For another thing, more students than ever are staying in school. From 1972 to 1994, the dropout rate for 16- to 24-year-old students fell from 14.6 percent to 10.5 percent. These kinds of numbers are rarely reported.

Instead, the President, governors, and education secretaries continue to issue "challenges to the nation" to adopt national standards and to test every fourth grader in reading and every eighth grader in mathematics. Now students are to be tested yearly, with the government spending $26.5 billion in 2002 (and $8 billion more next year) on testing alone, with K–12 students and schools and teachers being judged by the result. All that this does is guarantee that schools have an ongoing series of "testing weeks," four to eight standardized tests per year, valuable time taken away from instruction, so that the politicians' supporters will have "a nationwide test that will rank their children's ritzy schools with the ritzy schools in other rich suburbs" (Ohanian 1999, 6).

Measuring Accountability

We recently received a request to help a high school English department with its curriculum review process. The questions we were asked were: (1) What skills do you currently find lacking in your first-year students? (2) What books do you think your students should have read, but haven't? (3) What are the most common errors you find in first-year writing? These questions reveal the dissonance that results when behaviorist methods of evaluation are applied to a constructivist pedagogy of learning; that is, a deficiency model that views students' achievements in terms of shortcomings, inadequacies, and degrees of removal from a platonic-perfect performance. These views are linked to instruction that remediates not-yet mastered skills and is inadequate when trying to take some measurement of students in classrooms that support growth. Aimee Buckner (2002) advises focusing on what we know to be good teaching practices: "if we consider our students' needs from year to year, and our teaching is powerful and meaningful, then our students will pass the tests that inundate our classrooms" (215).

To shed some light on this dilemma we'd like to share a story that we first heard on the Internet, one forwarded through multiple email messages until all that we know of its source is an attribution to a John S. Taylor, a superintendent in a Lancaster County School District. It seems that during a routine checkup, a patient asked his dentist if he'd heard about a new state program to evaluate the effectiveness of dentists, allowing parents to make more informed decisions about whom to send their children to. The patient explained that the state would track the number of cavities found in each child aged 10, 14, and 18 in a given year and from that determine a cavity-to-patient score for every dentist, issuing a subsequent yearly report card of each dentist's rating, either excellent, good, average, below average, or unsatisfactory. The state, he said, feels this will encourage less effective dentists to improve and put those who don't improve in jeopardy of losing their licenses to practice.

Of course, when the dentist objected that this was not a fair method of judging good dentistry, the patient questioned the dentist's support of improved dental health for children and their parents' right to an informed choice. The dentist explained that there were too many variables, many of which were outside of the dentist's control. For example, a dentist who works in a rural area with a high percentage of patients from poorer homes (like those he serves) who visit the dentist only when there is a problem, would be unfairly compared to those whose patients are from upper-middle-class suburban neighborhoods, whose more educated parents understand the relationship between sugar and decay and believe in semiannual preventative checkups. When he brought up the fluoride issue— city water has it, well water doesn't, the patient accused him of making excuses. The dentist denied it vehemently and explained that his average cavity count would most likely be higher than that of other dentists, and he would end up being rated average or worse. Then the rating itself would further erode his standing, as the more prosperous parents, who believe this imperfect rating system actually measures his ability, might choose to go to someone with a higher rating, leaving him with only the poorer, more needy patients. This will cause his cavity-average score to worsen, making it increasingly difficult to attract good dental hygienists or other young but excellent associates to his dental practice. The patient accused him of overreacting to the laudable innovations initiated by a highly regarded committee of concerned civic leaders committed to improving dentistry in their state.

The dentist knew it was no use challenging the notion that dentistry is in need of improvement, so he suggested that a more accurate way to measure good dentistry might be to observe him at work, speak to his patients, and consider how much time he spends promoting good dental behavior, instead of considering one measurement, however simple to apply.

The patient countered that cavities are an absolute measurement, beyond dispute, one not open to subjective interpretation. In fact, he said, the state is willing to help. They'll pay to send a dentist who has been rated excellent to help troubleshoot problems for any dentists who are rated below average. In frustration, the dentist said, "In other words, the state will send a dentist with wealthy patients to show me how to treat the sort of dental problems that I've had much more experience with? This is so ill-conceived. How would teachers like it if the state decided to rate schools according to scores from a test of the students' progress, without any consideration of differences caused by outside factors, such as different home environments, tax bases, community profiles, and so forth?"

The patient could tell his dentist was getting upset, and even though, as the dentist picked up his drill, he was told to "open wide," the patient decided maybe he had better keep his mouth shut, if you know what we mean.

Ill-Conceived and Bizarre

The states and the federal government are indeed going ahead with ill-conceived evaluations based on one-shot measurements without consideration of the multitude of other factors that determine the quality of education being provided. As Aimee Buckner (2002) reminds us, "The people who are so high and mighty about these high-stakes tests don't know that Johnny's mom was arrested and sent to jail two weeks prior to the exam. They don't know that Jane is an A student who just found out her parents are getting a divorce. They don't know Jenny has worked hard all year and grown tremendously in the area of academics, but is petrified of taking this test" (215). Sometimes, reports about standardized tests are so bizarre that it's difficult to tell fact from fiction. For example, one teacher told us of a standardized reading test whose comprehension question involved a passage dealing with Stevie Smith. One of the last questions asked what Stevie's mother's name was. The correct answer was supposed to be the one whose last name ended in Smith. Unfortunately, a number of students in the class had mothers with names different from their own, and her students didn't make assumptions about what someone's mother's name might be. We have no way of verifying this story, but it sounds plausible. Any time tests are made by people who spend little or no time in classrooms, almost anything is possible.

Leaving Some Behind

Teachers and parents are well aware of the power of standardized testing. As students progress to secondary schools, standardized tests determine their future: grouping, grading, retention/ promotion, and entrance into higher education are all dependent on test scores. Many parents and teachers believed the 2001 Bush education promise that no child would be left behind and that testing "would make students buckle down—and might bring badly needed resources to schools with low scores" (Jehlen 2001). Yet, when two out of every five students failed a state's high-stakes test, its teachers were confused about what to do. "Should all these students be held back? The Ohio education department's Patti Grey [admitted that] this is not at all what the department had in mind when it originally set a target passing score. The idea was to help slow readers, not keep them back. 'We set the score high so more kids would get extra help,' she says. 'The legislature turned it into a retention score'" (Jehlen 2001). One politician believes that "before you start flunking students, you ought to at least make sure that each of them has the same opportunity to do well. . . . Many of these kids have teachers who aren't certified, decrepit buildings, heating that doesn't work, classes that are too big— never mind what goes on in their lives before they go to school and when they go home. We're not going to change any of that, but we're going to flunk them! These kids, some as young as eight, are going to be held back, and they're going to be utterly defeated. They'll be on their way to dropping out of school" ("A Senator" 2001).

According to a report by FairTest (the National Center for Fair and Open Testing), as standardized tests are used to determine eligibility for graduation, dropout rates increase especially for minority students in urban schools. The dropout rate soared in the years following the passing of the 1993 Education Reform Act. One researcher, Anne Wheelock, observes "a predictable push-out consequence of high-stakes tests . . . and it hits the most vulnerable students hardest. . . . As [standardized] testing fuels higher-grade retention rates, students are already dropping out in earlier grades. . . . Given the possibility of retaking a test that makes them feel stupid and the prospect of repeated humiliating failures, many students are likely to bow out of testing—and school—altogether" (Massey 2000). And even those who aren't dropping out or being retained are being hurt. Consider what will happen at an urban school in western Massachusetts in which only the top quarter of the students was able to pass a test that the class of 2003 will have to pass to graduate. Without their diplomas, the middle two quarters of the students who had historically been continuing with higher education will, in effect, be stymied in their chances to pursue a better education (Jehlen 2001).

As we mentioned earlier, large-scale assessments, like the SAT, are norm-referenced, which means that they are designed to compare students with each other. The tests are designed so that the results fall on a bell curve, with some students scoring high, some low, and the majority falling in the middle. The tests are piloted so that the questions are tested to make sure that the results fall into that range. It's impossible for all test takers to be in the upper half because the tests are designed to make sure that can't happen. A good example of a norm-referenced test is an IQ test, a test set up to spread the population out, with the middle score for the average person being arbitrarily set at 100, the more "intelligent" upper 2 percent of the population at one end (the Mensa end), around 160 or so, and the lower 2 percent at the opposite end, around forty. Another is the Pennsylvania System of School Assessment tests whose "scores range from 1000 to 1600 with the department [of education] assigning 1300 as the average scores in both math and reading" ("School Test Scores" 1999, 7). Most of the schools' averages that we saw reported went up or down about twenty points, but one school went from 1300 in reading last year to 1440, the highest in our area. What looks like quite an achievement in reading instruction could honestly be due to seven or eight of the poorest readers being absent the day of the test. A number of schools across the country have actually been accused of manipulating the scores in this fashion—barring those who are expected to do poorly from attending school on the days of the tests (Bracey 2000).

One of the most confusing aspects of large-scale norm-referenced tests is that the numerical score that is used as the average is arbitrarily chosen; there is no reason why the average score for the Pennsylvania System of School Assessment test is 1300 or IQ tests are 100. When we took SAT tests in high school, the joke used to be that you got 200 points for just signing your name. We didn't understand that the SAT scores were normed at an average score of 500 (back when it was created in 1941), and it was statistically unrealistic to hear of anyone scoring lower than 200. Hence, our joke. What we never knew was that by 1993, the average had shifted to 424 on the verbal section and 478 on the math section (Taylor and Walton 1998). The public's perception was that student performances were on the decline in verbal and math abilities. The test makers, who usually monitor the scores and select each year's questions, simply corrected the scoring so that the average was once again 500 for both sections. A student who scored 500 on both sections in 1994 would be perceived by his or her parents (and the general public) as outperforming the older sibling who scored 424 and 478 the year before, when in reality, they both produced similar performances. Again, we can only say what looks to be "objective" must still be interpreted.

While tests seem the least subjective form of measurement, the opposite is true. According to testing expert James Popham, standardized, norm-referenced "tests measure some things that teachers don't teach and don't measure some things that teachers do teach. They test some things that youngsters have learned outside of school, giving an inherent advantage to those from well-off, well-educated families" (Bracey 2000). One example that drives this home is the high correlation between being poor (eligibility for federally subsidized lunches) and doing poorly on tests. Furthermore, in a twist of logic, no more than 60 percent of the students can get a test question right, and no more than 40 percent can get it wrong, if a test question is to "behave right" in the statistical sense; that is, if it is to properly "spread out the scores." Yet, "most students should get most items right if the items tap what the teachers have emphasized, which, presumably, is what is important. Hence, commercial tests don't test at least some important content" (Bracey 2000).

We often hear of districts that tell their elementary teachers that the board expects every child in their district to be in the upper four stanines or in the upper 50 percent on the district's standardized tests, which are always norm-referenced tests like the Iowa or the California Achievement Tests. Such declarations are based on a misunderstanding of what such tests are measuring. If too many students get a certain question correct, that question will be changed or eliminated, even if it was an appropriate topic or question because that is the only way the bell curve can be maintained. So no matter who commands it, it is impossible for all children to be above average on this type of test.

Is it any wonder teachers have been told to "teach to the test?" They've been told to "raise the bar"; improve those scores; learn this core material; and remember, tests don't test thinking. Tests only know right from wrong answers. Still, we believe if we teach students to think, they should do well on these tests. Both of us are products of the New York State School System, which held state-level Board of Regents final exams every year. Kathleen felt the enormous pressure of those tests, although she was a good student. She remembers students spending the last weeks of classes in May and June going over old Regents exams, cramming their heads full of stuff that they hoped they'd recall. The exams were given on hot, late-June days in large sittings, so they could be scrupulously monitored. Often, while in the hall where the students would line up, waiting to file into the gym, Kathleen would have a friend hold her place, so she could be sick in the lavatory. Granted, the tests have changed in New York, but the pressures are still there.

Even more dangerous than the misconceptions about these types of tests is the effect competition in testing has on our moral values. "Generally, our society and our schools value competition over compassion. So often we hear that the main goal of schooling should be to prepare our students to compete in a global economy. The recent emphasis on testing and standards also stresses personal competition in schools. But do we want students who are clever and compete well on tests or students who have compassion for all forms of life and a sense of responsibility that goes beyond personal achievement? . . . Today the balance has swung the other way. We seem more concerned with testing what students have learned than with nurturing the learning process itself. From a holistic learning perspective, we need to balance learning and assessment rather than to favor one over the other" (Miller 1998/1999, 46).

Criterion-Referenced Testing

The other major type of standardized test is a criterion-referenced test, designed to assess what students know based on predetermined criteria. The scores on these tests are determined by how students meet the criteria. It is possible then, even expected, for most test takers to achieve a score that is average for their grade level; it is also possible (although not the primary purpose) for these tests to be used for comparison within a district to determine what percentage of students successfully met criteria or standards. A good example of a criterion-referenced test is the written examination given by the Department of Motor Vehicles for a license or driving permit (Calkins, Montgomery, and Santman 1998). The criteria for the written test is clearly outlined in the test preparation booklet and it is expected that most people who take the test will pass. Criterion-referenced tests have the potential of being helpful to our teaching and to student learning. Like any assessment tool, if learners and teachers are aware of the criteria that defines a task before them, they are more able to accomplish it. It is laudable when teachers are given a clear understanding of what they are expected to teach (although the decisions about how to teach should be theirs and students should also have a voice in what they would like to learn). Again, it is important that students are also given a clear understanding of the expectations of their teachers.

Problems with Standardized Testing

The problems and shortcomings of standardized tests have been well-documented in a variety of studies (Darling-Hammond, Ancess, and Falk 1995; Darling-Hammond 1989, 1991, 1994; Resnick and Resnick 1987; Wiggins 1993). "We have looked toward specialized agencies to provide precise, discrete, measured indicators of student performance on tests that reflect more the technical aspirations of psychometricians than the educational values of teachers" (Eisner 1992, 4). Because there is a push for standardization, or testing under conditions that are uniform, there is a tendency to test what is easiest to test or is easiest to measure, such as a student's reading speed. *Consumer Reports* found the same problem when it tried to make sense of "report cards" on managed health care:

> If you're looking for an HMO this fall, you can probably find the cheapest plan, but you can't find the best—one whose doctors always make timely and correct diagnoses, choose effective treatments, and avoid mistakes. That's because there are no good comparisons of health plans on measures like these. However, you may be able to find an HMO that answers your phone calls quickly, has reasonably short waits in doctors' offices, offers a large number of board-certified physicians, and gives you a wide choice of practitioners—indicators that the public has come to equate with good medicine in managed care. Often touted in "report cards," those dimensions, while desirable, have little to do with true quality. . . . "The public thinks the key to high quality care is quick access to a doctor," says Michael Millenson, a healthcare consultant with the firm of William M. Mercer. "That's only half. The other half is what the doctor does. It's amazing how we've ignored that." (Lieberman 1998, 35)

It's not too far a stretch to say we've done the same thing in education.

> While a host of other school data is readily available, the public has seized on test scores because they are succinct and easy to grasp. "It's one indicator. It's convenient. It's numerical," said William Britt, deputy superintendent of Clintondale Community Schools in Clinton Township [Michigan]. "But it's not enough." Catherine Taylor, associate professor of educational psychology at the University of Washington, Seattle, notes "the media and educational establishment have

'conspired' to teach people that numbers are more trustworthy than teachers.... that teachers are not to be trusted. Standardized tests are more trustworthy. People have been led to believe that test scores *mean* something. . . . But they don't tell you how effective the teachers are in a particular building, how challenging its classroom lessons are or how much progress its students have made." (Van Moorlehem 1998, 3)

Furthermore, test questions in such standardized tests are often perceived as narrow and misleading, provide little or no opportunity for higher-level thinking, and lack contextualization.

Bob Fecho (1998), a former classroom teacher of twenty-four years, takes issue with the misdirection standardized testing provides.

...On the one hand, public schools have so little positive press these days that any public indication of their worth needs to be celebrated and made known.... Pennsylvania schools are working hard and...scores on both the Philadelphia SAT 9 and the Pennsylvania System of School Assessment (PSSA) purport to be indicators of such, and, . . . if combined with other indicators, help to give us that positive picture. However, to place undue emphasis on the importance of these scores, to make these scores the indicator among indicators, to use these scores to disburse bonus funding, and to use these scores to compare vastly different schools operating under vastly different conditions is questionable practice, if not downright misleading and disheartening. (2)

And the tests create self-fulfilling prophecies—once a school is reported as low scoring, then parents who value education and provide in-home support will not move into those communities and the best of the newly certified teachers won't take jobs there. These tests are "scored without regard for educational resources, obstacles or opportunity. Educators say [standardized test] scores brand some schools and entire communities as inferior, creating a cycle that's hard to break. . . . [and] distorted as [these] scores may be, they are often used as the sole yardstick of school performance. Realtors use them to sell one neighborhood over another. Lawyers cite them in child custody battles. State officials use them to accredit schools" (Van Moorlehem and Newman 1998, 2).

Still, good teachers do question and try to fight test results with more authentic assessments, specifically data that has been collected over a period of time in authentic learning situations. But such data doesn't carry as much weight as the results of these standardized tests, and the child still must carry the weight of this classification in permanent records and be judged by it in years to come. Fecho (1998) believes test results are "problematic because we place the value of one test administered completely devoid of a context of study over the body of work done within the integrated curricular context of the classroom. . . . Although classroom work exists in very real and authentic ways in the lives of students and teachers, it seemingly has no weight in the eyes of politicians" (3). We know many students who do much better in the day-to-day activities of reading and writing and mathematics in the classroom but who score poorly on standardized tests. Does the school district throw out the test results as inaccurate or an inadequate measure of the child's true ability?

Sometimes it does (to an extent)—schools whose administrators respect the ability and judgments of classroom teachers sometimes use other data that the teacher has collected and uses the test scores as only one piece of the puzzle. Others, however, believe the test scores religiously. If a student does better in class than would be indicated by the test score, then the child is said to be an "overachiever." What a ridiculous term—what in the world is an overachiever? We've come to realize that this label is a good way to still blame the child for not fitting the system. In other words, the test is correct in its assessment of what the child cannot do, and when a child does somehow manage to do the impossible, then she is "overachieving." And as a student progresses through secondary school, the politics of testing is even more firmly established and test scores often determine life directions.

Fecho (1998) suggests that some students are smarter about test posturing than we give them credit for. One student he spoke with (a middle-class male, whose parents are educators) told him that "some of the readings [on the test] weren't important to him, but he knew what they wanted, so he gave them what they wanted." In contrast to this young man, one of Fecho's own students, "capable of interpreting complex text, synthesizing those texts, and responding in complex and thoughtful prose of his own, . . . also knew what the test makers wanted, but he refused to play by those rules. He ascribes to a culture which doesn't just go along to get along. . . . [He refused] to take the test for the testing sake." From this, Fecho concludes that "these large scale tests, taken alone, do not truly measure the complicated ways these students are growing as learners, nor are these other more local and authentic indicators given equal weight before the eyes of the public" (5–6).

A Matter of Respect

One aspect of teaching/learning that is sometimes left out is respect for the learner. Anne Wheelock has warned of students' refusal of "retaking a test that makes them feel stupid and the prospect of repeated humiliating failures." But the daily classroom experience can have just as strong an impact. Kathleen's dad never went to college or earned a degree, yet he taught himself cryogenic engineering and taught college graduates how to make breathing units for NASA extraterrestrial "outer space" and marine exploration. He was the kind of guy who watched the evening news every night, read magazines and newspapers, and taught his children the importance of staying aware of what was happening in the world. But he never considered himself smart. School had no place in his life, and as soon as he was old enough to enlist, he joined the army during World War II. Didn't his teachers understand his potential? Did they know how much he knew about the world of plants and animals? Ecology and forestry? Physics and engineering? Of course not, because those weren't part of their curriculum. In fact, the teachers in his life let him know how little they expected of him. We often heard him tell, years after it happened, the story of the history test he studied hard for (because it was interesting to him) and how he received a perfect score. Instead of congratulating him, his teacher accused him of cheating. Beyond the insult, the experience told Kathleen's dad that his teachers never expected him to get a good grade. Had that teacher bothered to find out, she would have discovered his love of American history and that he knew even more than her test asked about. This shows the ingredient missing in the mania for standardized testing, one essential in the teaching/learning process—the matter of respect for the learner. In many ways, Kathleen's dad overcame the obstacles to learning that school put before him, but even if times had been different, we're not sure he would've ever had thought of himself as *school* smart, because no one in his school life respected him enough to let him demonstrate what he knew. We still look at learning with such a limited perspective. We still report grades based on a competitive scale, comparing those students in a class who seem to learn easily what the curriculum deems important to those who seem unable to "get it," who seem lazy, or who seem not to care.

The Tyranny of Test Scores

So the testing frenzy continues. Education policies voted on and passed by Congress see one solution—testing. Let's test all students, every year, to determine what they have learned. By gosh, we'll keep teachers accountable that way. Secretary Rod Paige (2001) says it's the price we have to pay:

> In exchange for flexibility, of course, we must demand accountability. Parents and taxpayers and community leaders and state officials all need to know which schools are succeeding, and why, and which schools are failing, and what can be done. And they need to have the power to act on this information. They need access to objective annual tests that are aligned to state standards for what children in each grade are expected to know and be able to do. In Florida, [one school] I visited...uses testing very effectively to track the progress of each student, to tailor teaching to each child's strengths and weaknesses, and to make sure no child falls through the cracks. (4)

We've visited schools in several states that are falling victim to the testing madness. Usually urban schools whose test scores are being compared to affluent suburban schools are given alternatives—raise those test scores or your school will be "taken over" by the state and experts will show you how to do it. We need to remember what tests can and can't do. Tests aren't meant to compare students or teachers or schools, although they're sometimes used that way.

Not only are standardized tests politically powerful, they are most often misunderstood and misused. For example, recently the faculty at a nearby school were aware of an undercurrent of unrest: their students' test scores had again been lower than other schools in the district. Our university had expressly chosen to work with this school for the past few years because we endorsed these teachers' philosophy of learning. We believed these teachers would model for our students the kinds of constructivist approaches that result in children being actively engaged in learning. And yet the district administration, which was always suspicious of the pedagogical techniques used at this school, was quick to point to test scores as evidence that such approaches were unsound. The word was out: test scores must go up or instruction at the school would have to change.

What wasn't taken into consideration, however, were several facts:

1. Evidence that learning was taking place in this school was difficult to share in concise, compartmentalized charts or reports. Although teachers had plenty of evidence of such learning, the public believed test scores to be more "objective" evidence. The other evidence was difficult to quantify as a score that could be used to compare one student's accomplishments with others.

2. The teachers themselves were discouraged. Although they could see growth in many of their students, the test scores from year to year did not seem to show growth. What is demoralizing to secondary teachers in many states is witnessing growth in their students during the year, knowing that what they have learned will be measured in only one way—a timed test that can determine graduation. These tests damage not only those students who don't test well, but it minimizes the efforts of the teachers who taught them.

3. The school itself was located in a poor area of the city and the majority of its students qualified for free lunches. Research continues to show that socioeconomic and racial/ethnic backgrounds correlate highly with test performance (Slavin 1997/1998). "Districts with poorer or less-educated parents, high turnover rates or low per-pupil state aid tended to do worse than those whose students [have] had more educational advantages. That makes it tricky to compare districts using [standardized test] scores, experts

say, because you're looking more at who the district is teaching than how well they're being taught" (Newman 1998b, 1). Test questions often test students' understanding of items or operations found in a particular culture or in their background knowledge, and this bias gives students from one group an advantage over those of another. "Likewise, schools coping with factors such as severe poverty may be doing a superior job of educating students who start out behind wealthier counterparts. Poor parents, for example, may not be able to afford books, or home computers. Single, working parents may not have as much time to read to children. Parents who dropped out of high school may be too intimidated to approach educators about what's going on with their children in school" (Van Moorlehem and Newman 1998, 2). In addition to poverty, the *Detroit Free Press* reported that test results can be skewed by many outside factors, including: "The number of single parents; the number of households where no one is a high school graduate; the local unemployment rate, and school funds per pupil" (Newman 1998b, 1–2).

We still have a big problem with these high-stakes tests, as do most professional organizations such as NCTE, NCTM, IRA, and so on. Pass this one test or you don't graduate. Everything we know about assessing and evaluating learning tells us that this isn't a good way to evaluate what one knows. However, the point is that the tests are with us. Some state exams are asking for more than a regurgitation of facts and asks students to analyze, apply, and evaluate. Some are asking students to demonstrate thinking—to be third-story men and women, applying what they know, as Bellanca and Fogarty (1991) categorize it. So what does this mean to teachers? How do we prepare students for such tests? The answer—we teach them to think. We get them reading and writing and connecting and discussing and looking deeply into texts to discover possibilities. We set up classrooms of literate people who do what literate people do. They begin thinking like mathematicians, biologists, writers, and readers. In the process, they learn the skills these people need. They learn them because they need them now too, so they can enter the club of other literate people.

One first-year teacher in Florida, Shannon Dosh (2002), told us her experiences dealing with high-stakes tests.

> My dream burst . . . when the workbooks for the Florida Comprehensive Achievement Test (FCAT) arrived to prepare us for the school-wide state-mandated achievement test. I was torn between switching from a progressive strategy of "teaching for substance" to a traditional method of "teaching to the test." . . . I chose to focus on effective teaching principles to motivate and prepare my students for the test. . . .

As we rushed toward the testing dates, word leaked that I had not opened the "approved" workbooks, and the principal questioned me, demanding that I immediately implement these tools. She insisted that using the workbook was not "teaching to the test." My students became confused when I tried to explain the reasons we "must" use the workbooks....

But, tired of fighting closed minds, I was forced to put aside the current unit on *Treasure Island*, including daily sea logs written in response to oral readings, online Internet treasure hunts, and scurvy-day survival techniques. I went to extreme lengths in a effort to connect the FCAT material to my student's needs. (2–3)

Unfortunately, Shannon's contract was not renewed, although no explanation was given. She speculates that it could've been her conviction that

each student is a unique individual who may not fit the mold of one rigid learning strategy. Or perhaps ... because I embrace the diverse backgrounds of my students, which requires a constant reevaluation of classroom strategies, so that each child may reach their maximum potential and conquer the challenges they face each day.... I am certain that my decision not to "teach to the test" and to refuse to voluntarily incorporate the FCAT workbooks in a traditional manner into the classroom curriculum formed the basis for the principal's decision.... I leave, confident, knowing that over half of my students increased their STAR reading level during the year, even though I did not force them to read Accelerated Reader books and allowed them to choose literature that appealed to each individual. My students wrote heart-wrenching essays on the fourth quarter final exam, which explored their personal lives and established goal setting ideals. To the best of my knowledge, I am the only teacher who bypassed the traditional, quickly graded Scantron exam and administered a fully written, final exam that was actually read by the teacher. (9–11)

Shannon never learned her students' FCAT results but says she "wouldn't judge any school by a letter grade awarded by the state." She remains optimistic and hopes we can redirect a public "that is crying for instant results rather than the kind of long-term growth that leads to meaningful success for all students" (12).

So, Now What?

U.S. education isn't a dismal failure; we aren't losing the war, but our schools are failing some. Evaluation shouldn't be about determining who's failing and who's to blame, but determining who's floundering and how we intend to help. We need to make time in our regular course of teaching to help our students become test wise, and we have to do it in ways that make sense in our classrooms, through workshop approaches and problem-solving critical thinking. Two recent books give specific strategies to help children become prepared for these types of tests, *Children at the Center: A Workshop Approach to Standardized Test Preparation, K–8* (Taylor and Walton 1998) and *A Teacher's Guide to Standardized Reading Tests* (Calkins, Montgomery, and Santman 1998). Some of the suggestions include providing opportunities to practice, examine, manipulate, and reflect on common test patterns, formats, language, and conditions:

- Present test questions and solutions in different formats and explicitly discuss the differences. How many ways can something be asked? Teach students about question formats that are peculiar to standardized tests, such as the "Which of the following is NOT true?" type of question.
- Model choosing the one right answer or the best answer. Teach children to use the text, rather than their experience, to pick the answer. Also ask students to record what their thinking was as they worked through a question and what their reasoning was in choosing their answer. Even more importantly, follow this with a discussion. Teach students the importance of reading all the answer choices provided, rather than selecting the first one that appears to be correct.
- Practice distinguishing questions that ask for opinions and musings from those that ask for information. Class discussions may ask students for their opinions but similar language used in test questions is usually seeking one correct answer.
- Practice the elimination strategy. Tests frequently provide four choices: one that is completely wrong, one that is the opposite of the correct response, one that is close to the correct response, and one that is correct. Students can be taught how to eliminate the first two possibilities, but then they need help deciding between the remaining two possibilities. Some students will mistakenly avoid any answer containing words or phrases they are unfamiliar with (even though their other test strategies indicate that might be the correct response); others mistakenly believe that either of the two likely choices will be acceptable and simply pick one. These counterproductive test strategies can be corrected.
- Allow students to write multiple choice and true/false questions that connect with class discussions. Teach them how to ask "test-style" questions and provide likely answer responses. Use these to teach the difference between testing what is important and testing what is easiest to test.
- Give students practice working alone. In a constructivist classroom where decisions are socially negotiated, children are sometimes uncomfortable working on tests by themselves (Calkins, Montgomery, and Santman 1998, 105–122; Taylor and Walton 1998, 102–108).

By helping students understand what they will have to do, teachers will help them learn to be in control and to be informed test takers.

Additional Resources

The National Education Association (NEA) offers a set of practical classroom tips for students facing high-stakes tests. "Twelve Steps Teachers Can Take to Prepare Students for High-Stakes Tests" can be found, along with other useful materials, at *www.nea.org/issues/shorttakes/highstakes.html.*

The NEA resources also point out that "several sites compile state-by-state information on high-stakes tests. The University of Pennsylvania's list is very comprehensive: *www.gse.upenn.edu/cpre/docs/pubs/profiles.html.* Other excellent Web resources include the National Center for Research on Evaluation, Standards, and Student Testing at *http://cresst96.cse.ucla.edu* and the Education Commission of the States at *www.ecs.org* (look in Education Issues). FairTest, the National Center for Fair and Open Testing, at *www.fairtest.org,* is a good place to link up with other people working for alternatives to high-stakes tests" ("Resources" 2001).

Concluding Remarks

Perhaps the politicians and educators who find themselves at loggerheads over standardized testing would be wise to listen to the students. On their behalf, Annelise Schantz (2000) gave a valedictorian speech at her Hudson, Massachusetts, high school graduation that elicited a standing ovation from classmates. The Massachusetts governor, a supporter of high-stakes tests, was on the stage at the time Annelise delivered these remarks:

"So, I'm the valedictorian. Number one. But what separates me from number 2, 3, 4, 5, 6, 50, or 120? Nothing but meaningless numbers. What really is the difference between 3.8, 2.9, and 1.5? All these randomly assigned numbers reflect nothing about the true character of an individual. They say nothing about personality. Nothing about desire or will. Nothing about values or morals. Nothing about intelligence. Nothing about creativity. Nothing about heart. Numbers cannot and will not ever be able to tell you who a person really is. Yet in today's society we are sadly becoming more and more number oriented. Schools today are being forced to teach to the numbers. Children are no longer learning because it is interesting and fun; they are learning to pass the test so that the school will continue to be funded. New mandates across the country and in our own state incorrectly correlate test scores with the worth of teachers and schools. Not once do these new mandates take into account that schools in low income areas will never have as many books, long-term students, parent volunteers, or state-of-the-art facilities. How can anyone call these tests fair? Just as class rank and SAT scores say nothing about the true worth of a person, a child's or school's score on a test says nothing about the worth of the school or teachers....

"The already teetering learning process, made difficult by the social dynamics of school cliques, disrupted by a constant lack of funding and misplaced values, has been further torn apart by a few meddling politicians and yuppies who were bored and felt the need to create what they call a standard. Who cares that it is completely biased against those with learning disabilities and those in ESL programs. Who cares that the test itself is frighteningly ethnocentric in its rigid definition of what we should be learning. Who cares that all these numbers and standards only help to stamp out independent thought. All that matters is that the head *honchos* want some numbers that they can spew to the public to prove that they are so helpful to today's school children. Numbers, useless meaningless numbers. I doubt that a single one of these politicians has ever stopped to consider that we are not numbers. We are individuals. How dare they restrict us once more into useless categories of failing, proficient, advanced. Judging us by our competency on a biased test is perhaps the biggest injustice that the state could ever inflict upon us.

"Useless information about the double helix shape of DNA or the square root of negative one will not help anyone to survive. Last time I checked, the properties of diffusion and osmosis were interesting, but they still were of no help in reality. The battle of 1812 cannot help you prepare a healthy meal and common error C cannot help a jurist in a murder trial. Instead of realizing this, the bureaucracy that claims to be for the people continues to push for the advancement of uniform mediocrity in schools. Learning rote information never taught anyone to think. History, science, math, and English won't do you any good if you can't apply them. Formulaic thinking might help one to get good scores on tests, but it doesn't do jack in reality.

"When will society realize that the only useful skill that high school could ever teach us is the art of using our brain to think independently and express our ideas coherently? With the use of one's brain anything is possible, any problem solvable, any question answerable, any goal reachable. Unfortunately, it is the one thing that many students never learn because they are too busy trying to pass the tests.

"Schools are being turned into factories churning out brainless, mindless, opinionless hacks year after year. Any student that challenges the system is labeled a difficulty. Any teacher that pushes the limits and forces their students to actually use their brains is chastised and labeled extreme. In my five years, I have seen too many wonderful teachers lost or restricted to the box. I have seen too many extraordinary kids give up on school. But no one cares.

"The idea of MCAS [Massachusetts Comprehensive Assessment System] testing is similar to putting a Band-Aid on a severed limb. Not only is it pointless, it is a waste of time that could be much better spent. The solution to the poor education of children is not a uniform curriculum and it is certainly not a test. The solution lies in equal and adequate funding for all schools, so that teachers are paid what they are actually worth and budgets don't have to choose between paper for the copy machine or books for the students. . . .

"We hear GPA, class rank, SAT, test grade, midterms, finals, scholastic achievement, but never once do we hear 'never mind the grades, think about the learning, think about activism, think about life.' We celebrate those who have earned good grades but don't bother to consider if they are at all worthy of the praise. Does anyone care about the human beings behind the numbers?

"Perhaps I am bitter, but I have every right to be bitter and angry about the world that I see around me. My responsibility lies in that I must do something constructive with my anger. And I suppose that in the end I have school to thank for making me so unhappy, inadvertently giving me the fuel to take a stand in life and do something with what I have been given. And so I stand here today and forever, and refuse to be defined as a number."

For Further Exploration

1. How have standardized tests affected your life as a student? As a learner? How would you prepare your students to take standardized tests? How would taking such tests affect your curriculum?
2. Look at the standards for the teaching of reading and writing in your state. How do you think these standards came to define what's important to teach and learn? How could you address standards without letting them drive your curriculum?
3. Read *Hooray for Diffendoofer Day* to a group of high school students. Let them discuss the book in small groups. What is their reaction? How do they think it applies to their lives?
4. How would you respond to critics who lament the state of education in America today? What facts would you use to support your position?

Works Cited

"A Senator Challenges the Tests." 2001. *NEA Today* (January). Online.

Abrams, Jennifer. 2002. "Effective Monitoring During Class Time." *English Leadership Quarterly* 24(3): 8–10.

Applebee, Arthur N. 1992. "Stability and Change in the High School Canon." *English Journal* 81(5): 27–32.

Associated Press. 1998. "2.2 Million Teachers Needed: Education Secretary Emphasizes Quality." *Butler (Penn.) Eagle*, 16 September, 15.

Atwell, Nancie. 1998. *In the Middle: Writing, Reading, and Learning with Adolescents.* 2d ed. Portsmouth, NH: Boynton/Cook.

———. 1987. *In the Middle: Writing, Reading, and Learning with Adolescents.* Portsmouth, NH: Boynton/Cook.

———. 1985. "Everyone Sits at a Big Desk: Discovering Topics for Writing." *English Journal* 74(5): 35–39.

Bellanca, J. A., and R. Fogarty. 1991. *Blueprints for Thinking in the Cooperative Classroom.* 2d ed. Palatine, IL: IRI/Skylight Publishing.

Berlin, James. 1987. *Rhetoric and Reality.* Carbondale: Southern Illinois University Press.

Berliner, David C. 2001. "Our Schools vs. Theirs: Averages That Hide the True Extremes." *Washington Post,* 28 January, B3.

Berliner, David C., and Bruce J. Biddle. 1995. *The Manufactured Crisis: Myths, Fraud, and the Attack on America's Public Schools.* Boston: Addison-Wesley.

Bizzell, Patricia, and Bruce Herzberg. 1991. "A Brief History of Rhetoric and Composition." *The Bedford Bibliography for Teachers of Writing.* New York: St. Martin's.

Bloom, Benjamin. 1956. *Taxonomy of Educational Objectives: Handbook I: Cognitive Domain.* New York: McKay.

Blystone, Jane. 1997a. Email correspondence, January 5.

———. 1997b. Email correspondence, January 22.

Boon, Leslie. 2000. *Re: IB PROGRAM.* Email to listserv, December 14: *listmates @tempest.coedu.usf.edu*

Bracey, Gerald W. 2001. "Question Authority." *Phi Delta Kappan* 83(3): 191.

———. 2000. "The 10th Bracey Report on the Condition of Public Education." *Phi Delta Kappan*, October 15. Online.

Brewbaker, James. 1997. "On Tuesday Morning: The Case for Standards for the English Language Arts." *English Journal* 86(1): 76–82.

Britton, James, et al. 1975. *The Development of Writing Abilities 11–18*. New York: Macmillan.

Buckner, Aimee. 2002. "Teaching in a World Focused on Testing." *Language Arts* 79(3): 212–15.

Bush, George W. 2002. "Teacher Quality." *www.whitehouse.gov/infocus/teacherquality/*

Calkins, Lucy, Kate Montgomery, and Donna Santman with Beverly Falk. 1998. *A Teacher's Guide to Standardized Reading Tests: Knowledge Is Power*. Portsmouth, NH: Heinemann.

Cazden, Courtney. 1988. *Classroom Discourse: The Language of Teaching and Learning*. Portsmouth, NH: Heinemann.

Chambers, Rick. 1996. "Portfolio Writing and Learning: An Action Research Project." Ontario: Teachers College.

Chomsky, Noam. 1957. *Syntactic Structures*. The Hague: Mouton.

Christensen, Francis. 1978. *Notes Toward a New Rhetoric: Nine Essays for Teachers*. Rev. ed., ed. B. Christensen. New York: Harper & Row.

Cisneros, Sandra. 1991. "Eleven." *Woman Hollering Creek and Other Stories*. New York: Vintage.

Clinton, President William J. 1997. "State of the Union Address." 4 February. *http://library.whitehouse.gov/*

Crowley, Sharon 1998. *Composition in the University*. Pittsburgh: University of Pittsburgh Press.

Daniels, Harvey. 2002. *Literature Circles*. 2d ed. Portland, ME: Stenhouse.

———. 2001. Luncheon address at the annual National Conference of Teachers of English conference, Baltimore, 18 November.

Darling-Hammond, Linda. 1994. "Performance Based Assessment and Educational Equality." *Harvard Educational Review* 54: 5–30.

———. 1991. "The Implications of Testing Policy for Educational Quality and Equality. *Phi Delta Kappan* 73: 220–25.

———. 1989. "Curiouser and Curiouser: Alice in Testingland." *Rethinking Schools* 3(1): 17.

Darling-Hammond, Linda, J. Ancess, and Beverly Falk. 1995. *Authentic Assessment in Action*. New York: Teachers College Press.

Darling-Hammond, Linda, and L. A. Goodwin. 1993. "Progress Towards Professionalism in Teaching." In *Challenges and Achievements of American Education*, ed. G. Cawelti. Alexandria, VA: Association for Supervision and Curriculum Development.

Davies, Robertson. 1995. *The Cunning Man*. New York: Viking/Penguin.

Dewey, John. [1922] 1983. "Education as Religion." In *The Middle Works of John Dewey: 1899–1924*, ed. J. A. Boydston. Carbondale: Southern Illinois University Press.

Dosh, Shannon. 2002. "And by the Way, You're Fired." In *Welcome to Teaching: Advice from New Teachers*, ed. James Strickland. Portsmouth, NH: Heinemann.

———. 2000. "State Mandate." Email to listserv discussion, December 14: *listmates @tempest.coedu.usf.edu*

Dreyer, Diana. 1994. "When Models Collide." *English Leadership Quarterly* 16(1): 9–11.

Eisner, Elliot. 1992. "The Reality of Reform." *English Leadership Quarterly* 14(3): 2–5.

Elbow, Peter. 1973. *Writing Without Teachers*. New York: Oxford University Press.

Emig, Janet. 1971. *The Composing Process of Twelfth Graders*. Urbana, IL: National Council of Teachers of English.

Fecho, Bob. 1998. "Making Means or Making Meaning: The Mixed Messages of Large-Scale Assessment." Paper presented at annual meeting of National Council of Teachers of English, Nashville, TN, 20 November.

Fletcher, Ralph. 1996. *A Writer's Notebook: Unlocking the Writer Within You*. New York: Avon.

Flower, Linda, and John Hayes. 1980. "Identifying the Organization of the Writing Process." In *Cognitive Processes in Writing*, eds. L. Gregg and E. Steinberg. Hillsdale, NJ: Lawrence Erlbaum.

Foster, Xinia. 2000. "Re: Grading—Stacey." Email to listserv discussion, April 12: *golublist@tempest.coedu.usf.edu*

Golub, Jeffrey N. 2000. *Making Learning Happen*. Portsmouth, NH: Boynton/Cook.

———. 1994. *Activities for an Interactive Classroom*. Urbana, IL: National Council of Teachers of English.

Good, Thomas. 1981. "Teacher Expectations and Student Perceptions: A Decade of Research." *Educational Leadership* 38: 415–21.

Goodman, Ken. [1982] 1991. "Revaluing Readers and Writers." In *With Promise: Redefining Reading and Writing for "Special" Students*, ed. Susan Stires, pp. 127–34. Portsmouth, NH: Heinemann.

Goodman, Yetta. 1996. "Revaluing Readers While Readers Revalue Themselves: Retrospective Miscue Analysis." *The Reading Teacher* 49: 600–609.

———. 1992. "Bookhandling Knowledge Task." In *Whole Language Catalogue Supplement on Authentic Assessment*, eds. Ken Goodman, Lois Bridges Bird, and Yetta Goodman. Santa Rosa, CA: American School Publishers.

———. 1978. "Kid-watching: An Alternative to Testing." *National Elementary Principal* 57: 41–45.

Goodman, Yetta, Dorothy Watson, and Carolyn Burke. [1987] 1996. *Reading Miscue Inventory: Alternative Procedures*. Katonah, NY: Richard C. Owen.

Goodrich, Heidi. 1996/1997. "Understanding Rubrics." *Educational Leadership* 54(4): 14–17.

Graves, Donald. 1983. *Writing: Teachers and Children at Work*. Portsmouth, NH: Heinemann.

Gray, Esther N. 2001. "A Literacy Growth Spurt During Inquiry: Tommy's Story." *Language Arts* 78(4): 325–32.

Green, Joshua. 2000. "No Lectures or Teachers, Just Software" *The New York Times*, 10 August.

Guth, Hans. 1988. "Revitalizing Composition: The Unfinished Agenda." Promotional literature for *The Writer's Agenda*. Belmont, CA: Wadsworth.

Hansen, Jane. 1998. *When Learners Evaluate*. Portsmouth, NH: Heinemann.

Harris, Robert. 1997. "Evaluating Internet Research Sources." Accessed online June 17, 2002. *www.virtualsalt.com/evalu8it.htm*.

Hill, Bonnie Campbell, Nancy Johnson, and Katherine Schlick-Noe. 1995. *Literature Circles and Response*. Norwood, MA: Christopher-Gordon.

Huck, Charlotte. 1977. "Literature as the Content of Reading." *Theory into Practice* 16: 363–71.

Jago, Carol. 2000. *With Rigor for All*. Portsmouth, NH: Heinemann–Calendar Islands.

Jehlen, Alain. 2001. "Can the Standards Movement Be Saved?" *NEA Today* (January). Online.

Jonsberg, Sara Dalmas. 2000. "A Place for Every Student." *English Journal* 89(5): 28.

Johnson, Amy. 2002. "Reflections on Classroom Activities." Unpublished manuscript.

Kaywell Joan. 2002. "Re: What Do I Do?" Email to listserv discussion, January 24: *listmates@tempest.coedu.usf.edu*

King-Shaver, Barbara. 1992. "Process-Based Literature/Writing Examinations." *English Leadership Quarterly* 14(1): 6–7.

———. 1991. "Whole Language: Implications for Secondary Classrooms." *English Leadership Quarterly* 13(1): 4–5.

Kingsolver, Barbara. 1993. *Pigs in Heaven*. New York: HarperCollins.

Kirsch, Steven T. 2001. "Rod Paige Page." Accessed online February 22, 2002. *www.skirsch.com/politics/rod_paige_page.htm*

Klein, Stephen, Laura Hamilton, Daniel McCaffrey, and Brian Stecher. 2000. "What Do Test Scores in Texas Tell Us?" RAND Issue Paper. October 24. Accessed online March 8, 2002. *www.rand.org/publications/IP/IP202*.

Kohn, Alfie. 1999. *The Schools Our Children Deserve*. Boston: Houghton Mifflin.

———. 1993. *Punished by Rewards: The Trouble with Gold Stars, Incentive Plans, A's, Praise, and Other Bribes*. Boston: Houghton Mifflin.

Kotwica, Hollie. 2002. "Taking Risks." In *Welcome to Teaching: Advice from New Teachers*, ed. James Strickland. Portsmouth, NH: Heinemann.

Krumboltz, John, and Christine Yehn. 1996. "Competitive Grading Sabotages Good Teaching." *Phi Delta Kappan* 78(4): 324–26.

Kuhn, Thomas. 1963. *The Structure of Scientific Revolutions*. Chicago: University of Chicago Press.

Lamott, Anne. 1994. *Bird by Bird: Some Instructions on Writing and Life*. New York: Random House.

Landsberg, Michele. 1999. "Book Offers Clear and Calm Lesson on Learning." *Toronto Star*, 18 September.

Lemieux, Brittanny. 2000. "Re: Grading—Stacey." Email to listserv, April 12: *goleublist@tempest.coedu.usf.edu*

Leo, John. 1996. "Shakespeare vs. Spiderman." *U.S. News and World Report* 120: 61.

Lieberman, Trudy. 1998. "In Search of Quality Health Care." *Consumer Reports* (October): 35.

Lowry, Lois. 1993. *The Giver*. Boston: Houghton Mifflin.

Macrorie, Ken. 1988. *The I-Search Paper: Revised Edition of Searching Writing*. Portsmouth, NH: Boynton/Cook.

Mahoney, Jim. 2002. *Power and Portfolios*. Portsmouth, NH: Boynton/Cook.

Mandrell, Liz. 1997. "Zen and the Art of Grade Motivation." *English Journal* 86(1): 28–31.

Marcus, Stephen. 1991. "Invisible Writing with a Computer: New Sources and Resources." In *The English Classroom in the Computer Age: Thirty Lesson Plans*, ed. W. Wresch, 9–13. Urbana, IL: National Council of Teachers of English.

Martin, Barbara. 2001. "Re: Calling on Students." Email listserv discussion, September 4: *goleublist@tempest.coedu.usf.edu*

Massachusetts Comprehensive Assessment System (MCAS). 1998 "Grade Ten, English Language Arts, 1998 Session One, Reading Selection #1. Massachusetts Department of Education." Accessed online March 8, 2002. *www.doe.mass.edu/mcas/2001/retest/ela.asp*

Massey, Joanna. 2000. "Dropout Rate Up as MCAS Looms." *New Bedford (Mass.) Standard Times*, 8 October. Accessed online. *www.s-t.com/daily/10-00/10-08-00/a01sr003.htm*

Mayher, John, Nancy Lester, and Gordon Pradl. 1983. *Learning to Write/Writing to Learn*. Portsmouth, NH: Boynton/Cook.

McAndrew, Donald A., and Thomas J. Reigstad. 2001. *Tutoring Writing*. Portsmouth, NH: Boynton/Cook.

Miller, John P. 1998/1999. "Making Connections Through Holistic Learning." *Educational Leadership* 56(4): 46–48.

Miller, Suzanne. 1991. "Room to Talk: Opening Possibilities with the At-Risk." *English Leadership Quarterly* 13(2): 10–11.

Morkes, John, and Jakob Nielsen. 1997. "Concise, SCANNABLE, and Objective: How to Write for the Web." Accessed online. *www.useit.com/papers/webwriting/writing.html*

Murray, Donald M. 1978. "Internal Revision: A Process of Discovery." In *Research on Composing*, eds. Charles Cooper and Lee Odell. Urbana, IL: National Council of Teachers of English.

NCTE/IRA Joint Task Force on Assessment. 1996. "Standards for the Assessment of Reading and Writing." Accessed online. *www.ncte.org/idea/assess/asses-in.html*

Newman, Heather. 1998a. "Fair Assessment of Students: A Thorny Issue." *Detroit Free Press*, 21 January, 1.

———. 1998b. "Test Results Can Be Skewed by Many Outside Factors." *Detroit Free Press*, 7 May, 1–2.

Ohanian, Susan. 1999. *One Size Fits Few: The Folly of Educational Standards*. Portsmouth, NH: Heinemann.

Paige, Rod. 2001. "Back-to-School Address: Remarks as Prepared for Delivery by the U.S. Secretary of Education." Talk given to the National Press Club, Washington, DC, 4 September.

Parker, Jennifer. 2000. "Re: Grading—Stacey." Email to listserv discussion, April 12: *golublist@tempest.coedu.usf.edu*

Peters, Linda. 2001. "Rime of the Ancient Mariner." Email to listserv discussion, January 25: *listmates@tempest.coedu.usf.edu*

Piaget, Jean. [1954] 1971. *Psychology and Epistemology*. Translated by A. Rosin. New York: Grossman.

Pinker, Steven. 1994. *The Language Instinct: How the Mind Creates Language*. New York: HarperCollins.

Popham, James. 1988. "Texas Educational Assessment of Minimum Skills—Reading Skills Test." In *Educational Evaluation*, 2d ed., pp. 141–43. Englewood Cliffs, NJ: Prentice Hall.

Postman, Neil, and Charles Weingartner. 1967. *Teaching as a Subversive Activity*. New York: Delacorte Press.

Powers, Margo. 2002. "Re: Vocabulary." Email to listserv discussion, January 27: *listmates@tempest.coedu.usf.edu*

Probst, Robert. 1992. "Five Kinds of Literary Knowing." In *English Language Instruction*, ed. Judith Langer, pp. 54–77. Urbana, IL: National Council of Teachers of English.

Resnick, Daniel P., and Lauren B. Resnick. 1987. "Understanding Achievement and Acting to Produce It: Some Recommendations for NAEP." Papers commissioned by the Study Group on the National Assessment of Student Achievement, cited in Appendix B of "The Nation's Report Card."

"Resources." 2001. *NEA Today* (January). Online.

Rodrigues, Dawn, and Ray Rodrigues. 1986. *Teaching Writing with a Word Processor, Grades 7–13*. Urbana, IL: National Council of Teachers of English/ERIC.

Rogers, Carl. 1969. *Freedom to Learn*. Columbus, OH: Merrill.

Romano, Tom. 1987. *Clearing the Way: Working with Teenage Writers*. Portsmouth, NH: Boynton/Cook.

Romberg, Thomas A. 1993. "NCTM's Standards: A Rallying Flag for Mathematics Teachers." *Educational Leadership* 50(2): 36–41.

Rose, Mike. 1995. *Possible Lives: The Promise of Public Education in America*. New York: Penguin.

———. 1980. "Rigid Rules, Inflexible Plans, and the Stifling of Language: A Cognitivist Analysis of Writer's Block." *College Composition and Communication* 31: 389–401.

Rosenblatt, Louise M. 1978. *The Reader, the Text, and the Poem: The Transactional Theory of the Literary Work*. Carbondale: Southern Illinois University Press.

Savin, Teresa. 2002. "Motivation: What Doesn't Work Is Easy." In *Welcome to Teaching: Advice from New Teachers*, ed. James Strickland. Portsmouth, NH: Heinemann.

Schantz, Annelise. 2000. Graduation speech, Hudson, Massachusetts, 4 June.

Scholes, Robert. 1998. *The Rise and Fall of English*. New Haven, CT: Yale University Press.

Schwartz, H. 1984. *SEEN* [computer program]. Iowa City, IA: Conduit.

Selfe, Cynthia, and Billie Wahlstrom. 1983. *Wordsworth II* [computer program]. Houghton, MI: Michigan Technological University.

Seuss, Dr., and Jack Prelutsky. 1998. *Hooray for Diffendoofer Day*. Illustrated by Lane Smith. New York: Alfred A. Knopf.

Shames, Laurence. 1995. *Sunburn*. New York: Hyperion.

Siebert, S., R. Dowding, S. Quigley, M. Bills, and R. Brooke. 1997. "Between Student and Teacher Roles: Negotiating Curricula During Teacher Training." In *Sharing Pedagogies: Students and Teachers Write About Dialogic Practices*, ed. Gail Tayko and John Paul Tassoni. Portsmouth, NH: Boynton/Cook.

Silberman, Charles. 1970. *Crisis in the Classroom: The Remaking of American Education*. New York: Random House.

Skinner, B. F. 1953. *Science and Human Behavior*. New York: Macmillan.

Slavin, Robert E. 1997/1998. "Can Education Reduce Social Inequity?" *Educational Leadership* 55(4): 6–10.

Smith, Frank. 1994. *Understanding Reading*. 5th ed. Hillsdale, NJ: Lawrence Erlbaum.

———. 1988. *Joining the Literacy Club: Further Essays into Literacy*. Portsmouth, NH: Heinemann.

St. Michel, Terrie. 1997. Personal correspondence, January 5.

Stephanopolis, George. 2000. *ABC News* television broadcast, March 11.

Strickland, James. 1997. *From Disk to Hard Copy: Teaching Writing with Computers*. Portsmouth, NH: Boynton/Cook.

———. 1990. "Supervision and Evaluation." *CSSEDC Quarterly* 12(3): 1.

———. 1987. "Computers, Invention, and the Power to Improve Student Writing." *Computers and Composition* 4(2): 7–26.

———. 1984. *Free/Quest* [computer programs]. Slippery Rock, PA: Slippery Rock University.

Strickland, Kathleen, and James Strickland. 1998. *Reflections on Assessment: Its Purposes, Methods, and Effects on Learning*, Portsmouth, NH: Boynton/Cook.

———. 1993. *UN-Covering the Curriculum: Whole Language in the Secondary and Post-Secondary Classroom*. Portsmouth, NH: Boynton/Cook.

Tattersall, Kathleen. 1996. "Why Are So Many of Us Suspicious of Success?" *The London Times*, 16 August, 28.

Taylor, Kathe, and Sherry Walton. 1998. *Children at the Center: A Workshop Approach to Standardized Test Preparation, K–8*. Portsmouth, NH: Heinemann.

Tchudi, S. 1985. *Language, Schooling, and Society*. Portsmouth, NH: Boynton/Cook.

Tierney, R., M. Carter, and L. Desai. 1991. *Portfolio Assessment in the Reading-Writing Classroom*. Norwood, MA: Christopher-Gordon.

Troy, Frosty. 2000. "Dunces of Public Education Reform." *Progressive Populist*, 3 December. Accessed online. *www.populist.com/00.20.troy.html*

Van Moorlehem, Tracy. 1998. "Home Sales, Custody Fights Hinge on Exam." *Detroit Free Press*, 19 January, 3.

Van Moorlehem, Tracy, and Heather Newman. 1998. "Testing MEAP Scores: Comparing Raw Results Has Some Pitfalls." *Detroit Free Press*, 19 January, 2.

Vygotsky, L. 1978. *Mind and Society*, ed. M. Cole, V. J. Steiner, S. Scribner, and E. Souberman. Cambridge, MA: Harvard University Press.

Walker, Amy Lynne. 2001. Weaving a Literacy Tapestry: A Teacher-Research Case Study of One Fifth Grade Student in a Transactional Special Education Classroom. Unpublished dissertation, Indiana University of Pennsylvania.

Walsh, Kenneth T. 2001. "The Morning After the Ball: Inauguration of President Bush." *U.S. News & World Report* 130(4): 12.

Watson, John B. [1912] 1957. *Behaviorism*. Chicago: University of Chicago Press.

Weaver, Connie. 1994. *Reading Process and Practice: From Socio-Psycholinguistics to Whole Language*. 2d ed. Portsmouth, NH: Heinemann.

Weber, Chris. 2002. *Publishing with Students: A Comprehensive Guide*. Portsmouth, NH: Heinemann.

Wells, Gordon. 1986. *The Meaning Makers: Children Learning Language and Using Language to Learn*. Portsmouth, NH: Heinemann.

White, Edward M. 1985. *Teaching and Assessing Writing*. San Francisco: Jossey-Bass.

Wieland, S. 1990. "Leading Classroom Discussions." *English Leadership Quarterly* 12(4): 1–3.

Wiggins, Grant. 1993. "Assessment: Authenticity, Context, and Validity." *Phi Delta Kappan* 75(3): 200–14.

———. 1989. "A True Test: Toward More Authentic and Equitable Assessment." *Phi Delta Kappan* 70(8): 703–13.

Wilcox, Bonita. 2002. "Alternative Assessment." *English Leadership Quarterly* 24(3): 1–2.

Wilhelm, Jeffrey D. 1995. *"You Gotta BE the Book": Teaching Engaged and Reflective Reading with Adolescents*. Urbana, IL: National Council of Teachers of English.

Wresch, William, Donald Pattow, and James Gifford. 1989. *Writing for the Twenty-First Century: Computers and Research Writing*. New York: McGraw Hill.

Zemelman, Steven, and Harvey Daniels. 1988. *A Community of Writers: Teaching Writing in the Junior and Senior High School*. Portsmouth, NH: Heinemann.

Index

Abrams, Jennifer, 150, 156
Accelerated Reader, 42, 204
anecdotal records, 38, 142, 145
anticipation guides, reading, 50–52,
      76–77
Applebee, Arthur, 7
assessment, 38, 40, 42, 76, 94, 139–145,
      148, 157–58, 162, 166, 168,
      170–76, 180, 197–200
   alternative, 142
   authentic, 142, 162
   performance, 143
   qualitative techniques, 145
Atwell, Nancie, 22, 80, 93, 94, 95, 99,
      100, 101, 106, 109
authentic learning, 2, 9, 15, 142, 199

behavioral paradigm, 4–11, 192
Bellanca and Fogarty, three classes of
      verbs, 155, 203
Berlin, Jim, 43
Berliner, David, 180, 185, 186, 188
Bills, Melanie, 8, 9, 92
Bloom, Benjamin, 6
Blystone, Jane, 141, 169–74
Boon, Leslie, 83, 87
Bracey, Gerald W., 11, 189, 195, 196
Brewbaker, James, 179
Burke, Jim, 18
Bush, George, 177
Bush, George W., 6, 185, 188, 190, 194

California, educational policies in, 13,
      47, 150, 187
Cazden, Courtney, 23
Chambers, Rick, 106, 168, 170, 173
checklists, 142–48
Chomsky, Noam, 11, 137
Christensen, Francis, 122
Cisneros, Sandra, 20
classroom management, 21–23
Clinton, William J., 6, 177, 198
collaborative learning, 20, 89, 93, 133,
      135, 138, 144, 158
community, learning, 9, 12, 19–26, 29,
      42, 93, 111, 117, 133–38
computers, 116–21, 131–37, 169, 203
   word processing, 116–26, 131
computers, network connectivity, 133
conferencing. See writing strategies
Conger, Joette, 157
constructivist approaches to teaching,
      6–17
Core Knowledge movement, 45, 184
Cosgrove, Neil, 148
covering the curriculum, 16
Crowley, Sharon, 43, 44
Crucible, The, 37
cultural literacy, 8, 45, 46

Dandoy, Bob, 56, 60, 113
Daniels, Harvey, 12, 20, 60, 73, 75, 80,
      94, 105, 167

David Copperfield, 48
deficit model of learning, 4
dentist analogy, the, 192–93
Department of Education, United
    States, 177, 191
Dewey, John, 6
DiMarco, Danette, 134
Directed Reading Thinking Activity,
    63, 78
discussion, 14, 22–29, 31, 35, 50, 52,
    64–67, 74, 77, 95, 104, 132, 134
  assigning roles, 29
  facilitating, 28
  listserv, 134
  small group, 28
distance learning, 136
Dosh, Shannon, 46, 203, 204
Dreyer, Diana, 163

editing, 92, 96, 110–12, 119, 122, 125,
    145, 147
Eisner, Elliot, 141, 180, 181, 198
Elbow, Peter, 83, 84
evaluation, 29, 40, 42, 50, 76, 139–41,
    148, 152, 162, 165–70, 173, 175,
    192

FairTest, 195, 206
Fecho, Bob, 199, 200
Finding Forrester, 21
Fletcher, Ralph, 85, 86, 87
Florida Comprehensive Achievement
    Test, 203, 204
Foster, Xinia, 156
Frankenstein, 48
freewriting, 8, 83–88, 91, 118, 119, 137
Frost, Robert, 24, 26

Giver, The, 74, 127
Golub, Jeff, 11, 12, 13, 23, 156
Goodman, Kenneth, 1
Goodman, Yetta, 15, 139
Goodrich, Heidi, 152

grading, 41, 139, 142, 150, 156,
    160–68, 174, 175, 194
  competitive, 166
  proofs of purchase evaluation,
    156–57
Graves, Donald, 80, 99, 117, 168
Great Expectations, 57
Great Gatsby, The, 7, 47
group work, 20, 26–29, 35, 48, 56, 60,
    73–77, 104, 105, 134, 156

Hamlet, 7, 44, 50
Hansen, Jane, 141
Harvard, entrance exam, 43–44
Higher Order Concerns (HOCs), 100,
    107, 110
Huckleberry Finn, 7, 37

inquiry-based classrooms, 19
Internet, 31–33, 91, 117–18, 124, 129,
    131, 135, 192, 204
  reliability, 32
interviews, 36, 131, 145
I-Search research, 30

Jago, Carol, 47
Jane Eyre, 48
jigsawing, reading strategy, 48
Johnson, Amy, 50–55, 57–59, 65–70,
    76–77, 97–99
journals, 40, 74, 85

Kaywell, Joan, 56
kidwatching, 15, 76, 139
King, Martin Luther, Jr., 131
King-Shaver, Barbara, 48, 158,
    159
Kohn, Alfie, 13, 165, 181
Kotwica, Hollie, 5
Kuhn, Thomas, 5, 6

Labov, Willliam, 22
Lamott, Anne, 79, 91, 101, 107

language learning beliefs, 11–13, 17,
    124
Laubach, Rebecca, 126
Lemieux, Brittanny, 156
listening, active, 27
listserv. *See* discussion
literacy club, the, 36, 76
literature circle, roles. *See* roles,
    literature circles
literature circles, 29, 73–77
literature studies, replace reading, 43
Lord of the Flies, 7
Lower Order Concerns (LOCs),
    110

Macbeth, 3, 4, 5, 7, 44, 62
Mahoney, Jim, 20–21, 37, 60, 106–107,
    109, 113–14, 120, 168–72,
    174–75
Marcus, Stephen, 119
Martin, Barbara, 23
Massachusetts Comprehensive
    Assessment System, 160, 208
McAndrew, Donald, 100, 105, 110
Miller, Suzanne, 35
minilessons, 31, 81, 84, 109, 129
Moby Dick, 62, 154
Morrison, Laurie, 126
Murray, Donald, 80

National Council of Teachers of
    English, 44, 139, 160, 166, 178,
    180, 185, 203
National Council of Teachers of
    Mathematics, 177
Neal, Maureen, 167, 173, 174
network connectivity, 133

Odyssey, The, 7, 47, 132
Of Mice and Men, 7, 73
Ohanian, Susan, 177, 184, 185, 186,
    187, 192
online writing labs (OWLs), 138

Paige, Rod, Secretary of Education,
    187–88, 201
parading. *See* writing strategies
peer response, 134, 150, 171
Pennsylvania System of School
    Assessment, 195, 196, 199
Peters, Linda, 13
Piaget, Jean, 6, 47
Pigs in Heaven, 47, 71, 75
Pinker, Steven, 12
Poe, Edgar Allan, 27, 132
Popham, James, 142, 196
portfolios, 144, 148, 152, 167–76
PowerPoint slides, 125–29
Powers, Margo, 56
prewriting. *See* writing strategies
Probst, Robert, 16, 47
process orientation to teaching, 15
proofs of purchase. *See* grading
publishing, on the Internet, 124

questioning
    calling on students, 23
    in transactional classrooms, 24
    in transactional classrooms, 26
    known-answer questions, 23, 24, 154
    the IRE model, 23, 35

readers' theatre, 62
reading. *See also* anticipation guides
    as literature study, 43
    book talks, 64, 74
    graphic organizers, 67
    levels guides, 65–67
    place for in students' lives, 38
    predictions, 4, 50, 52, 54, 55, 63, 64
    understanding students as readers,
        36, 40
reading logs, 40–43
reading, independent, 41
Red Badge of Courage, The, 16
Reid, Louann, 179
Reigstad, Thomas, 100, 105, 110

reporting, 139–41

research paper, the, 19, 30, 31, 33, 34, 79, 114, 130

revision, 107, 108, 119, 121, 138

Rodrigues, Dawn and Ray, 125

roles

    literature circles, 74–75

    small group discussion, 29, 75, 77

Romeo and Juliet, 7, 57, 67, 68, 69, 154

Rose, Mike, 108, 183

Rosenblatt, Louise, 16, 46, 73, 117

rubrics, 148–54, 176

SAT test scores, 15, 160, 191, 195, 196, 199, 207, 208

Savin, Teresa, 92, 113, 164

Scarlet Letter, 7

Schantz, Annelise, 206–208

Schrank, Roger, 137

Seuss, Dr., 186

Skinner, B. F., 6

Smith, Frank, 4, 8, 36, 41, 76, 77, 116, 194

software programs, 117, 118, 124, 125, 132, 136, 137

spell checkers, 112, 122, 124

standardized tests, 57, 141, 182, 186, 194, 197, 199, 202

    criterion-referenced, 197

    norm-referenced, 195

    strategies to help students prepare, 205–206

    teaching to the test, 159

Standards for the English Language Arts, The, 178–79

status of the class, 94, 145

Steiger, Laura, 23, 108

story impressions, pre-reading, 52, 53–55, 59

story schema, 46

Strickland, James, 117, 118, 125, 126, 134, 157, 167, 174, 175

Strickland, Kathleen, 126, 157, 167, 174, 175

student-centered learning, 1, 13, 14, 19, 25, 67, 94, 99, 117, 142, 169, 186

Sustained Silent Reading (SSR), 63

technology, 32, 116–37, 138, 184

testing

    authentic, 154

    constraints of, 158–59

Texas, educational policies in, 13, 188

To Kill a Mockingbird, 7

traditional approaches to teaching, 5–17

Troy, Frosty, 188–91

trust and risk, 1–3

vocabulary instruction, 55–59, 62, 75–78

Vygotsky, Lev, 6, 107

Walker, Amy, 20

Watsons Go to Birmingham, The, 48

Weaver, Constance, 13, 22

websites, 112, 136

Wieland, Sharon, 19, 25

Wiggins, Grant, 3, 142, 143, 144, 152, 155, 156, 157, 198

Wilcox, Bonita, 165

Wilhelm, Jeff, 48

workshop approaches to teaching, 15

Wresch, Bill, 32

writer's notebook, 85–86, 115, 135, 170–72

writers' workshop, 79

    elements of, 82

writing process, 80, 81, 95, 110, 125, 147, 158

writing strategies

    brainstorming, 4, 119

    brainstorming, 87–90

clustering, 90, 91
conferencing, 31, 36, 94–95, 103
cumulative sentences, 120–21
guidance files, 125–27
modeling, 106
nutshelling, 84
outlining, 120

parading, 106–107, 110, 111
paragraphing, 121
peer conferencing, 103, 134
prewriting, 81–83, 88–91, 108, 125,
    138

Zemelman, Steven, 12, 20, 80, 94, 105